ISBN: 9781313173803

Published by:
HardPress Publishing
8345 NW 66TH ST #2561
MIAMI FL 33166-2626

Email: info@hardpress.net
Web: http://www.hardpress.net

THE SCOTT EXHIBITION

MDCCCLXXI.

CATALOGUE OF THE EXHIBITION

HELD AT EDINBURGH, IN JULY AND AUGUST 1871,

ON OCCASION OF THE COMMEMORATION

OF THE CENTENARY

OF THE BIRTH OF

SIR WALTER SCOTT.

EDINBURGH: MDCCCLXXII.

TABLE OF CONTENTS.

First Division.

BUSTS, PORTRAITS, ETC., OF SIR WALTER SCOTT.

Second Division.

A SERIES OF ILLUSTRATIONS IN PHOTO-LITHOGRAPHY, FROM THE EXHIBITED BUSTS AND PORTRAITS OF SIR WALTER SCOTT.

ADDITIONAL ILLUSTRATIONS.

Third Division.

MANUSCRIPTS AND EARLY EDITIONS OF SCOTT'S WRITINGS.

Fourth Division.

HISTORICAL AND PICTORIAL ILLUSTRATIONS OF SCOTT'S WORKS.

INDEX.

PREFACE.

In the Summer and Autumn of 1870 preparations were set on foot by the Border Counties Association, a Society which had existed for some years in Berwick, Roxburgh, Selkirk, and Dumfries, for the celebration of the Hundredth Anniversary of the birth of Sir Walter Scott. It was at first intended to hold this celebration within the bounds of the Associated Border Counties, but the scheme of the Association gradually enlarging itself, it was resolved to make the event National instead of Local, and the Scottish Capital its scene. As President of the Association, Lord Jerviswoode naturally became Chairman of the Committee by which the plan of the Festival was devised and matured. In course of conversation with his Lordship, in the spring of 1871, Sir William Stirling Maxwell remarked that a Loan Exhibition of Pictures, MSS., and other Relics and Works of Art, for the illustration of the life and labours of Sir Walter Scott, would form an interesting and appropriate feature of the Commemoration. Lord Jerviswoode approving of the hint, Sir William, a few days afterwards, on the 8th April, wrote him a letter, of which what follows is the larger portion :—

"I beg to offer a suggestion regarding the approaching commemoration of the Centenary of the birth of SIR WALTER SCOTT.

"The scheme of a Scott Exhibition to be held in Edinburgh in August is perhaps but a small portion of what it may be found possible to accomplish. But if it is to be successfully realized, it ought to be made known, and the preliminary steps taken, without loss of time.

"There was held at Florence in May 1865 a commemoration of the sixth centenary of the birth of Dante, consisting of a series of *feste* lasting for three days. The political circumstances of Italy at that time gave a significance and an interest to the commemoration of the birth of the greatest of Italians, which, happily for us, are wholly wanting to any similar proceedings in honour of the greatest of Scotchmen. But what Dante was and is to Italy and Florence, Scott was and is in many ways to Scotland and Edinburgh; and I believe that a Scott Exhibition in 1871 would be no less successful and interesting than was the *Esposizione Dantesca* of 1865. How ample were the materials which Italy could bring together to illustrate the life of her great poet may be judged by the fact that the Catalogue, or rather the Catalogues, for there were three, form a handsome octavo volume of pp. 112, 70, and 36 respectively—one of the most valuable of recent additions to the ever-growing 'Biblioteca Dantesca.' Each Catalogue represents a department of the Exhibition—the first describing the MSS. of the works of Dante and original documents connected with his history; the second, the editions of his works; and the third, various objects of art, which were divided into three groups:—(1.) Portraits and Medals of Dante; (2.) Works connected with his life; and (3.) Works illustrating his writings.

"Now if Italy, swept for so many centuries by conquerors and collectors, could assemble so many relics of Dante, who died in 1321, surely we ought to have no difficulty in doing something of the same kind for Scott, who died in 1832. The single disadvantage under which we seem to labour is the shortness of the time left for preparation. The managing committee of the Dante Exhibition, opened on the 14th May 1865, appears to have held its first meeting on the 11th May 1864, while our Exhibition must be opened within three months from the present time. Still, with the large experience that many of our countrymen have had of recent exhibitions, the thing surely may be done, if it shall appear to be worth doing.

"Following the Florentine precedent, we should first turn our attention to the Scott MSS. That unwearied hand (recorded in the well-known anecdote) which was seen night after night[1] in the bow window of Castle Street adding to a pile of written sheets, was too famous for many of these sheets to find their way to the fire. I believe the MSS. of most of Scott's chief works are still carefully preserved, there having been within my recollection two or three sales of which they formed the chief attraction. His letters also exist in many family archives, and in large numbers. As a young man he prepared the minutes of the Speculative Society, of which Lockhart notices the careless spelling. A complete set of the first edition of his publications, from the *Bürger Ballads*, in 1796, to *Castle Dangerous* in 1831, would easily, I should think, be collected from our Scotch libraries; and to them might be added specimens of the more ornate editions, of Continental and American reprints, and of the translations into foreign languages.

"Of the portraits of Scott there must be many, beginning, perhaps, with the miniature which he sent in 1797 to the lady who became his wife, and comprising some of the best works of Raeburn, Chantrey, Allan, Watson Gordon, Grant, and Colvin Smith. The engraved portraits must be legionary in number. Around Scott himself might be grouped the portraits of his relatives and intimate friends, and of the more famous contemporaries who enjoyed his personal friendship. Historical portraits, and relics connected with his works, or pictorial compositions suggested by them, would perhaps open a field too wide to be dealt with within the time and space at our command. But even within the narrower limit indicated, I believe an Exhibition might be formed of a very interesting and instructive character, well worthy of the notice even of 'the famous wits, native and hospitable,' who may be expected to meet in Edinburgh in August.

"The Dante Exhibition was formed and displayed under the auspices and authority of the Superintendent-General of the Tuscan Archives. That functionary and a committee was responsible for the selection of the objects exhibited and for the order of the Exhibition. It is of great and obvious importance that our Exhibition should take place under the care of some official person, or body of persons, whose resources should afford a sufficient guarantee for the safety of the various precious things we seek to assemble, and for their presentation to the public view in a convenient and worthy manner.

[1] Lockhart's *Life of Scott*, London, 1845. 8vo, p. 256 (June 1814).

"Perhaps it may be needful to raise a guarantee fund to meet the expenses of the undertaking; though I cannot suppose these will be very large, or doubt that some public building will open its doors to the Exhibition. Indeed, I am inclined to hope that a Scott Exhibition may not only meet its own expenses, but also afford some surplus towards any public and beneficent work by which it may hereafter be determined to commemorate the first centenary of the birth of Scott."

The idea finding favour with the friends whom Lord Jerviswoode consulted, the above extract from Sir William Stirling Maxwell's letter was published in the *Edinburgh Courant* of Thursday, 4th May, and in other newspapers, and communications were opened with Mr. Hope Scott, the Duke of Buccleuch, and other possessors of memorials of Scott. The success which attended their communications was such as to encourage further proceedings, and the formation of a Committee is as follows:—

At a Meeting held in the Signet Library on Friday the 19th day of May 1871—

Present,—SIR WILLIAM STIRLING MAXWELL of Keir and Pollok, Bart.;
ARCHIBALD CAMPBELL SWINTON, Esq. of Kimmerghame;
DAVID LAING, Esq.; and
JAMES DRUMMOND, Esq., R.S.A.

SIR WILLIAM STIRLING MAXWELL was called to preside.

It was unanimously resolved to organize a Loan Exhibition commemorative of the Centenary of Sir Walter Scott. That the objects of Exhibition should consist of,

1. Portraits of Sir Walter Scott, whether Paintings, Drawings, Statues, Busts, Fine Impressions of the best Prints;
2. Specimens of his Autograph Writings, including some of the Original Manuscripts of the Waverley Novels;
3. Pictures or other Works of Art, illustrating his Writings and Personal History;

And that the Exhibition should continue open from the 15th day of July till Saturday the 12th of August inclusive.

It was reported to the Meeting that promises of Loans had already been received from the Royal Collection at Windsor, from the National Portrait Gallery, and from various private individuals.

It was further reported that permission had been obtained from the Honourable The Board of Manufactures to hold the Exhibition in the eastern galleries of the National Gallery.

The Meeting then proceeded with the formation of the Committee of Management; and having in view the expediency of limiting the members, with a view to facilitate the arrangements for the Exhibition, selected the following Noblemen and Gentlemen from a number of others who had expressed themselves interested in the success thereof, viz.:—

His Grace The DUKE OF BUCCLEUCH AND QUEENSBERRY, K.G.
The Right Hon. The EARL OF STAIR, K.T.
The Hon. CHARLES BAILLIE, LORD JERVISWOODE.
The Right Hon. JOHN INGLIS, LORD JUSTICE-GENERAL.
The Right Hon. SIR WILLIAM GIBSON CRAIG of Riccarton, Bart.
SIR HUGH HUME CAMPBELL of Marchmont, Bart.
SIR WILLIAM STIRLING MAXWELL of Keir and Pollok, Bart.
SIR J. NOEL PATON, R.S.A.
JAMES BALLANTINE, Esq.
ADAM BLACK, Esq. of Priorbank.
JAMES DRUMMOND, Esq., R.S.A.
DAVID LAING, Esq.
ARCHIBALD CAMPBELL SWINTON, Esq. of Kimmerghame.

SIR WILLIAM STIRLING MAXWELL to be Convener, and Mr. H. W. CORNILLON, S.S.C., Secretary for the Exhibition.

The draft of an Advertisement announcing the Exhibition, and requesting the loan of Objects of Exhibition, was thereafter drawn up and adjusted, and Mr. Cornillon was instructed to insert the same in Saturday's newspapers. He was also instructed to procure estimates for fitting up the cases and arranging the Exhibition.

It was then resolved that a Guarantee Fund of £400 should be provided to meet such expenses of the Exhibition as might not be covered by the money taken at the doors, and the Chairman reported that sums amounting to £110 had already been promised.

The Advertisement of the Exhibition, of which the draft was prepared at the above meeting, was immediately published in the Newspapers, and privately circulated by the members of the Committee amongst those who seemed likely to be able and willing to aid in the undertaking. It was so nearly in the words of the Minute printed above that it is unnecessary to reprint it here. SIR GEORGE HARVEY, President of the Royal Scottish Academy, and JAMES T. GIBSON CRAIG, Esq., were added to the Committee; and it was announced that communications might be addressed either to SIR WILLIAM STIRLING MAXWELL, 10 Upper Grosvenor Street, London; DAVID LAING, Esq., Signet Library, Edinburgh; or to H. W. CORNILLON, Esq., Secretary, 67 George Street, Edinburgh. The Guarantee Fund was promptly filled up, but the financial results of the Exhibition were such as to preclude any need for recourse to it.

Meetings of the Committee were subsequently held on 31st May, 14th June, 22d June, 27th June, and almost daily thereafter till the opening of the Exhibition; but it does not appear necessary to print the record of their deliberations. It may, however, be mentioned that the Committee resolved itself into the following Sub-Committees:—

Sir William Stirling Maxwell, Bart., . James T. Gibson Craig, Esq., ... James Drummond, Esq., R.S.A., . . . David Laing, Esq., ...	*For Portraits.*
Lord Jerviswoode, ... David Laing, Esq., ... Archibald Campbell Swinton, Esq., . . .	*For Manuscripts.*
Sir George Harvey, *P.*R.S.A., ... Sir J. Noel Paton, R.S.A., ... James Ballantine, Esq., ... James Drummond, Esq., R.S.A., ...	*For Paintings and Illustrations.*
Sir William Stirling Maxwell, Bart., . . James T. Gibson Craig, Esq., ... James Drummond, Esq., R.S.A., . . .	*For Engraved Portraits and other Illustrations.*

All arrangements being complete, the Scott Exhibition was opened on the 15th of July, and remained open until the 19th of August. The hours were from nine A.M. to five P.M., and during the Centenary week the Exhibition was kept open in the evening as well, from six P.M. to eight P.M.

It consisted, as detailed in the present Catalogue, of—

Portraits of Sir Walter Scott.

Specimens of his Autograph Writings.

Pictures and other Works of Art illustrating his Writings.

Miscellaneous Objects.

The highest price of admission was One Shilling, Sixpence being charged for Catalogues.

The highest number of Visitors who were present on any one day was 880, and the lowest 168. Upwards of 12,000 persons visited the Exhibition during the period it was open.

On the 28th of August a meeting of the Committee was held, when the following financial statement was read and approved:—

Receipts—		
Receipts for Admission, Catalogues, and Season-tickets, . .		£690 3 7
Expenditure—		
Printing, Catalogues, Circulars, Season-tickets, etc., .	£130 18 6	
Advertising, ...	64 19 2	
Expenses connected with Cases, fitting up Exhibition, and returning Objects of Loan, ...	191 8 2	
Insurance, etc., ...	17 1 10	
Allowance to Secretary, ...	50 0 0	
Do. to Superintendent of Galleries and Wages to Staff, ...	84 5 11	
Postages, Telegrams, Porterages, and Miscellaneous Disbursements, ...	9 10 10	
		548 4 5
Surplus, . .		£141 19 2

The original Catalogues of the Exhibition as sold at the doors, in consequence of the unavoidable haste with which they were prepared, were not what the Committee would have wished them to be. As the types were kept standing, corrections were made from time to time, but there were defects of arrangement which could not be cured by any process short of reprinting the whole.

A Meeting of the Committee was therefore held at the Signet Library, on the 14th September 1871, to consider the question of reprinting the Catalogue, with Illustrations, and such corrections and additions as should appear necessary to make it a worthy record of the Exhibition.

There were present—

Sir William Stirling Maxwell—*in the Chair.*
James T. Gibson Craig, Esq.
James Ballantine, Esq.
James Drummond, Esq., R.S.A.
David Laing, Esq.

It was unanimously resolved to reprint the Catalogue, with such Illustrations as the resources of the Committee permitted; the size to be quarto, and the printers Messrs. Constable.

A series of Photographs, taken during the Exhibition by Mr. Alexander M'Glashon. from the most important Portraits of Sir Walter Scott, and from pages of some of his Original MSS., were submitted to the Committee, and of these a selection suitable for publication was made.

The cost of these Illustrations, to be printed by the Carbon Process, on good paper, was estimated by Mr. M'Glashon at 20s. per 100 copies, and of the Facsimile of MSS., to be executed in photo-lithography, at 5s. per 100 copies.

It was agreed by the Committee to accept this estimate, and to intrust the executing of the Illustrations to Mr. M'Glashon on the above terms; it being understood that when the requisite number of impressions had been taken, the Negatives should be destroyed.

It was also estimated by the Committee that the number of copies of the Catalogue that would be required would be Six Hundred, of which Two Hundred would be required for presentation to the persons who had co-operated, as lenders or otherwise, in the Exhibition, and Four Hundred would remain for sale.

A Sub-Committee for the preparation of the Catalogue, with full powers to revise the text, determine on the Illustrations, and make all the arrangements necessary for the publication of the work, was appointed, consisting of—

Sir William Stirling Maxwell;
James Drummond, Esq., R.S.A.; and
David Laing, Esq.,

who have accordingly acted as Editors of the present volume.

Their desire has been to make their work an inventory, as complete as circumstance and opportunity permit, of the Memorials of Sir Walter Scott existing on the Hundredth Anniversary of his birth.

In some few cases where objects of peculiar interest have been brought under their notice, it has been thought right to record them in the Catalogue, and to give them a place among the Illustrations, although, from being discovered too late, or other causes, it was found impossible to include them in the Exhibition.

The Editors have seen no reason to depart from the estimate of the Committee, that 600 copies—200 for presentation and 400 for sale—will be a sufficient impression.

They have to express their thanks to their colleagues in the Committee, and other friends, for aid kindly afforded, and especially to those who, like Mr. Hope Scott, Sir Robert Peel, Sir Francis Grant, President of the Royal Academy, Mr. J. P. Knight, R.A., Mr. F. Richardson, and Mr. G. S. Hillard, have favoured them with communications which add much interest and value to their volume.

The expense of preparing and printing this Illustrated Catalogue has considerably exceeded the sum which the Exhibition placed at the disposal of the Committee. From its sale, therefore, no great profit can be expected. But if, after payment of the expenses, a sufficient sum should remain in the hands of the Committee, they propose to employ it in striking a Medal for a "Scott Prize" in connexion with the University of Edinburgh.

W. S. M.

KEIR, *November 6, 1872.*

First Division.

BUSTS, PORTRAITS, ETC., OF SIR WALTER SCOTT.

I.—BUSTS, SCOTT MONUMENT, TAPESTRY, ARMOUR, ETC.

II.—ORIGINAL PORTRAITS.

III.—FAMILY PORTRAITS, AND SCOTT'S PERSONAL FRIENDS.

IV.—ENGRAVED PORTRAITS, MEDALLIONS, AND BUSTS.

CATALOGUE.

ENTRANCE HALL.

I.—BUSTS, SCOTT MONUMENT, TAPESTRY, ARMOUR, ETC.

BUSTS.

1. SIR WALTER SCOTT, Bart. Bust in Plaster. The first of forty-five Casts from Chantrey's marble bust of 1820, now at Abbotsford. These Casts were made under the superintendence of the Sculptor. (See the Photo-Lithographic Illustrations, No. I.)

Lent by — *Sculptor.*

ALLAN A. MACONOCHIE, ESQ. — SIR FRANCIS CHANTREY, R.A.

2. SIR WALTER SCOTT, Bart. Bust in Bronze, executed by the Artist for Robert Cadell, Esq., from the Original Bust modelled in the year 1820.

REV. R. H. STEVENSON. — SIR FRANCIS CHANTREY, R.A.

3. SIR WALTER SCOTT, Bart. Bust in Marble, executed or remodelled in 1828. In the possession of Sir Robert Peel, Bart. (See Title-page; and Illustrations, No. II.)

SIR FRANCIS CHANTREY, R.A.

4. SIR WALTER SCOTT. Bust in Marble, 1822. (See Illustrations, No. III.)

MRS. BURN CALLENDER. — SAMUEL JOSEPH, R.S.A.

5. SIR WALTER SCOTT. Bust in Parian Composition. Reduced from Chantrey's, 1820.

MR. JOHN T. ROSE.

6. SIR WALTER SCOTT, a small Statuette in Plaster from the seated figure carved in Freestone.

After JOHN GREENSHIELDS.

7. Sir Walter Scott, Bart. Bust in Marble, executed in 1831. (See Illustrations, No. IV.)

Lent by — *Sculptor.*

Mr. W. Cross. — Lawrence Macdonald, R.S.A.

8. Sir Walter Scott. Composition from Mr. Steell's Statue in the Scott Monument. A small Statuette in Parian, in 1849.

Association for the Promotion of the Fine Arts. — John Steell, R.S.A.

9. Sir Walter Scott. Statuette in Marble, reduced from the original Statue in the Scott Monument. (See Illustrations, No. V.)

James Hay, Esq. — John Steell, R.S.A.

10. The Bannatyne Club Testimonial, in Silver. Presented to the Secretary in 1861, containing a Statuette of Sir Walter Scott, the Founder of the Club. (See Illustrations, No. VI.)

David Laing, Esq. — Peter Slater.

11. Medallion: date uncertain.

Mr. Henry Laing. — J. Henning.

John Henning, a self-taught artist, was born at Paisley in 1771. He came to Edinburgh, as a modeller of busts, in 1802, but latterly removed to London, where he died, April 8, 1851, in his eightieth year.

12 and 13. Sir Walter Scott. Two Bronze Medals.

Sir J. Noel Paton, R.S.A., and A. Campbell Swinton, Esq. — Stothard, *after* Chantrey.

14. The same Medal, cast in Silver.

Sir William Stirling Maxwell, Bart.

15. Impressions of Medals and Seals of Sir Walter Scott.

Mr. Henry Laing.

16. Sir Walter Scott. Medal.

Mr. W. MacDonald.

17. Impression from a Seal of the face of Sir Walter Scott, cut by Laurence Butters, seal engraver, Edinburgh. The Seal is the property of James T. Gibson Craig, Esq.

18. A Silver Prize Medal, presented by Sheriff Trotter in 1843 to the Dux of the Dumfries Grammar School. A head of Sir Walter Scott, in profile, is chased upon it.

John Blacklock, Esq.

THE SCOTT MONUMENT.

Immediately after the death of SIR WALTER SCOTT, a universal feeling was expressed that a Monument should be erected to his memory in his native city. For this purpose public meetings were held, committees appointed, and efforts made to raise subscriptions. When about £7000 had been collected, a difference of opinion prevailed as to the kind of Monument that should be fixed upon. At a general meeting of the Subscribers, held on 11th December 1835, it was wisely resolved, "That it be an instruction to the Committee that no Architectural Monument should be adopted of which a STATUE cannot form a part." It was further resolved to throw the matter open to general competition; and accordingly, in March 1836, the Sub-Committee advertised for designs for a Monument that should combine a Statue with Architecture, the cost of which should not exceed £5000, and they offered fifty guineas to each of three plans, which, in their judgment, should possess the greatest merit. In due time the Committee received no fewer than fifty-four plans, comprising twenty-two Gothic structures, eleven statues, more or less accompanied by architecture, fourteen Grecian temples, five pillars, one obelisk, and one fountain. In this competition one of the premiums was given to GEORGE KEMP, under the assumed name of *John Morvo*, whom no one had ever heard of; and afterwards his improved Design (No. 21) was adopted in connexion with the Statue by Mr. JOHN STEELL. When the necessary arrangements had been completed, the foundation-stone of the Monument was laid on Scott's birthday, the 15th August 1840, with all due masonic honours, public processions, banquets, etc. The inauguration of the Monument when completed (at an expense of £15,650) was celebrated in a like manner on the 15th August 1846.—(*Abridged from the Scottish Herald*, Nov. 6, 1846.)

19. THE ADVERTISEMENT for Designs for the Scott Monument, in September 1837, a copy written by George Kemp; and Letter from Sir Thomas Dick Lauder, in December that year, in reference to Kemp's first Design.

Lent by
MRS. KEMP.

20. 'THE FIRST IDEA' of the Scott Monument, a Sketch sent by George Kemp, 1837, signed 'John Morvo.'

MR. JAMES BALLANTINE.

21. THE ELABORATE DRAWING SENT IN COMPETITION FOR THE PROPOSED SCOTT MONUMENT IN 1838.

GEORGE KEMP, *Architect.*

Kemp's original Competition Drawing for the Monument. It exhibits St. George's Church in the background, as it was first proposed to have been erected in the centre of Charlotte Square. This Drawing was recently bought from his family for the Trustees of the Scott Monument, to form part of 'The Scott Museum,' when the present Exhibition closed. The room for this purpose is now fitting up at the expense of the 'Trustees of the Monument.'

22. THE SCOTT MONUMENT. Another Drawing by George Kemp, by whom it was presented to Mr. John Dick in 1840.

Lent by

MRS. DICK. GEORGE KEMP.

23. THE SCOTT MONUMENT. This Drawing was made by George Kemp, and presented by him to Mr. Donaldson. Now the property of Mr. Thomas Bonnar.

MR. BONNAR. GEORGE KEMP.

[After the close of the Exhibition this very careful Drawing was sent by Mr. Bonnar to a friend of his in the United States, who carried it to Chicago, where it unfortunately was destroyed during the great conflagration.]

24. THE SCOTT MONUMENT. A Drawing.

DR. A. PATERSON. GEORGE KEMP.

25. MODEL OF THE SCOTT MONUMENT. Lent by Mrs. Dick to the Industrial Museum, Edinburgh, and by her permission now exhibited.

THOMAS C. ARCHER, ESQ., DIRECTOR OF THE MUSEUM OF SCIENCE AND ART. GEORGE KEMP.

George Kemp was employed by the Committee for the Monument to make this Model for the masons to work from. It was afterwards presented by the Committee to their Secretary, Mr. John Dick, by whose family it has been deposited on loan, in the Industrial Museum, Edinburgh.

26. A DESIGN FOR THE SCOTT MONUMENT. A Drawing.

MR. W. D. CLARK. DAVID ROBERTS, R.A., *H.*R.S.A.

TAPESTRY, ARMOUR, ETC.

27. SEVEN PIECES OF FLEMISH TAPESTRY from the Murthly Collection. The first four having borders of fruit and flowers, very rich in colour, and well designed. On each is B.B., with either a heart or lozenge between the letters, and either G.P. or P.V.D.BORCHT.

1.	Apollo and the Muses, . . .	B.B.	G.P.
2.	Hunting Scene, ...	B.B.	G.P.
3.	Hunting Scene, ...	B.B.	G.P.
4.	Hunting Scene, ...		G.P.
5.	Diana preparing for the Chase, .	B B.	P.V.D.BORCHT.
6.	Neptune and Amphitrite, . .	B.B.	P.V.D.BORCHT.
7.	The Forge of Vulcan, . . .	B.B.	P.V.D.BORCHT.

Lent by

THE EARL OF BREADALBANE.

28. ANOTHER PIECE OF FLEMISH TAPESTRY.

Flora and Attendants, . . . B.B. P.V.D.BORCHT.

MESSRS. BONNAR & CARFRAE.

29. THREE SUITS OF ARMOUR—

Fluted Suit, Cap-à-pie, about 1500.

Plain Suit, Cap-à-pie, about 1550.

Pageant Suit, Cap-à-pie, for a boy—richly etched and parcel gilt.

SIR J. NOEL PATON, R.S.A.

30. SUIT OF ARMOUR.

HENRY G. WATSON, ESQ.

31. TROPHY of Target, Basket Hilts, Sporrans, Dirks, and other Highland Weapons.

JAMES DRUMMOND, ESQ., R.S.A.

1. This Target is characterized by more than usual symmetry of design in the Celtic ornamentation upon the leather, and has in addition embossed at its centre a double-headed eagle displayed, the cognizance of the Lord of the Isles. There are three richly engraved flat powder-horns. One of these is especially curious, having on it the monogram of Sir George Mackenzie, with a rude attempt at his portrait,—the costume evidently of the time of Charles I. He is dressed in a flat bonnet and feather, a slashed jerkin and Vandyke frill, with the belted plaid and trews worn at the same time. His attendant gillie, who is blowing a great horn, has no cap on, a skin coat or doublet reaching nearly to the knees, which are bare, and hose. Both sides of this horn are covered with ornament. It may have been the property of Sir G. Mackenzie, afterwards Lord Tarbat and Earl of Cromarty.

2. Two Lochaber axes, one from Killiecrankie, the other from Drumossie Moor.

3. Dirk, the handle richly carved, the back of the blade ornamented by an inlaying of brass engraved with running ornament, surmounted by a crown, and having two mottoes engraved on the blade, one on each side,—'*A Soft ansuer tourneth away wrath;*' the other, '*Thy King and Countries Cause defend though on the spot your Life should end.*'—J. D.

32. TROPHY of Helmets, Swords, Rapiers, Daggers, Cross-bows, Wheel-locks, and other weapons, with an Iron Mask.

Lent by

MR. J. DRUMMOND, R.S.A.

1. The Iron Mask 'has originally been a helmet of the 16th century, the Beavor and Vizor of which (being in one piece) have been riveted to the under or chin part, the side joints have also been unfastened, and the ends filed away, their place being supplied by two rude hinges at the brow, and thus forming a sort of rude box, which is held close by two strong hasps, which may be fixed by a padlock or chain;' thus forming an instrument of torture of the most barbarous nature, with small openings for breathing; certainly, for food, none. (See *Proceedings of the Society of Antiquaries of Scotland*, vol. viii. p. 428.)
2. Frame-work of skull-cap, of steel, for using under velvet or leather cap.
3. Four Cross-Bows, the stock of one of which is carved with much delicacy, and is in other respects complete, having the Windlass and Quarrels. Another, a Chinese one, has a double chamber capable of holding fourteen bolts, two of which are propelled at each discharge.
4. Wheel-lock Fowling-Piece of the 16th century, elaborately inlaid with ivory.
5. A set of Bandoliers, with Primer and Powder-Flask.
6. A Chamfron with Neckpiece, richly engraved.
7. A Dagger, the handle of ivory, quaintly carved with the heads of St. George and the Dragon, the head and paws of the latter surmounting a shield, charged with three Lions passant-gardant, this having been the royal arms of England previous to 1340, at which time Edward III. quartered the French shield, semée-de-Lys, on his Great Seal; on the opposite side, the head of St. George, having his gorget composed of grotesque masks.—J. D.

33. THE BOURBON SHIELD.

MR. WILLIAM MACDONALD.

Of iron, richly engraved, having in the centre an armed knight mounted on a horse, fully caparisoned, and under it 'Le Duc de Bourbon au Tournai.' The shield of arms of the Bourbon Condé branch of the family is engraved below this, and three other coats of arms, one at each angle.

34. THE STOCK AND HORN.

MR. J. DRUMMOND, R.S.A.

He tuned his pipe and reed sae sweet,
  The burds stood listening by;
E'en the dull cattle stood and gazed,
  Charmed wi' his melody.

The Broom o' the Cowdenknowes.

A musical instrument composed of the *stock*, which is the hind thigh-bone of a sheep, or a piece of elder, with stops in the middle; the *horn*, the smaller end of a cow's horn; and an oaten reed.—J. D.

35. BAGPIPES, formerly the Property of Sir Walter Scott, and used by his Piper, John Bruce, called *John of Skye*, in 1818. (See Lockhart's *Life of Scott.*)

Lent by

J. WOLFE MURRAY OF CRINGLETIE, ESQ.

36. SIR WALTER SCOTT'S STUDY CHAIR (from his house, No. 39 North Castle Street, Edinburgh).

THE SOCIETY OF ANTIQUARIES OF SCOTLAND.

37. SIR WALTER SCOTT'S WALKING-STICK, given by him to William Laidlaw, and by William Laidlaw to Dr. Charles Mackay.

CHARLES MACKAY, LL.D.

38. THORN cut by Sir Walter Scott at Abbotsford in 1830, and given by him to John Leycester Adolphus, Esq., Author of *Letters on the Authorship of Waverley.* Lond. 1821.

MRS. ADOLPHUS.

39. TARTAN DRESS in which Sir Walter Scott received His Majesty George IV. at Holyrood, in August 1822.

ALEXANDER NICHOLSON, ESQ.

---

40. CAPTAIN BASIL HALL, R.N. Bust in Marble. Exhibited in London, at the Royal Academy, 1840.

Sculptor.

SIR WILLIAM STIRLING MAXWELL, BART. S. JOSEPH, R.S.A.

CAPTAIN BASIL HALL, R.N., son of Sir James Hall of Dunglas, Bart., was born at Edinburgh, December 31, 1788. His first work, 'Voyage to Corea, 1818,' brought him prominently before the public. He died 11th September 1844. As an intimate friend of Sir Walter Scott, he left a graphic account of the domestic life of the great Novelist in his MS. 'Abbotsford Journal,' from December 29, 1824, to January 10, 1825, published by Mr. Lockhart in the *Life of Sir Walter Scott.* See also the concluding chapter, "Sir Walter Scott's embarkation at Portsmouth in the Autumn of 1831," of Hall's *Fragments of Voyages and Travels*, Third Series, 1833.

41. George Kemp, Architect, a Bust modelled from the life by the late Alexander Handyside Ritchie, A.R.S.A., and carved in marble by John Hutchison, R.S.A., by whom it has been presented to the Trustees of the Scott Monument, to be placed in the Museum there.

Lent by — *Sculptor.*

The Artist. — John Hutchison, R.S.A.

George Meikle Kemp was born at a farm, on the property of Newhall, among the Pentlands, where his father was a shepherd, in the year 1796. At an early age he was sent to learn the trade of a joiner, but had always a predilection for architecture, and missed no occasion of acquiring knowledge in that direction. Working at his trade, he wandered through England, France, and Flanders, making plans and elevations of every noteworthy building that came in his way. Fortunately, in 1837, an opportunity occurred of applying the information thus gained in preparing his successful competition design for the Scott Monument. Kemp had previously exhibited in the Scottish Academy Exhibition, 1830, a drawing of Melrose Abbey; in 1837, another of the interior of Roslin; and in 1839, one of his drawings of the Scott Monument. While superintending the erection of this great work, the life of the Artist was brought to a sudden and most disastrous termination. On his way home to Morningside, on the evening of the 6th of March 1844, after attending a meeting in connexion with the Structure, he missed his road to a canal-bridge, owing to the extreme darkness, fell in, and was drowned.

42. Jeanie Deans. The original Model.

The Artist. — William Brodie, R.S.A.

43. Statuette of Diana Vernon.

The Artist. — George E. Lawson.

44. Dominie Sampson—'Prodigious!'

The Artist. — George E. Lawson.

---

45. A Mask, in Plaster, of Sir Walter Scott's Head, taken after his Death in September 1832. (See Illustrations, No. XXI.)

James R. Hope Scott, Esq.

II.—ORIGINAL PORTRAITS OF SIR WALTER SCOTT, Bart.

Born at Edinburgh, August 15, 1771.
Died at Abbotsford, September 21, 1832.

---

46. Walter Scott. Known as the Bath Miniature, from its having been executed in 1777, while at Bath, in the sixth year of his age. (See Illustrations, No. VII. a.)

Lent by — *Painter.*

David Laing, Esq. — Unknown.

47. Walter Scott, Esq. A Miniature, sent by himself to Miss Carpenter shortly before their marriage in 1797. (See Illustrations, No. VII. b.)

James R. Hope Scott, Esq., Q.C. — Unknown.

48. Walter Scott, Esq., Advocate. Painted in 1805 for Mrs. Scott. (See Illustrations, No. VIII.) 4 ft. × 3 ft. 3 in.

William E. Green, Esq. — James Saxon.

Engraved by James Heath, A.E., for *The Lady of the Lake*, 1810, 4to.

49. Walter Scott, Esq. Painted in 1808 for Mr. Constable. (See Illustrations, No. IX.) 6 ft. × 4 ft. 10 in.

The Duke of Buccleuch, K.G. — Sir Henry Raeburn.

Engraved by C. Turner and Others.

50. Walter Scott, Esq. A Drawing in Water-colours, in 1815. Etched by the Painter in 1817. (See Illustrations, No. X.) Size of head 3½ in.

Mrs. Nicholson. — William Nicholson, R.S.A.

51. Walter Scott, Esq. Another Drawing in Water-colours. The position of the Head somewhat altered, and no objects introduced in the background. Head 3 in.

W. C. C. Erskine, Esq. — William Nicholson, R.S.A.

52. WALTER SCOTT, Esq. Painted in 1818. Study for a Painting of the Discovery of the Scottish Regalia. 1 ft. 10 in. × 1 ft. 5 in.

Lent by | *Painter.*

MISS JAMES, LONDON. | ANDREW GEDDES, A.R.A.

Engraved by F. C. LEWIS.

The occasion when this Portrait was painted was the discovery, on the 4th of February 1818, of the Regalia of Scotland in the Castle, Edinburgh. The search was made by the Officers of State, under a Royal Warrant, dated October 1817.

Drawings were then made by various artists of the ancient Crown, the Sceptre, the Sword of State, etc., to be sent to London to the Prince Regent. At the same time, Mr. Geddes employed himself in making spirited sketches in oil of the chief persons who were present, as studies for an historical painting of this discovery. Sir Walter Scott at that time prepared a *Description of the Regalia*, Edinburgh, 1819. This was reprinted, with Illustrations, in his *Provincial Antiquities*, Vol. i., London, 1826.

ANDREW GEDDES, a native of Edinburgh, born 1788, was one of the early members of the Scottish Academy, and A.R.A. in 1832, having latterly settled in London, where he died, May 5, 1844.

53. WALTER SCOTT, Esq. Painted in 1818, for Mr. Murray of Albemarle Street, London. 3 ft. × 2 ft. 3 in.

JOHN MURRAY, ESQ. | THOMAS PHILLIPS, R.A.

"The costume was, I think, unfortunately selected—a tartan plaid and open collar. This gives a theatrical air to what would otherwise have been a very graceful representation of Scott in the forty-seventh year of his age. Mr. Phillips (for whom Scott had a warm regard, and who often visited him at Abbotsford) has caught a true expression not hit upon by any of his brethren—a smile of gentle enthusiasm. The head has a vivid resemblance to Sir Walter's eldest daughter, and also to his grandson, John Hugh Lockhart.—A duplicate was added by the late Earl Whitworth to the collection at Knowle."—LOCKHART.

Engraved in 1822 by S. W. REYNOLDS and Others.

Mr. PHILLIPS, the eminent portrait painter, was born, October 18, 1770, admitted R.A. in 1808, and died April 20, 1845.

54. WALTER SCOTT, Esq. Painted in 1820 for the Marchioness of Abercorn. (See Illustrations, No. XI.) 3 ft. × 2 ft. 4 in.

LORD NAPIER. | JOHN WATSON (GORDON).

55. SIR WALTER SCOTT, Bart. Painted in 1820 for George IV. (See Illustrations, No. XII.) 5 ft. × 4 ft. 3 in.

HER MAJESTY THE QUEEN. | SIR THOMAS LAWRENCE, *P*.R.A.

Engraved by J. HENRY ROBINSON.

56. Sir Walter Scott, Bart. Painted in 1822. (See Illustrations, No. XIII.) 1 ft. 5 in. × 1 ft. 2 in.

Lent by — *Artist.*

Sir William W. Knighton, Bart. — Sir David Wilkie, R.A.

Engraved by E. Smith.

57. Sir Walter Scott, Bart. Painted in 1822 for Lord Montagu. (See Illustrations, No. XIV.) 2 ft. 6 in. × 2 ft.

The Earl of Home. — Sir Henry Raeburn, R.A.

58. Sir Walter Scott, Bart. Painted in 1824 for Mr. Murray. 1 ft. 3½ in. × 1 ft. ½ in.

John Murray, Esq. — Gilbert Stuart Newton, R.A.

Engraved by W. Finden.

Gilbert Stuart Newton, R.A., was born at Halifax, Nova Scotia, in 1794. He was nephew of Gilbert Stuart, Portrait Painter at Boston, who was best known, by the name of American Stuart, from his full-length portrait of Washington. Newton was admitted R.A. in 1832, and died August 5, 1835.

59. Sir Walter Scott, Bart. 2 ft. 2½ in. × 2 ft.

J. P. Raeburn, Esq. — Sir Henry Raeburn, R.A.

Engraved by William Walker.

60. Sir Walter Scott, Bart. Painted in 1828 for the Lord Chief Commissioner Adam. 2 ft. 6 in. × 2 ft. 1 in.

W. P. Adam, Esq., M.P. — Colvin Smith, R.S.A.

61. Sir Walter Scott, Bart., sitting to James Northcote, R.A. Painted in 1828. 4 ft. 2 in. × 3 ft. 2 in.

Sir William W. Knighton, Bart. — James Northcote, R.A.

This Portrait of Sir Walter Scott was painted for Sir William Knighton, by James Northcote, in 1828. Allan Cunningham, in his Life of the artist, has given an account of its progress (*British Painters*, vol. vi. p. 123). It may be preferable, however, to quote Sir Walter's own words in his Diary, May 9, 1828:—"This day, at the request of Sir William Knighton, I sat to Northcote, who is to introduce himself in the same piece in the act of painting me, like some pictures of the Venetian school. The artist is an old man, low in stature, and bent with years—fourscore at least; but the eye is quick and the countenance noble. A pleasant companion, familiar with recollections of Sir Joshua, Samuel Johnson, Burke, Goldsmith, etc. His account of the last confirms all that we have heard of his oddities." "*May* 11.—Another long sitting to the old wizard Northcote. He really resembles an animated mummy." This picture presents anything but a fortunate likeness.

James Northcote was born in 1745, admitted R.A. in 1786, and died at London, July 23, 1831, aged eighty-six.

62. SIR WALTER SCOTT, Bart. Painted in 1829. (See Illustrations, No. XV.) 2 ft. 6 in. × 2 ft. 1 in.

Lent by — *Painter.*

THE ARTIST. — COLVIN SMITH, R.S.A.

63. SIR WALTER SCOTT, Bart. Painted in 1829 for the Royal Society of Edinburgh. (See Illustrations, No. XVI.)
4 ft. 7 in. × 3 ft. 8 in.

THE COUNCIL OF THE ROYAL SOCIETY. — JOHN GRAHAM (GILBERT), R.S.A.

Engraved by J. THOMPSON.

64. SIR WALTER SCOTT, Bart. Cabinet Portrait. 3 ft. × 2 ft. 4 in.

JOHN BLACKWOOD, ESQ. — SIR WILLIAM ALLAN, *P.*R.S.A., R.A.

Engraved on a small scale by W. FINDEN.

65. SIR WALTER SCOTT, Bart. Study of his Head. (See Illustrations, No. XVII.) 2 ft. 6 in. × 2 ft.

HENRY G. WATSON, ESQ. — SIR JOHN WATSON GORDON, *P.*R.S.A., R.A.

66. THE AUTHOR OF WAVERLEY in his Study. Cabinet Portrait painted in 1831 for Robert Nasmyth, Esq., F.R.C.S.E.
2 ft. 8 in. × 2 ft. 2 in.

THE TRUSTEES OF THE NATIONAL PORTRAIT GALLERY, LONDON. — SIR WILLIAM ALLAN, *P.*R.S.A., R.A.

Engraved by JOHN BURNET.

67. SIR WALTER SCOTT, Bart. Painted in 1830 for Mr. Cadell.
4 ft. 2 in. × 3 ft. 3 in.

THE DOWAGER LADY LISTON FOULIS. — SIR JOHN WATSON GORDON, *P.*R.S.A.

Engraved on a small scale by JOHN HORSBURGH.

68. SIR WALTER SCOTT, Bart. Cabinet Picture painted for Lady Ruthven in 1831. 2 ft. 5 in. × 2 ft.

THE DOWAGER LADY RUTHVEN. — SIR FRANCIS GRANT, *P.*R.A., *H.*R.S.A.

Engraved by THOMAS HODGETTS.

69. SIR WALTER SCOTT in his Study in Castle Street, Edinburgh, writing. Cabinet Portrait. 3 ft. 2 in. × 2 ft. 4 in.

HENRY G. WATSON, ESQ. — SIR JOHN WATSON GORDON, *P.*R.S.A., R.A.

Engraved by R. C. BELL for the Royal Association for the Promotion of the Fine Arts in Scotland.

70. SIR WALTER SCOTT, Bart. 2 ft. 6 in. × 2 ft.

SIR WILLIAM STIRLING MAXWELL, BART. — SIR JOHN WATSON GORDON, *P.*R.S.A., R.A.

71. Sir Walter Scott, Bart. A full length of Scott, in his ordinary walking costume in the country. Painted about 1830.

7 ft. 10 in. × 4 ft. 8 in.

Lent by — *Painter.*

Sir William Stirling Maxwell, Bart. — James Hall.

James Hall, a younger son of Sir James Hall of Dunglass, Bart. He passed Advocate in 1821, but instead of practising at the Bar he devoted himself to Art. He was well known in London as an old student and an occasional Exhibitor in the Royal Academy. He was a particular friend of Wilkie and Geddes, and many of the English artists of the time. He died during a visit to his sister, Lady Russell, at Ashestiel, October 26, 1854, aged 57. This Portrait of Scott is specially alluded to in 1831 by his brother, Captain Basil Hall (*Fragments, etc.*, Third Series, vol. iii. p. 315).

72. Sir Walter Scott, Bart. Painted for Mr. Wells shortly after Sir Walter's death. (See Illustrations, No. XVIII.) 4 ft. 11 in. × 4 ft.

William Wells, Esq., M.P. — Sir Edwin Landseer, R.A., *H.*R.S.A.

73. Sir Walter Scott, Bart. A duplicate of No. 66, with Dog looking the reverse way. Painted in 1835, for the Speculative Society, Edinburgh. 4 ft. 3 in. × 3 ft. 3 in.

The Speculative Society. — Sir John Watson Gordon, *P.*R.S.A.

74. Sir Walter Scott, Bart. A Miniature in Enamel from the Portrait by Sir Thomas Lawrence.

Henry G. Bohn, Esq. — William Essex.

Mr. Essex of H.M. Household, was appointed Enamel Painter in Ordinary. This with Nos. 97 and 107 were in one frame. These three Enamels, then in the possession of Thomas de la Rue, Esq., were in the Exhibition of Portrait Miniatures at the South Kensington Museum, in June 1865.

75. Sir Walter Scott in the character of Peter Paterson. A Drawing in Chalks.

John Blackwood, Esq. — Robert Scott Lauder, R.S.A.

---

76. The Abbotsford Family. Painted for Sir Adam Ferguson in 1817. (See Illustrations, No. XIX.) 1 ft. 3 in. × 11 in.

Mrs. Ferguson. — Sir David Wilkie, R.A.

Engraved by R. Graves, A.R.A., W. Greatbach, and J. Smith.

77. Sir Walter Scott, Bart., his Family and Friends. Painted in 1825 from Miniatures. 4 ft. 8 in. × 3 ft. 2 in.

Lent by — *Artist.*

Mrs. Stewart Watson. — W. Stewart Watson.

William Stewart Watson, son of Captain Andrew Watson, was born in 1800, and educated, like some of his relations, as an artist, although not attaining to the same distinction. He was the nephew of George Watson, President of the Scottish Academy, and cousin-german of Sir John Watson Gordon, R.A., who also filled the chair as President of the R. S. A. Mr. Stewart Watson died at Edinburgh in November 1870.

78. Sir Walter Scott and his Friends at Abbotsford. (See Illustrations, No. XIX.) 5 ft. 3 in. × 3 ft. $9\frac{1}{2}$ in.

Alexander Dennistoun, Esq. — Thomas Faed, R.A., *H.*R.S.A.

79. Gala Day at Abbotsford. Unfinished Sketch in Oil Colour. 1 ft. 3 in. × 11 in.

Robert Horn, Esq. — Sir William Allan, *P.*R.S.A., R.A.

80. Gala Day at Abbotsford. Sketch in Sepia. (See Illustrations, No. XX.) 1 ft. 2 in. × 8 in.

James T. Gibson Craig, Esq. — Sir William Allan, *P.*R.S.A., R.A.

81. A Scene at Abbotsford during the Last Days of Sir Walter Scott. 3 ft. 2 in. × 2 ft. 2 in.

W. Logan White, Esq. — Gourlay Steell, R.S.A.

82. His Majesty George IV. received by the Nobles and People of Scotland, upon his entrance to the Palace of Holyrood House, on the 15th of August 1822. On panel 4 ft. 2 in. × 6 ft.

HER MAJESTY THE QUEEN. — Sir David Wilkie, R.A.

In this grand Painting Sir Walter Scott is introduced as the Historian or Bard. According to Allan Cunningham, it was finished in 1830, at an expense of sixteen hundred guineas.

Engraved by W. Greatbach in the Series of Engravings from the Royal Pictures in *The Art-Journal* for March 1858.

III.—FAMILY PORTRAITS AND SCOTT'S PERSONAL FRIENDS.

---

83. Dr. John Rutherfoord (Maternal Grandfather of Sir Walter Scott).
2 ft. 8½ in. × 2 ft. 3 in.

Lent by — *Artist.*

Dr. Daniel Rutherford Haldane. — C. A., 1756.

Dr. John Rutherford, one of the founders of the Medical School of Edinburgh, was born in 1695. He studied at Leyden, under the celebrated Boerhaave, and took his degree of M.D. at Rheims, July 21, 1719. Having settled in Edinburgh, he was admitted a Member of the Royal College of Physicians in 1724, and elected Professor of the Practice of Physic in the University of Edinburgh, February 9, 1726. He resigned the Chair in 1766, and died November 6, 1776. Sir Walter Scott in his Diary says, "Dr. Rutherford was twice married. His first wife, of whom my mother is the sole surviving child, was a daughter of Sir John Swinton of Swinton, a family which produced many distinguished warriors during the middle ages, and which, for antiquity and honourable alliances, may rank with any in Britain." This is confirmed by the Marriage-Contract of his daughter with Walter Scott, Writer to the Signet, in 1758. In the next Division a facsimile of the signatures will be given.

On examining the portrait, the initials "C. A." joined as a monogram prove that it was painted by Cosmo Alexander, an eminent portrait-painter in Edinburgh.

83*. Portraits of Walter Scott, Writer to the Signet, and of Anne Rutherford, Sir Walter Scott's parents, are at Abbotsford, and have been Engraved. See p. 39.

84. Mrs. Scott, the Mother of Sir Walter Scott. A Miniature.

William MacDonald, Esq. — P. Paillou.

Died December 1819, aged about 80.—When this Miniature, named as above, was recently acquired by the present proprietor, he received a letter in which Mr. Charles Mackintosh Mackay states that it was done "by the celebrated Italian artist Pailleu." That gentleman further adds, "It was painted for the late General Macintosh of Dunchattan (who was a relative of Scott's), and was presented by him to my father some twenty years ago: that is the history of the Painting."

Mr. George Chalmers in 1818 employed "Mr. Pailou, a very ingenious artist," to paint a composition miniature portrait of Mary Queen of Scots, which was engraved for his *Life of Queen Mary.*

85. LIEUT.-COLONEL SIR WALTER SCOTT, Second Baronet of Abbotsford. A full length. Painted from a Miniature.

Lent by — *Artist.*

THE DOWAGER LADY SCOTT OF ABBOTSFORD. — COLVIN SMITH, R.S.A.

WALTER, eldest son of Sir Walter Scott, was born October 28, 1801. He succeeded to the Baronetcy in September 1832. He entered the army, and died Lieut.-Colonel of the 15th Hussars, near the Cape of Good Hope, on his return from India, February 8, 1847. Lady Scott conveyed his remains to this country, and they were interred at Dryburgh.

86. THE BREAKFAST-ROOM AT ABBOTSFORD (September 1832). Figure of Miss Anne Scott, kneeling.

HER MAJESTY THE QUEEN. — SIR WM. ALLAN, *P.*R.S.A., R.A.

87. JOHN GIBSON LOCKHART, Advocate. 2 ft. 6 in. × 2 ft.

JOHN MURRAY, ESQ. — HENRY W. PICKERSGILL, R.A.

Born 1794. Died 1854.

Engraved in Vignette by G. T. DOO, F.R.S.

HENRY WILLIAM PICKERSGILL, R.A., was born in London in 1782; became a student at the Royal Academy in 1805; elected an Associate in 1822; and R.A. in 1826. After the death of Thomas Phillips, R.A., he was much employed in painting full-length portraits.

88. JOHN GIBSON LOCKHART. (See Illustrations, No. XXII.) 12 in. × 10 in.

J. R. HOPE SCOTT, ESQ., Q.C. — SIR FRANCIS GRANT, *P.*R.A., *H.*R.S.A.

Engraved by JAMES FAED.

89. JOHN GIBSON LOCKHART. 3 ft. 4½ in. × 2 ft. 7 in.

JOHN BLACKWOOD, ESQ. — ROBERT SCOTT LAUDER, R.S.A.

Engraved by ROFFE.

90. (SOPHIA SCOTT) MRS. LOCKHART. A Drawing in Water-colours.

J. R. HOPE SCOTT, ESQ., Q.C. — WM. NICHOLSON, R.S.A.

Engraved by G. B. SHAW; as well as the similar Portrait, at Abbotsford, of Miss ANNE SCOTT, also by NICHOLSON. Miss ANNE SCOTT died June 25, 1833; her Sister, MRS. LOCKHART, May 17, 1837.

---

91. JOHN LEYCESTER ADOLPHUS, Barrister-at-Law, Inner Temple. A Drawing in Water-colours. Head 3½ in.

MRS. ADOLPHUS. — W. F. W. (W. F. WITHERINGTON, R.A.?)

Died at London, December 24, 1862, aged 67.

92. JAMES BALLANTYNE, Printer. 1 ft. 2 in. × 1 ft.

Lent by *Artist.*

REV. RAYMOND BLATHWAYT. UNKNOWN.

Born at Kelso, 1772. Died in January 1833.

93. JOHN BALLANTYNE, Bookseller. 2 ft. 1 in. × 2 ft. 5 in.

JOHN BALLANTYNE, ESQ., R.S.A. UNKNOWN.

Born at Kelso, 1774. Died in June 1821.

94. ALEXANDER THOMSON BALLANTYNE, Printer. 2 ft. 5½ in. × 2 ft. 1 in.

ROBERT BALLANTYNE, ESQ. J. BALLANTYNE, R.S.A.

Born at Kelso, 1776. Died 1847.

95. WILLIAM BLACKWOOD, Bookseller and Publisher.

4 ft. 1½ in. × 3 ft. 3½ in.

JOHN BLACKWOOD, ESQ. SIR WILLIAM ALLAN, *P.*R.S.A., R.A.

Born at Edinburgh, 1776. Died 1834.

96. HARRIET, DUCHESS OF BUCCLEUCH, the Early Patroness of Sir Walter Scott. 4 ft. 10 in. × 3 ft. 6½ in.

THOMAS BONNAR, ESQ. WILLIAM BONNAR, R.S.A.

Engraved in mezzotint by THOMAS DICK, and published in 1842 by Alexander Hill, Princes Street, Edinburgh. 2 ft. 1 in. × 1 ft. 6 in.

WILLIAM BONNAR, R.S.A., was born in the year 1800, at Edinburgh, where he died in 1853. He was a painter of scenes in Scottish life, but latterly devoted much of his time to painting portraits, many of which were engraved in mezzotint by his two sons, both promising Artists, now deceased, William and Thomas Bonnar.

97. GEORGE GORDON NOEL, LORD BYRON. Enamel, after Thomas Phillips, R.A.

H. G. BOHN, ESQ. W. ESSEX.

Born 1788. Died 1824.

In one frame with No. 73.

98. ROBERT CADELL, Bookseller and Publisher. 3 ft. × 2 ft. 4 in.

REV. R. H. STEVENSON. SIR JOHN WATSON GORDON, *P.*R.S.A., R.A.

Born in East Lothian, 1788. Died 1849.

99. ARCHIBALD CONSTABLE, Bookseller and Publisher.

4 ft. 1½ × 3 ft. 3½ in.

THOMAS CONSTABLE, ESQ. SIR HENRY RAEBURN, R.A.

Born at Kellie, in Fife, in 1775. Died 1827.

Engraved by G. T. PAYNE in mezzotint, and on a smaller scale in line by THOS. DOBBIE.

100. WILLIAM ERSKINE, Advocate, raised to the Bench, by the title of Lord Kinnedder. A Drawing in Water-colours. Head 3 in.

W. C. C. ERSKINE, ESQ. WILLIAM NICHOLSON, R.S.A.

Born 1770. Died in August 1822.

101. LADY FORBES OF PITSLIGO.

Lent by — *Painter.*

RIGHT HON. LORD CLINTON. — GEORGE SAUNDERS.

This Lady, celebrated in the Life of Sir Walter Scott as *his First Love*, was the daughter of Sir John and Lady Jane Stuart Belsches, Bart., of Invermay. She married Sir William Forbes of Pitsligo in 1797, and died in 1810.

102. JAMES HOGG, 'The Ettrick Shepherd.' 4 ft. 1½ in. × 3 ft. 3½ in.

JOHN BLACKWOOD, ESQ. — SIR JOHN WATSON GORDON, *P.*R.S.A., R.A.

Born 1772. Died 1835.

Engraved by S. HOLLYER.

103. FRANCIS JEFFREY (Lord Jeffrey), Advocate, and a Lord of Session. 3 ft. × 2 ft. 3½ in.

THE ARTIST. — COLVIN SMITH, R.S.A.

Born 1773. Died 1850.

Engraved by WILLIAM WALKER.

104. CHARLES MACKAY, Actor, Edinburgh Theatre. 2 ft. 5 in. × 2 ft.

MRS. MACKAY. — SIR JOHN WATSON GORDON, *P.*R.S.A., R.A.

105. CHARLES MACKAY in the character of Bailie Nicol Jarvie. 2 ft. 6 in. × 1 ft. 1 in.

MRS. GLOVER. — DANIEL MACNEE, R.S.A.

106. HENRY MACKENZIE, Author of *The Man of Feeling*, etc. 4 ft. 1½ in. × 3 ft. 3½ in.

COLVIN SMITH, ESQ. — COLVIN SMITH, R.S.A.

Born at Edinburgh, 1745. Died 1831.

Engraved by J. HORSBURGH.

107. THOMAS MOORE. Enamel, after Sir Thomas Lawrence, *P.*R.A.

H. G. BOHN, ESQ. — W. ESSEX.

Born 1779. Died 1852.

In one frame with No. 73.

108. DANIEL TERRY, Comedian. A Drawing in Water-colours. Head 3 in.

ADAM BLACK, ESQ. — WM. NICHOLSON, R.S.A.

An intimate friend of Sir Walter Scott, who settled in Edinburgh, and became a great attraction in Henry Siddons's Company in 1809. He afterwards removed to London, as joint manager of the Adelphi Theatre, where he died in 1828.

109. THOMAS THOMSON, Advocate, Deputy Clerk-Register. 1 ft. 7 in. × 1 ft. 2½ in.

LOCKHART THOMSON, ESQ. — ROBERT SCOTT LAUDER, R.S.A.

Born at Dailly, in Ayrshire, 1768. Died 1852.

Engraved by GEORGE BAIRD SHAW.

110. PROFESSOR JOHN WILSON. 4 ft. 1¼ in. × 3 ft. 3 in.

Lent by — *Painter.*

JOHN BLACKWOOD, ESQ. — SIR JOHN WATSON GORDON, *P.*R.S.A., R.A.

Born at Paisley, 1785. Died 1854.

Engraved by LUMB STOCKS, A.R.A.

111. PROFESSOR JOHN WILSON. In Crayons.

A. CAMPBELL SWINTON, ESQ. — JAMES SWINTON.

---

112. GEORGE M. KEMP, Architect of the Scott Monument.

1 ft. 1½ in. × 1 ft. 10½ in.

THOMAS BONNAR, ESQ. — WILLIAM BONNAR, R.S.A.

Born 1796. Died 1844.

The three following Nos. were sent for Exhibition, as Scott Portraits, and admitted, although sufficient information was not given to enable the Committee to judge of their authenticity.

113. SIR WALTER SCOTT, as a Boy. A Miniature. Purchased in Italy a few years ago.

JAMES YOUNG, ESQ. — UNKNOWN.

114. WALTER SCOTT in his Boyhood, and his pretty Nurse.

JAMES RENNY, ESQ. — ALEX. NICHOLSON.

A modern fancy picture, and undoubtedly misnamed. It also was erroneously attributed in the Catalogue to William Nicholson, R.S.A.

115. SIR WALTER SCOTT as a Country Lad, with a brown Can in his hand.

ADAM BLACK, ESQ.

Some years ago Messrs. A. & C. Black were persuaded to purchase this as a youthful portrait of Walter Scott. Soon after the opening of the Exhibition it was satisfactorily proved to have been misnamed, and was withdrawn from the Catalogue. It was ascertained, in fact, that it was a fancy picture drawn by JOHN BEUGO, an eminent engraver in Edinburgh, and a member of the Associated Artists. The same figure, in full length, was exhibited in York Place, Edinburgh, in April 1813, with the title, 'No. 74. THE PEASANT BOY, by J. BEUGO.' This painting is still in the possession of Mr. Beugo's daughter, Mrs. Scott, widow of John Scott, Esq., of the Customs, Leith.

THE SCOTT MONUMENT.

It was obviously impossible to obtain for the Loan Exhibition all the Original Busts and Portraits of Scott, so widely dispersed, and, in some cases, the present proprietors unknown. Nor was it thought advisable to swell out the collection, and to incur much trouble and risk, as well as expense, by applying for repetitions or duplicate Portraits by the same Artist.

It may, however, not be saying too much, that the preceding pages include nearly all the best and most authentic Portraitures that are known; and, considering the limited time which the COMMITTEE had for carrying out the objects of the Exhibition, the success far exceeded their expectations, in having so many Paintings and other works of Art of inestimable value intrusted to their care, including works of the most eminent Painters and Sculptors of the time. This was no doubt mainly owing to what may be esteemed a patriotic desire of the proprietors to avail themselves of such a favourable occasion of honouring the memory of our illustrious Countryman.

It may nevertheless be useful to subjoin a few notices of some important Busts and Paintings (exclusive of the repetitions alluded to) that were not actually Exhibited.

I.—SCULPTURE.

MR. LOCKHART in his List of Portraits and Busts of Sir Walter Scott, says, "Sir Walter's good nature induced him to sit, at various periods of his life, to other Sculptors (than Chantrey) of inferior standing and reputation. I am not aware, however, that any of their performances but two (those by JOSEPH and MACDONALD) ever reached the dignity of marble."

(1.) In the Exhibition at the Royal Institution, Edinburgh, in 1821, there was a Bust of Walter Scott, Esq., by WILLIAM SCOULAR, an artist who had a studio both in Edinburgh and London. It was esteemed a good likeness, although described at the time as requiring to be softened down. In the Royal Scottish Academy Exhibition, 1839, No. 502, there was a Statue in marble of Sir Walter, by Scoular.

WILLIAM SCOULAR, a native of Edinburgh, was born in 1796, became a pupil of the Royal Academy, and exhibited talents for the higher department of Sculpture. In 1817 he gained the gold medal; and in 1825 he also was the "Gold Medal Student," to whom the travelling allowance for three years was awarded by the Royal Academy. The models which secured these prizes were afterwards finished in marble and exhibited. He died at London in the year 1854.

(2.) The Bust of Sir Walter Scott by CHANTREY, cast as a trial in Bronze, mentioned at the foot of p. 45, has been presented, in the name of the Family of Mr. Allan Cunningham, by his son, COLONEL FRANCIS CUNNINGHAM, to the Museum of the SCOTT MONUMENT, Edinburgh.

The following is a note by the Sculptor, respecting his original marble Bust, in the volume of Cooper's Letters, in the British Museum:—

"BELGRAVE PLACE, 31*st March* 1830.

"MY DEAR SIR,—In compliance with your request, I have the pleasure to inform you that I modelled the Bust of Sir Walter Scott in the year 1820, and in the year 1828 the original marble Bust was placed in the Library at Abbotsford. I believe it has not been engraved.—Very truly yours, FR. CHANTREY.

"*To* ABM. COOPER, Esq."

A Photograph of the second marble Bust by Chantrey, belonging to Sir Robert Peel, is given as No. II. of the Illustrations, p. 47.

(3.) The Statue in freestone by JOHN GREENSHIELDS, 1830, described by Mr. Lockhart, is now in the Under Library of the Faculty of Advocates. See No. XXI. of the Illustrations, p. 85.

(4.) A posthumous Bust of Sir Walter Scott by HENRY WESTMACOTT, Sculptor, at that time a resident in Edinburgh, was in the Scottish Academy's Exhibition of 1833, No. 320. The same Bust in marble was in the Exhibition of 1836, No. 333. Also, No. 343, "A Model of a Cenotaph, to be executed in American granite, and surmounted by a Bust in marble, in memory of the Bard of Abbotsford, to be erected by Subscription at New York, United States, H. WESTMACOTT, H."

(5.) SIR WILLIAM ALLAN, President, exhibited at the Scottish Academy, 1838, No. 426, a "Modelled Sketch of Sir Walter Scott and his Dog."

(6.) A Medallion Head of Sir Walter Scott, with bare neck, and tartan plaid round his shoulders, in bronze, by DAVID CRAWFORD. See No. 225. This Artist, formerly Seal Engraver in Edinburgh, and now living in Glasgow, had the advantage of a sitting from Scott in preparing his Medal, in the possession of Mr. J. DRUMMOND, R.S.A.

(7.) In the Exhibition of the Royal Scottish Academy, 1839, No. 503, was a "Head of the Statue of Sir Walter Scott in the Monument at Glasgow, by James Ritchie." The Scott Monument, designed by David Rhind, Architect, and erected in the centre of George Square, Glasgow, is a lofty pillar in the form of a Grecian Doric Column, about eighty feet in height, with a colossal figure on the top, of Sir Walter, in a shepherd's cloak. The figure was modelled by JOHN RITCHIE (brother of A. H. R.), a Sculptor of considerable promise, who died at Rome, December 1, 1850.

(8.) In the Exhibition of the Royal Scottish Academy, 1843, No. 592, was a "Model of the Statue of Sir Walter Scott in Sheriff's robes, executed in freestone, and erected in the Market Place of Selkirk," by ALEXANDER HANDYSIDE RITCHIE. See page 88.

II.—PORTRAITS.

(1.) WALTER SCOTT, Esq. A full-length by RAEBURN, painted in 1809. It is a repetition, with some variations, of that of 1808. See Illustrations, No. IX. The Committee to their regret found that this Painting, with some others, preserved at ABBOTSFORD, could not with any propriety have been removed from the walls at a season when the House and its Collections were accessible to visitors from all quarters of the globe.

The Abbotsford Portrait by RAEBURN (5 ft. 11 in. x 4 ft. 10 in.), represents Sir Walter Scott, with his hat off, sitting on a piece of broken rock. There are two dogs with him, one of which is looking up into his face, and almost leans on his right shoulder, the other, a bull terrier, is lying on the ground near his left foot. He holds a red note-book in his left hand, and a pencil in his right. At the background of the figure are trees, and in the distance a winding stream. He is dressed in a green coat, grey pantaloons, and Hessian boots, a white waistcoat and cravat; no shirt-collar is shown. He is leaning forward, and is in deep thought. The chin rather leans into the cravat, and the mouth slightly compressed.

The background of the Painting, as described by Mr. Lockhart (see p. 61), represents the Valley of the Yarrow, in place of Hermitage Castle, and the mountains of Liddesdale.

Sir Henry Raeburn, the distinguished Portrait-Painter, was born at Stockbridge, near Edinburgh, March 4, 1756. He was elected an Associate in 1814, and a Royal Academician in 1815. During George the Fourth's visit to Edinburgh he obtained the honour of knighthood, and was appointed His Majesty's Limner for Scotland. He died July 8, 1823.

(2.) On applying to Lord Polwarth for an account of Scott's portrait by Thomas Phillips, R.A., at Mertoun House, Berwickshire, it appears from his Lordship's obliging reply, that it was a second repetition of Mr. Murray's portrait, 1818 (exhibited as No. 53), probably by the younger (Henry) Phillips. His Lordship would have lent it for the Scott Exhibition, had he thought it an original. There are in Mertoun House several Family Portraits by the elder (Thomas) Phillips, R.A.

(3.) The Illustration No. XXIV. is accompanied with a detailed account of the half-length Portrait painted by C. R. Leslie, R.A., in 1824, for Mr. Ticknor of Boston, New England.

(4.) "A small head was painted in 1826 by Mr. Knight, a young artist, patronized by Terry. This juvenile production, ill-drawn and feeble in expression, was engraved for Mr. Lodge's great work."—Lockhart.—An interesting letter from the Artist himself, relating to this Portrait, will be found at page 199 of the present Volume.

IV.—ENGRAVED PORTRAITS, BUSTS, ETC., OF SIR WALTER SCOTT.

WITH a few exceptions, as specified in the List of Contributors, this series of Engraved Portraits was the joint contribution of Sir WILLIAM STIRLING MAXWELL, Bart., and JAMES DRUMMOND, Esq., R.S.A. The following Catalogue was prepared by Mr. Drummond.

In describing these Prints, the position of the head is noted thus:—If the head is towards the right side, *i.e.* the right side of the person portrayed, it is marked *r.*; if left, *l.* full or front-face, *f.f.*; *s. r.* or *s. l.*, simply that it is somewhat or slightly turned to *r.* or *l.*

The measurements given are in inches to the size of the picture or engraved part; it so frequently happens that the inscription is cut or torn away, particularly in old and scarce prints, that this is considered the safer mode. In those which are vignetted, if more than the head is given, they are so described, but only the size of the head given.

116. WALTER SCOTT, 1777. Ætat. 6. Engraved by J. Horsburgh from an Original Miniature. Edinburgh: Published by Robert Cadell; London: John Murray, and Whittaker & Co. 1839.

In a frame, 3 in. × 2⅝ in., *r.*

(1.) Prefixed as the Engraved Title of *Life of Sir Walter Scott, Bart.*, second edition, vol. i., 1839; and (2.) in 1871, post 8vo.

117. WALTER SCOTT, Esq. Saxon, *pinxt.*; Heath, *sculpt.* Published by Ballantyne & Co., Edinburgh; and Longman, Hurst, Rees, & Orme, London. March 1, 1810.

r., 8¼ in. × 6½ in.

Engraved for *The Lady of the Lake*; Edinburgh, 1810, 4to.

JAMES HEATH, an eminent engraver, was born in 1765, admitted to the class of Associate Engravers in the Royal Academy, London, in 1791. He died in 1835.

118. WALTER SCOTT, Esq. Engraved by Charles Turner from the Original Picture by Raeburn, in the possession of Archibald Constable. Published 1810.

A proof impression having the Harp mark. Lent by MR. GIBSON CRAIG. Mezzotint. Full length, seated, *s.r*, 18 in. × 12½ in.

CHARLES TURNER, born in 1773, was admitted an Associate of the Royal Academy, London, in 1828. He died in 1857.

119. Sir Walter Scott, Bart. Painted by Sir H. Raeburn, R.A. Engraved by R. Cooper. Published by A. Constable & Co., Edinburgh; Longman, Hurst, & Co., J. Murray, and Hurst, Robinson, & Co., London.

Full figure, seated. Line and stipple, *s.r.*, $3\frac{5}{8}$ in. × $2\frac{7}{8}$ in.

120. Sir Walter Scott, Bart. Sir Henry Raeburn, 1808. Horsburgh. Engraved for *Life of Scott*, 1837, Abbotsford Edition, Poetry, and People's Edition of Novels.

121. Sir Walter Scott. 1808. Painted by Sir H. Raeburn. Engraved by J. Horsburgh for *The Life of Sir Walter Scott, Bart.*, Second Edition, vol. iv. Edinburgh: Published by Robert Cadell; and Whittaker & Co., London. 1839.

s. r., $4\frac{1}{8}$ in. × $3\frac{1}{4}$ in.—John Horsburgh, an excellent line engraver, and much respected, died in Edinburgh, September 25, 1869, aged 79.

122. Walter Scott, Esq. Engraved by Colin Campbell, Edinburgh, 1817.

Full figure, seated. This is Raeburn's Picture reversed (No. 113), with the dog left out, and in its place a large Scots thistle and Sir Walter's hat. At his foot a pen and inkholder. Line, *s. l.*, $4\frac{1}{2}$ in. × $3\frac{1}{2}$ in.

123. Walter Scott, Esq. From an Original Picture by H. Raeburn, Esq., in the possession of Mr. Constable of Edinburgh. Drawn by W. Evans, Engraved by C. Picart. Published December 21, 1811, by T. Cadell & W. Davis, Strand, London.

Vignette, with hands introduced. Stipple, *s. r.*, $2\frac{1}{2}$ in.

In *The British Gallery of Contemporary Portraits* (1809-1822), Vol. ii.; London, 1822, folio.

This and the following fourteen are either head sizes or vignetted, and are all taken from Raeburn's Portrait, No. 113.

124. Walter Scott, Esq. Engraved for the *New Monthly Magazine* by Henry Meyer. Published November 1, 1818, by Henry Colburn, Conduit Street.

Head size. Vignette, with border. Stipple, *s. r.*, $5\frac{1}{4}$ in. × $4\frac{1}{2}$ in.

125. Walter Scott, Esq. Raeburn, *pinxit.* C. Heath, *sculpsit.* Published January 1, 1820, by Archibald Constable & Co., Edinburgh; and Longman, Hurst, Rees, Orme, & Brown, London.

Head size. Stipple, *s. r.*, $3\frac{1}{2}$ in. × 3 in.

126. Sir Walter Scott, Bart. Raeburn, *pinxit.* W. T. Fry, *sculpsit.* Published January 1, 1821, by Archibald Constable & Co., Edinburgh; and Longman, Rees, Orme, & Brown, London.

Head size. Stipple, *s. r.*, $3\frac{1}{2}$ in. × $2\frac{3}{4}$ in.

127. Sir Walter Scott, Bart. Roffe, *sculpt.* Published by J. Limbird, 143 Strand.

Vignette, in stipple. *s. r.*, 1⅝ in.

128. Sir Walter Scott, Bart. Engraved by Holl from an Original Drawing.

Vignette, with fur collar. Stipple, *s. l.*, 1¾ in.

129. Sir Walter Scott, Bart. J. R. West, *sculpt.*

Vignette, hands introduced, *s. r.*, 2 in.

130. Mr. Scott. W. & D. Lizars, *sculpt.* Vignette. Engraved for *Peter's Letters to his Kinsfolk*, vol. ii. Printed for William Blackwood, Edinburgh; T. Cadell & W. Davis, London; John Smith & Son, Glasgow. 1819.

s. r., 1¾ in.

131. Sir Walter Scott, Bart.

Vignette, hand with book. Stipple, *s. r.*, 1¼ in.

132. Sir Walter Scott, Bart. No Engraver's name.

Head size. Line, *s. r.*, 2¾ in. × 2½ in.

133. Walter Scott. No Engraver's name.

Vignette. Stipple, *s. l.*, 1¾ in.

134. Sir Walter Scott. No Engraver's name.

Vignette. Line, *s. l.*, 2 in.

135. Sir Walter Scott, Bart.

In a small oval frame, introduced as an ornament on a harp. Line, *s. r.*, ⅞ in.

136. Sir Walter Scott.

Outline, head size, *s. r.*, 1¾ in.

137. Sir Walter Scott.

Head size, slightly shaded, *s. r.*, 1⅝ in.

138. Walter Scott, Esq. No. 4 in a set of Twelve Portraits of Advocates "who plead without Wigs." I. Kay, 1811.

These Medallion Portraits are engraved on one plate. In the collected Edition of the *Edinburgh Portraits*, by John Kay (b. 1742, d. 1830), published at Edinburgh, by Hugh Paton, 1839, this plate forms No. CLVI., and is a companion to No. CL., of Twelve Advocates "who plead with Wigs on."

139. Walter Scott. W. N., *ft.* 1817. An etching by William Nicholson, R.S.A. (The copy exhibited, lent by Mr. J. T. Rose, had the Autograph of Sir Walter Scott, and the words, "I beg your acceptance of a specimen of Edinburgh art, which I hope you will like.")

Vignette, hand resting on stick, and dog looking up in his master's face. Highland armour on wall. *s. l.*, 2⅛ in.

140. Sir Walter Scott, Bart., *P.*R.S.E. Engraved by J. Thomson from an Original Picture.

Vignette. Stipple, from Nicholson's portrait, *s. l.*, 1⅝ in.

141. The Abbotsford Family. Painted by Sir David Wilkie, R.A. Engraved by Robert Graves, A.R.A.

This print, published as a separate plate, contains a group of eight figures, which was painted in 1817 for Sir Adam Ferguson. 15 in. × 11½ in.

142. Sir Walter Scott and his Family. Painted by Sir David Wilkie R.A. Engraved by W. Greatbach. London: Published in the *Art Journal* and in the *Wilkie Gallery*, for the Proprietors, by George Virtue, 28 Ivy Lane.

8 in. × 6½ in.

143. The Abbotsford Family. Sir David Wilkie, R.A. John Smith.

5 in. × 3⅞ in. Vol. xii. Abbotsford Edition, and xxv. Library Edition.

144. Sir Walter Scott and his Family. A Photograph, in a volume of *The Great Works of Sir David Wilkie.* Twenty-six Photographs, etc. London. 1868. 4to.

145. Sir Walter Scott, Bart. T. Phillips, R.A. S. W. Reynolds. Published by T. Phillips, R.A., 1822.

Mezzotint, *r.*, 3⅞ in. × 3 in.

This picture was painted in 1818, and represents Sir Walter in a plaid, with a Highland bonnet in his hand.

146. Sir Walter Scott, Bart. Published November 1, 1820, by T. Boys, 1 Ludgate Hill. Engraved with permission of John Murray, Esq., from a Painting by T. Phillips, Esq., R.A., by W. T. Fry.

In a richly-designed octagonal frame. Stipple, *r.*, 4 in. × 2½ in.

147. Sir Walter Scott. R. Cooper, *sculp^t^.* Published by W. Crawford, jun., 124 Cheapside.

In an ornamental frame. Stipple, *r.*, 4¼ in. × 3¼ in. This is from Phillips's portrait, with the dress altered.

148. Sir Walter Scott, Bart. London: William Darton, 58 Holborn Hill. 1822.

After T. Phillips. Stipple, vignette, *r.*, 1⅛ in.

149. Walter Scott, Esq. From a stolen Sketch by T. Arrowsmith.

Vignette. Line and stipple, *l.*, 2¾ in. In the act of writing; Advocate's gown on.

150. Walter Scott. A. Geddes, *del^t^.* F. O. Lewis, *sculp^t^.* London: Published by Carpenter & Son, Old Bond Street. 1824.

Vignette. Stipple, in imitation of pencil drawing, *s. r.*, 3 in. Autograph in facsimile.

151. WALTER SCOTT. The Portrait Engraved by Woolnoth and the Emblematical Design by Hawksworth. Published by Sherwood, Gilbert, & Piper, Paternoster Row, November 12, 1825.

In a richly-designed Gothic frame, with designs from his Poems, and a profusion of other ornament. The Portrait after Geddes, *s. r.*, 1 in. Prefixed as a frontispiece to *The Spirit of the Public Journals*, for the year 1825, small 8vo, with a printed description, pp. v.-vii.

152. SIR WALTER SCOTT, Bart. Knight & Lacey, London. 1828.

In a frame. Vignetted. Stipple. After Geddes, *s. r.*, 1 in.

153. SIR WALTER SCOTT, Bart. W. Read, *sc.*

In a frame. The head after Geddes, but looking up; one of the hands is also introduced, holding a book. Stipple, *s. r.*, ⅞ in.

154. SIR WALTER SCOTT, Bart. In the *Leisure Hour* for July 1871.

Profile. Woodcut, from a Sketch by Robert Scott Moncrieff, Advocate, taken in the Parliament House, between 1816 and 1820.

A Photograph from this sketch is given as No. XII. in the volume recently published, *The Scottish Bar Fifty Years Ago: Sketches of Scott and his Contemporaries.* By the late Robert Scott Moncrieff, Esq., Advocate. With Biographical Notices by G. B. [George Burnett.] Edinburgh, 1871. Royal 4to.

155. SIR WALTER SCOTT, Bart. From an Original Sketch by Mr. Slater, in the possession of Sir Robert Henry Inglis, Bart. Engraved by R. W. Sievier. London: Published August 10, 1821, by J. Slater, No. 70 Newman Street; and by Messrs. Longman & Co., Paternoster Row.

Vignette. Stipple, *r.*, 3 in.

156. SIR WALTER SCOTT, Bart. From the Original Picture in His Majesty's Gallery, Windsor Castle. Painted by Sir Thomas Lawrence, *P.*R.A. Engraved by John Henry Robinson.

Half-length, seated; port-crayon in right hand, left elbow resting on arm of chair; table with MSS., on which is written *Lay of the Last Minstrel*, *Waverley*, *s. l.*, 11¾ in. × 9¾ in.

157. SIR WALTER SCOTT, Bart. Sir Thomas Lawrence, *P.*R.A. William Humphrey. London: Published January 1, 1844, by H. Graves & Co., Printsellers to Her Majesty, 6 Pall Mall.

From the same Picture. Mezzotint, *s. l.*, 7½ in. × 6 in.

158. SIR WALTER SCOTT, Bart. From the Picture in the Royal Collection. Sir T. Lawrence, *pinx*t. J. Horsburgh, *sculp*t. London: James S. Virtue.

Engraved for the *Art Journal*, vol. iv., 1858; *s. l.*, 10 in. × 8¼ in.

159. SIR WALTER SCOTT, Bart. Copy of Robinson's Print (No. 156), but neither Painter's nor Engraver's name given.

s. l., 4 in. × $3\frac{1}{4}$ in.

160. WALTER SCOTT. Laurens, *pinxt.* Belnos, *del.* Publié à Paris, par Vor. Morlot, 2 Rue de Louvois. New York: Published by Bailly, Ward, & Co.

A copy of Robinson's Portrait in lithography, done in reverse, but of the same size.

161. SIR WALTER SCOTT, Bart. Engraved by J. Thomson from a Drawing by J. Partridge. Published February 18, 1823, by J. Robins & Co., Ivy Lane, Paternoster Row, London.

Vignette. Stipple. Head looking up, *s. l.*, $1\frac{5}{8}$ in.

162. SIR WALTER SCOTT, Bart. Engraved by William Walker from a Picture by Sir Henry Raeburn, R.A. Dedicated, by permission, to the King, by His Majesty's most dutiful subject and servant, William Walker. Published 1st October 1826, by W. Walker, 3 Great King Street, Edinburgh; and 18 Norton Street, Portland Road, London; Deposà à la Bibliothèque, et se vend à Paris, chez Shroth, Rue de la Paix, No. 18.

This is engraved in a composite style of line and stipple, and is a powerful and effective Print. From the Picture in the possession of the Raeburn family at Charlesfield, Mid-Calder, *s. r.*, 11 in. × $9\frac{3}{4}$ in.

163. SIR WALTER SCOTT, Bart. Painted by Sir Henry Raeburn. Engraved by E. Mitchell. From an Original Picture by Sir Henry Raeburn. Dedicated, with permission, to His Most Gracious Majesty William the Fourth by His Majesty's most obliged and very humble servant, Edward Mitchell.

In a frame border. Line. From Raeburn's Portrait, as above, at Charlesfield, *s. r.*, $12\frac{1}{4}$ in. × $10\frac{1}{4}$ in.

164. WALTER SCOTT. Mauraisse, *ft.* 1826. Lith. de C. Motte.

From Raeburn's Portrait, but reversed, and having a plaid over shoulder. Vignette in Lithography, *s. l.*, $3\frac{3}{4}$ in.

165. SIR WALTER SCOTT. From a Picture by Sir Henry Raeburn.

Woodcut. Engraved for *The Graphic*, August 15, 1871, *s. r.*, $10\frac{1}{2}$ in. × $8\frac{3}{4}$ in.

166. SIR WALTER SCOTT, Bart. W. H. Weisse, *fect.* Lith. Est. of Fr. Schenck, Edinburgh.

A Lithograph, reversed from Raeburn's Portrait. Vignette, *s. l.*, $3\frac{3}{4}$ in.

167. SIR WALTER SCOTT, Bart. Branston & Wright, *sculpt.* Woodcut. "Yours truly, W. SCOTT," in facsimile.

Vignette. Plaid over shoulders, head reversed, *s. l.*, $2\frac{1}{2}$ in.

168. SIR WALTER SCOTT.

Small oval. Head reversed as in the above, *s. l.*, 1½ in.

169. SIR WALTER SCOTT, Bart. Painted by D. Wilkie, R.A. Engraved by Edward Smith. London: Published June 1, 1831, by Moon, Boys, & Graves, Printsellers to the King, 6 Pall Mall.

From the Picture painted in 1824. Cloak with fur collar, and book in hand. Line, *l.*, 9½ in. × 7⅝ in.

170. SIR WALTER SCOTT, Bart. D. Wilkie, R.A. E. Smith.

Same as above, *l.*, 3¾ in. × 2¾ in.

171. SIR WALTER SCOTT, Bart. Painted by G. S. Newton, R.A. Engraved by W. Finden. From the Original Picture painted for Mr. Murray in 1824. London: Black & Armstrong. Facsimile of handwriting, "Very truly yours, WALTER SCOTT. Abbotsford, 3 Sept. 1824."

Vignette. Stipple, *l.*, 1¾ in.

172. SIR WALTER SCOTT. G. S. Newton, R.A. J. B. Bird. Facsimile of Autograph. A. Fullarton & Co., London and Edinburgh.

Engraved for *The Scottish Nation*, a Biographical History of the People of Scotland, by William Anderson. Vol. III. 1863, royal 8vo. Vignette, *l.*, 1¾ in.

173. SIR WALTER SCOTT. B. Holl. Presented gratis on Friday, March 1, 1833, to the purchasers of No. 1 of *The Critic: a New Liberal, Impartial, and Independent Review of Books, the Drama, and the Fine Arts.* Published at the Penny National Library Office, 369 Strand.

This is Newton's Portrait, with slight alterations, *l.*, 1⅝ in.

174. SIR WALTER SCOTT. Painted by C. R. Leslie, R.A. Engraved by M. J. Danforth. Published by Longman, Rees, Orme, Brown, & Green. 1829.

Line, *s. r.*, 3⅞ in. × 3 in.

175. SIR WALTER SCOTT, Bart. Painted by C. R. Leslie, R.A. Engraved by G. H. Phillips. From the Original Picture by Mr. Leslie, formerly in the possession of Mr. Constable of Edinburgh, and now in the Collection of Alaric A. Watts, Esq. Published by Charles Tilt, 86 Fleet Street, September 1833. The same Engraving afterwards had the imprint of another publisher—London: Published February 17th, 1864, by W. Tegg, Pancras Lane.

This Portrait was painted in 1824. It is half-length, sitting; hand resting on stick: coat of arms in the background. Mezzotint, *s. r.*, 13 in. × 10 in.

176. Sir Walter Scott, Bart. Engraved by W. Read. Published by Thomas Ireland, jun., 57 South Bridge Street, Edinburgh.

After Leslie's Portrait, the background altered, *s. r.*, 4 in. × $3\frac{1}{8}$ in.
In the *Life of Scott*, by George Allan. Edinburgh, 1834. 8vo.

177. Sir Walter Scott, Bart. Neither engraver nor publisher's name.

A poor copy. Danforth's Print, after Leslie.

178. Sir Walter Scott, Bart.

Head, in oval frame, surmounted by coat of arms, below view of Abbotsford, in a frame; the whole surrounded by an ornamental border. Lithograph, *s. r.*, 2 in. After Leslie.

179. Sir Walter Scott, Bart. One of a Series of Members of the Scottish Bench and Bar. Engraved by T. Gaugain after B. W. Crombie. Published by A. Constable & Co., Edinburgh; and Hurst, Robinson, & Co., London. 1825.

Profile, $1\frac{1}{8}$ in. The same heads, with the Key, 'Etched by Benj. W. Crombie.'

180. Sir Walter Scott, Bart. From the Original, painted by Knight, in the possession of Mr. Harding. Engraved by H. T. Ryall. London: Published June 1, 1833, by Harding & Lepard, Pall Mall, East.

r., $4\frac{7}{8}$ in. × $3\frac{7}{8}$ in.
In the original edition of Lodge's Portraits, vol. iv. London, 1833. Folio.

181. Sir Walter Scott, Bart. Ob. 1832. From the Original, by J. P. Knight, Esq., in the possession of Mr. Harding. Engraved by H. T. Ryall.

In an ornamental frame, with pen in hand, *r.*, $7\frac{1}{4}$ in. × 6 in.
The same Engraving prefixed to the *History of Scotland*, by Thomas Wright, vol. iii.

182. Sir Walter Scott, Bart. Ob. 1832. Knight, *pinx.*

In the small edition of Lodge, by H. G. Bohn. Vol. viii. 1850. 12mo.

183. Sir Walter Scott, Bart. Lithographed by Richard Lane, A.R.A., from a Picture by J. P. Knight.

184. Sir Walter Scott, Bart. Painted by J. Graham, Esq. (J. Graham Gilbert, R.S.A.) Engraved by J. Thomson. Fisher & Son, London. 1832. With Autograph.

Engraved for *The National Portrait Gallery*, vol. iii., *l.*, $4\frac{1}{2}$ in. × $3\frac{1}{2}$ in.

185. Sir Walter Scott, Bart. Gatti. Napoli, R. Lithografia Militare. 1829.

An exaggerated portrait in lithography, with a wide flowing collar, and a plaid broached over the shoulders.

186. Sir Walter Scott, Bart. John Watson Gordon, 1830. John Horsburgh. Published 1831, by Robert Cadell, and Moon, Boys, & Graves, London.

Half-length, sitting, and resting both hands on his walking-stick. The Eildon Hills in the background, his dog Maida by his side. *f.f.* 4 in. × 3⅛ in.

In Vol. 33 of the 48 vol. Edition, and Vol. i. of the Centenary Edition.

187. Sir Walter Scott, Bart. T. Crawford, 1838.

f.f. 3½ in. × 2½ in.

188. Sir Walter Scott, Bart. Head and shoulders, taken from Watson Gordon's (No. 66).

Vignetted. Stipple, *f.f.*, 1⅜ in.

189. Sir Walter Scott, Bart. Head in oval. Also after No. 66.

f.f. 2 in.

190. Sir Walter Scott. Sir John Watson Gordon. H. Robinson. From the original in the possession of the Publishers. Blackie & Sons, London, Edinburgh, and Glasgow.

Vignette. Stipple, *r.*, 1½ in. This is from a different Portrait than the above, and was engraved for Robert Chambers's *Lives of Eminent Scotsmen.* 1837. 8vo.

191. The Author of Waverley. B. W. Crombie, *ft.* London, 1831. Published by R. Ackermann, 96 Strand.

A full-length, walking by a burn. A coloured lithograph in profile.

192. The Author of Waverley in his Study. W. Allan, A.R.A., *pinxt.* E. Goodall, *sculpt.*

Sitting by a window writing. 4¼ × 3¼ in.

193. The Author of Waverley. Published by J. Fraser, 215 Regent Street, London. Engelmann, Graf, Coindet, & Co. Lithog., 14 Newman Street. Autograph in facsimile, "Yours truly, Walter Scott." (From a Sketch made at Cork, in August 1825, by Daniel Maclise, R.A.)

Full-length figure, walking with his Lowland bonnet in his hand, dressed in his green shooting-jacket, accompanied by two dogs. Outline. This forms No. VI. of "The Gallery of Illustrious Literary Characters," in *Fraser's Magazine*, November 1830, p. 412.

194. Sir Walter Scott, Bart., in his Study at Abbotsford. Painted by William Allan, R.A. Engraved by John Burnet.

Engraved from the original Picture in the possession of R. Nasmyth, Esq., F.R.C.S., and most respectfully dedicated to His Grace the Duke of Buccleuch, by his obliged servant, William Allan. The impression exhibited, lent by Mr. Laing, was one of a few thrown off with the owner's name spelled Naysmith.

Sir Walter is represented sitting reading a Royal Proclamation, his dog Maida at his feet. 17 in. × 13¼ in.

John Burnet, the engraver of this plate, was a man of various accomplishments. He was a painter of no mean power, many of his pictures being engraved. The principal of these being Greenwich Pensioners, painted and engraved by him as a companion to Wilkie's Chelsea Pensioners, of which he was also the engraver. He likewise engraved the Reading of the Will, and others of Wilkie's principal works. He was the author of *Practical Hints on Painting*, and other works on Art, all now standard works in their department. He was born at Musselburgh in 1781, and died at London in 1868.

195. Etching by Sir William Allan of the above Picture. No name or inscription.

4¼ in. × 3¼ in.

196. Sir Walter Scott, Bart. Painted in his Study at Abbotsford in 1831, whilst dictating his last novel, *Count Robert of Paris*. This Print is respectfully dedicated by permission to Sir Walter's friend, The Lady Ruthven (for whom the original Picture was painted), by her Ladyship's most obedient humble servants, Colnaghi & Co. Painted by F. Grant, Esq. Engraved by Thomas Hodgetts. London, Oct. 1835. Published by Colnaghi & Co., Printsellers in Ordinary to His Majesty, and to H.R.H. the Duchess of Kent, No. 23 Cockspur Street, Charing Cross.

17¼ in. × 13½ in.

In this Picture Sir Walter is sitting with an open book on his knee, which he is holding with left hand, while his other, which he rests upon a table, is holding a pen. Two dogs are his companions.

197. Sir Walter Scott in his Study, 39 Castle Street. Painted by Sir John Watson Gordon, P.R.S.A., R.A. Engraved by Robert C. Bell. This was engraved for the Royal Association for the Promotion of the Fine Arts in Scotland.

Line, *l.*, 9½ in. × 7½ in.

198. Sir Walter Scott, Bart. Drawn and engraved by R. M. Hodgetts. London: Published by Martin Colnaghi, and William Swinton, Edinburgh.

Mezzotint, *s.r.*, 9¼ in. × 7½ in. Half-length seated, resting both hands on his walking-stick.

299. Sir Walter Scott, Bart. Published by A. Hutton, from a Picture painted by Mr. Henry and engraved by R. Hodgetts, jun.

Mezzotint, *l.* 13½ in. × 10½ in. Seated and resting his head upon his right hand, a dog looking up in his face.

200. Walter Scott. Naples, 16th April 1832. Vin. Morani, *fecit.* nel 1832. Lit., A. Ledoux.

Upper part of body, reading a book, which is resting upon another, entitled *Codice dei Longobardi.* Surrounded by a cloud. Lithograph, *r.* 2 in.

201. Walter Scott. Proto e Masta, P. Napoli, Lita Fergola, e De Falco, 1832.

Head and hand, cloak over shoulders. Lithograph. Vignette, *r.* 4 in.

202. Walter Scott. Hayez del. Milano, Litog. Vassalli.

Evidently a copy from the above, same size, but reversed.

203. Sir Walter Scott's Armoury at Abbotsford. From a Painting by Lieut.-Col. Henry Stisted. Pr. by Graf & Soret, 14 Newman Street. Published by R. Ackermann, 96 Strand, London.

Sir Walter is sitting at a table by the window, reading. Lithograph. 10¼ in. × 7¾ in.

204. Sir Walter Scott, Bart. Head in outline. Woodcut, profile. After G. S. Newton, R.A.

1¾ in. Used for the Prospectus of the Waverley Novels, Library Edition.

205. Sir Walter Scott, Bart. A composition made up of various Portraits of Sir Walter, placed against the front of a book-case. His favourite deerhounds lying in front of it. 1. Miniature, 1777; 2. Sir W. Allan, 1831; 3. Chantrey's Bust, 1820; 4. Sir J. W. Gordon, 1830. Drawn by H. Corbould. Engraved by W. Finden. R. Cadell, Edinburgh.

Frontispiece Library Edition and Vol. II. Abbotsford Waverley.

206. Sir Edwin Landseer's Studio.

An engraving in Mezzotint. A dog of a small breed lying on a table, beside it some game and modelling tools. In the background a bust of Sir Walter Scott.

207. The Author of Waverley. A Portrait, the head covered with a curtain, within the frame. Engraved by A. Wilson, Edinburgh. Prefixed to *Illustrations of the Author of Waverley.* By Robert Chambers. Second Edition, Edinburgh, 1825. John Anderson, Jun. 12mo.

The First Edition has a head called Rob Roy.

Family of Sir Walter Scott, Bart. Engraved for Lockhart's *Memoirs of the Life of Sir Walter Scott, Bart.* Ten Vols. Second edition. Robert Cadell, Edinburgh; John Murray, and Whittaker & Co., London. 1839. 12mo.

208. Walter Scott, surnamed Beardie, Great-Grandfather of Sir Walter Scott. Engraved by G. B. Shaw from the Original at Abbotsford.

209. Walter Scott, Writer to the Signet, Father of Sir Walter Scott. Engraved by G. B. Shaw, from a Picture at Abbotsford.

210. Anne Rutherford, Mother of Sir Walter Scott. Engraved by G. B. Shaw, from a Picture at Abbotsford.

211. Lady Scott. Saxon, *pinxit.* G. B. Shaw, *sculp.*

212. Mrs. J. G. Lockhart, Eldest Daughter of Sir Walter Scott. Engraved by G. B. Shaw. Painted by Nicholson.

213. Anne Scott, Second Daughter of Sir Walter Scott. Engraved by G. B. Shaw. Painted by W. Nicholson.

214. John G. Lockhart. W. Allan, R.A. G. B. Shaw.

215. Sir Walter Scott, Bart. Engraved by G. B. Shaw from the Marble Bust by Sir F. Chantrey in the Library at Abbotsford. With Autograph, "Walter Scott, Edinr., 17 November 1828." Edinburgh: Published by Robert Cadell, 1848. Lockhart's *Life of Scott*, Vol. i.; also in Vol. viii. of Life published in 1839; and Roxburgh and Crown edition of Life.

216. Sir Walter Scott, Bart. From the Statue by Greenshields, 1830-31. In the possession of Mr. Cadell, Edinburgh. Engraved by Geo. B. Shaw. On pedestal 'Sic Sedebat.' Lockhart's *Life of Scott*, vol. ii. 1848.

---

217. Sir Walter Scott. From a Bust by Chantrey. Engraved by W. Holl. London: Published by Charles Knight & Co., Ludgate Street. From the *Gallery of Portraits with Memoirs*, Vol. vii. London, 1837.

218. The Author of Waverley. Engraved by Thompson from a Bust by Chantrey. *Court Journal* of 6th October 1832.

219. Sir Walter Scott, Bart. Lithographed from Chantrey's Bust by John Ballantyne, R.S.A., by whom it was also published.

220. Sir Walter Scott. From the Bust by Chantrey. Wood engraving done for the *Illustrated London News*, August 5th, 1871.

221. Walter Scott. Engraved by A. Collas' Patent Process. Medallion in a very elaborately designed frame. From *The Authors of England.* Published by Charles Tilt. London, 1838.

222. Sir Walter Scott. Medallion head, in a specimen plate given with the Prospectus of an Edition of the *Trésor de Numismatique de Glyptique*, to be re-issued by Bossange, Barthés, and Lowell, London. (1834.)

223. Sir Walter Scott, Bart. Medallion Portrait after the Bust by Chantrey by Stothard. Engraved by J. Bate.

224. Sir Walter Scott. Medallion after Chantrey. Engraved by Tacey. The Ornament by Mitau, after H. Corbould.

225. Walter Scott. From a Medal by David Crawford, Die, Stamp, and Seal Engraver, Glasgow. Ruled by machinery by T. S. Woodcock, Brooklyn, N.Y.

226. Sir Walter Scott, Bart. From Statue in his Monument at Edinburgh, by John Steell, R.S.A. Lithographed by J. Sutcliffe.

227. Colossal Statue of Sir Walter Scott, Bart. A Woodcut from the Statue in the Monument at Edinburgh.

228. Sir Walter Scott. From Steell's Statue. Prefixed to *Life of Scott*, by the Rev. George Gilfillan. Edinburgh, 1870. post 8vo.

229. SIR WALTER SCOTT, Bart. Statuette, being the upper portion of a Testimonial in Silver, presented by the Members of the Bannatyne Club to the Secretary. It was modelled by Peter Slater. A Lithograph. (See Illustrations, No. VI.)

230. SIR WALTER SCOTT AND HIS FRIENDS AT ABBOTSFORD.

Painted by THOMAS FAED, R.S.A. Engraved by JAMES FAED. Published January 2, 1854, by James Keith, 60 Princes Street, Edinburgh. See Illustrations, No. XXX.

Size of Plate, 2 ft. 4½ in. × 1 ft. 8½ in.

ADDITIONAL ENGRAVED PORTRAITS.

230. (2.) SIR WALTER SCOTT, Bart. Lithograph from the Picture by Sir Henry Raeburn, R.A. Published at the Centennial Birthday of the Author of *Waverley*, 15th August 1871. Gustav W. Seitz, Wandsbeck. 12 in. × 15 in.

230. (3.) SIR WALTER SCOTT, Bart. (1820.) In Profile. On one plate with others, of Canning, Wollaston, and Crabbe, after Sir F. Chantrey, R.A.

Being plate 10 of *Lithographic Imitations of Sketches by Modern Artists*, by R. J. Lane, A.R.A. London, 1832.

230. (4.) SIR WALTER SCOTT, Bart. Drawn on Stone by Richard J. Lane, A.R.A. From a Picture painted at Abbotsford by J. Knight, in the possession of J. Hughes, Esq. Printed by Engelmann, Graf, Coindet, & Co., and published by them at 92 Dean Street, Soho, December 10, 1828. *v.*, 4 in. × 3⅛ in.

RICHARD JAMES LANE, the distinguished Lithographer, an Associate of the Royal Academy in 1827. Among the most important and characteristic of his style, may be mentioned "High Life" and "Low Life," after Sir Edwin Landseer, R.A.

230. (5.) SIR WALTER SCOTT AND HIS FAVOURITE DOG MAIDA. From an Original Sketch. On Stone by J. R. Hamerton. London: Published by J. M'Cormack, 147 Strand. 1832.

Vignette, *s. l.* Size of head, 2¼ in.

Second Division.

A SERIES OF ILLUSTRATIONS

FROM

THE EXHIBITED BUSTS AND PORTRAITS

OF

SIR WALTER SCOTT.

In giving a series of Illustrations from the exhibited Busts and Portraits of SIR WALTER SCOTT, the Committee were desirous that these should include his likeness at different periods of life, and more especially any that might not have previously been engraved. The state of several of the Paintings, unfortunately, rendered this a difficult task, either from cracking or lowering in tone, so that in some instances the negatives for Photographs had to be laid aside as quite unsuitable. In the case, therefore, of Nos. VIII. and IX., it was found necessary to have recourse to early impressions of the excellent engravings made from the paintings some sixty years ago; and of No. X., to adopt the finished etching by the artist himself in preference to either of the water-colour drawings.

In place, also, of illustrating the Catalogue with ordinary Photographs, requiring to be mounted on Bristol boards, etc., and involving much extra expense, the Committee resolved to have the impressions taken by a new Process of Photo-Lithography, called Albert-type, which is permanent, and not liable to the changes to which ordinary Photographs are almost invariably exposed.

In carrying out this resolution, before the Exhibition was closed, there were careful Photographs from the original Busts or Portraits taken by Mr. ALEXANDER M'GLASHAN, and from which he prepared the plates for printing, under the inspection of Mr. DRUMMOND, R.S.A. If, therefore, these impressions want the brilliant effect of first-rate Photographs, they have, at least, the advantage of permanence, and of exhibiting the actual state of the originals, without any attempt to improve them by subsequent touching up of the plates, and thus transmitting the features and expression as given by the pictures, in a way to which no engraving could pretend.

D. L.

I.

BUST BY CHANTREY. 1820. (No. 1.)

In the Catalogue of the Second Public Exhibition, 16 York Place, 1809, No. 46 was a frame containing fifteen Medallion portraits, in enamel, by John Henning, the chief sculptor in Edinburgh at that time. One of the fifteen was Walter Scott, Esq. There may have been other medallion heads; but it seems agreed on all hands that Sir Walter Scott first sat for a bust to Chantrey in 1820.

It was during Sir Walter Scott's visit to London in March 1820 to receive his Baronetcy, that, upon Chantrey's special request, he sat 'for that bust' (says Mr. Lockhart) 'which alone preserves for posterity the cast of expression most fondly remembered by all who mingled in his domestic circle.' Allan Cunningham's account of these sittings is well known. In No. II. we shall quote Sir Francis Chantrey's own statement contained in a letter to Sir Robert Peel in 1838. From this artist's letter it will be seen that Chantrey had also superintended a limited number of casts for Sir Walter's friends, when the original bust was finished. From one of these (said to be the first) the present Photograph has been taken. But the plaster cast fails in representing the beautiful texture of the marble. The bust itself from one of these casts has been often pirated, and copies of it dispersed in all quarters of the globe.

The original marble bust of 1820 is now a principal ornament in the collection of Abbotsford. A duplicate of it, by Chantrey himself, was made for the Duke of Wellington, and sent to Apsley House in 1827. It was also cast in Bronze for Mr. Cadell. This fine bust formed No. 2 of the present Exhibition, but its dark colour rendered it unsuited for a Photograph. It is understood that a trial-cast of this bust in bronze was taken; and it was presented by the Artist to Allan Cunningham. It is now in the possession of his son, Colonel Francis Cunningham.

II.

SECOND BUST BY CHANTREY. 1828. (No. 3.)

Sir Francis Chantrey sculptured in 1828 a bust, as Mr. Lockhart expresses it, possessing the character of a second original, who placed it some years later, probably in 1837, in the gallery of Sir Robert Peel, at Drayton Manor. As this bust could not be obtained at the time of the Scott Exhibition, the present Sir Robert Peel responded to a request made by Sir William Stirling Maxwell, by allowing photographs of it to be taken by Mr. W. T. Hulland at Tamworth. One of these, as a profile view, will serve for a medallion head on the title-page of this Catalogue. Another, a front view, is here given, and may justly be reckoned a most admirable likeness.

The history of its execution is contained in the following letter from the eminent Sculptor himself, as given in Mr. Lockhart's *Life of Scott*, 1839; and compared with the *Recollections of Chantrey*, by George Jones, R.A., 1849:—

To the Right Hon. Sir Robert Peel, Bart., Whitehall.

Dear Sir Robert, Belgrave Place, *26th January* 1838.

I have much pleasure in complying with your request, to note down such facts as remain on my memory concerning the bust of Sir Walter Scott, which you have done me the honour to place in your collection at Drayton Manor.

My admiration of Scott, as a poet and a man, induced me, in the year 1820, to ask him to sit to me for his bust—the only time I ever recollect having asked a similar favour from any one. He agreed, and I stipulated that he should breakfast with me always before his sittings, and never come alone, nor bring more than three friends at once, and that they should be all good talkers. That he fulfilled the latter condition, you may guess, when I tell you that on one occasion he came with Mr. Croker, Mr. Heber, and the late Lord Lyttelton. The marble bust produced from these sittings was moulded; and about forty-five casts were disposed of by me among the poet's most ardent admirers. This was all I had to do with plaster casts. The bust was pirated by Italians; and England and Scotland, and even the Colonies, were supplied with unpermitted and bad casts to the extent of thousands, in spite of the terror of an Act of Parliament!

I made a copy in marble from this bust for the Duke of Wellington. It was sent to

Apsley House in March 1827, and it is the *only* duplicate of my bust of Sir Walter that I ever executed in marble.

I now come to your bust of Scott. In the year 1828, I proposed to the Poet to present the original marble as an Heirloom to Abbotsford, on condition that he would allow me sittings sufficient to finish another marble from the life for my own studio. To this proposal he acceded; and the bust was sent to Abbotsford accordingly, with the following words inscribed on the back:—THIS BUST OF SIR WALTER SCOTT WAS MADE IN 1820 BY FRANCIS CHANTREY, AND PRESENTED BY THE SCULPTOR TO THE POET, AS A TOKEN OF ESTEEM, IN 1828.

In the months of May and June in the same year, 1828, Sir Walter fulfilled his promise; and I finished, from his face, the marble Bust now at Drayton Manor—a better sanctuary than my studio, else I had not parted with it. The expression is more serious than in the two former Busts, and the marks of age *more* than eight years deeper.

I have now, I think, stated all that is worthy of remembering about this Bust, save that there is no fear of piracy, for it has never been moulded. . . .—I have the honour to be, Dear Sir, your very sincere and faithful servant, F. CHANTREY.

Sir Francis Chantrey, R.A., Sculptor, was born at Norton, near Sheffield, April 7, 1782; came to London to study as a sculptor; was elected a Royal Academician in 1818; obtained the honour of knighthood from King William IV. in St. James's Palace, July 1, 1835; and died November 25, 1841.

III.

BUST BY JOSEPH. 1823. (No. 4.)

This marble bust was made for Mr. Burn Callander of Prestonhall, a few miles from Edinburgh, about the year 1823. It appears in the Catalogue of the Scottish Academy's Exhibition for 1825.

Samuel Joseph, Sculptor, was probably born in London about the year 1788. He became a pupil in the Royal Academy, and so distinguished himself, to use the words of his friend Mr. Allan of Glen (afterwards Lord Provost of Edinburgh, 1829-1831), 'that in a fair and arduous competition in the Royal Academy of London, he had gained all the medals in its various schools in succession, up to the last and highest, the gold one, given for the best composition in Sculpture.' This was in 1815. His name occurs in the Academy's Exhibition Catalogues for 1811 and subsequent years.

At the advice of Mr. Ferguson of Raith and other gentlemen, Joseph came to Scotland, and took up his residence in Edinburgh about 1821. He was much employed, and was one of the first in this country in recent times to advance the art of Sculpture. Several of his busts were exhibited at Edinburgh between the years 1822 and 1835. He resolved, however, to return to London; and on that occasion the Scottish Academy (of which Joseph was one of the original members) entertained him at dinner on April 28, 1828.

Mr. Joseph died at London in July 1850. Of his works, the marble statue of Wilberforce in Westminster Abbey, and of Wilkie in the National Gallery, London, are best known. His busts, however, for a fine perception of character and graceful modelling, have been more generally admired. In the National Gallery of Scotland, his two admirable marble busts of Sir David Wilkie and Lord Brougham are sufficient to perpetuate his name as a sculptor.

IV.

BUST BY MACDONALD. 1831. (No. 7.)

Mr. Lockhart pronounces a very decided opinion regarding this marble bust, when he says, that "it was modelled by Mr. Lawrence Macdonald, in the unhappy winter of 1830. The period of the artist's observation would alone have been sufficient to render his efforts fruitless. His bust may be, in point of execution, good; but he does not seem to me to have produced what any friend of Sir Walter's will recognise as a likeness." From a letter written by Mr. George Combe, and printed in the *Phrenological Journal*, 1839, it appears that this bust was actually modelled at Abbotsford by Mr. Macdonald in January 1831. The statement respecting it is as follows, dated Edinburgh, August 10, 1838 :—

"In January 1831, Mr. Lawrence Macdonald, sculptor, now settled in Rome, lived for several days at Abbotsford, and modelled a bust of Sir Walter Scott. Mr. Macdonald was then a practical phrenologist. He knew that no bust, authentic in the measurements, of Sir Walter's head existed; and he bestowed every possible attention to render his work a true representation of nature. He assured me that he measured the size of the head in different directions with callipers, and preserved the dimensions in the clay; while he modelled every portion of the surface with the utmost care, so as to exhibit the outlines and proportions as exactly as his talents could accomplish. Sir Walter sat four hours at a time to him, dictating a romance all the while to his amanuensis, Mr. Laidlaw. Sir Walter's vigour, both bodily and mental, had by that time declined; and his features had lost part of their mental expression. The bust bears evidence in the features of this decay of power; but there is no reason to believe that the disease had at that time existed so long as to cause any diminution of the skull. This bust, therefore, forms the best record which now exists of the dimensions and relative proportions of the different parts of Sir Walter Scott's head; and as it is in my possession, I present you with the following measurements, and note of the size of the organs. It will be seen that the head was really large."

Sir Walter Scott came from Naples to Rome in April, and left on his return home May 11, 1832. If during that interval the artist was enabled to avail himself of the opportunity at Rome to obtain one or more sittings, it might well be called an *unhappy* period.

The Sculptor, who is a native of Trinity-Gask, Perthshire, still resides at Rome, having settled there permanently about the year 1832, and has revisited Scotland only on a few rare occasions.

The bust itself was obtained by Mr. George Combe from his friend the Sculptor, and at the sale of Mr. Combe's effects it was acquired by the present proprietor.

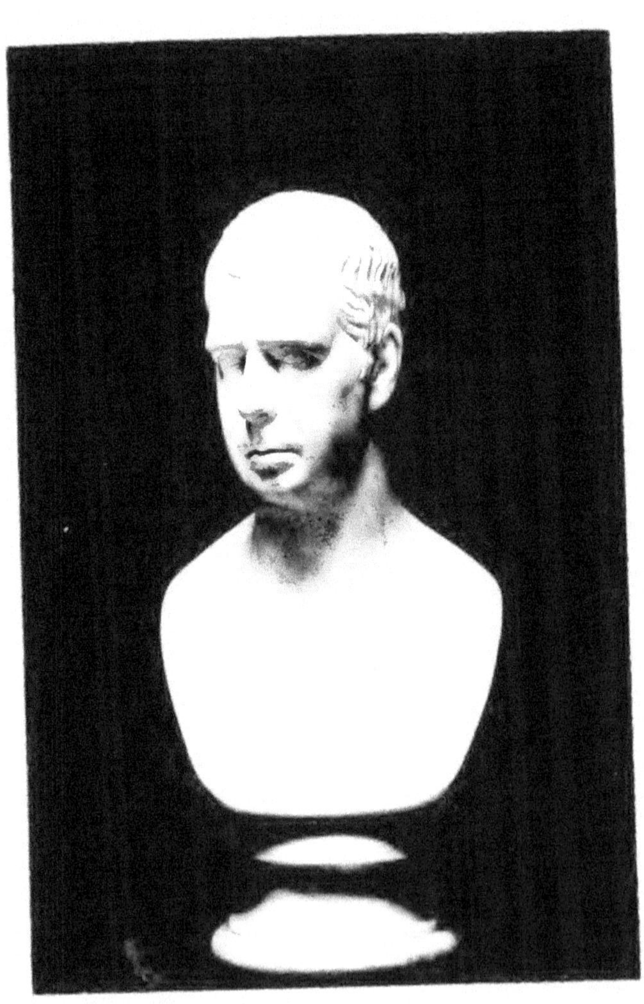

V.

STATUETTE BY STEELL. 1849. (No. 9.)

A MODEL for the noble Statue of Sir Walter Scott, which so fitly adorns the Scott Monument in Edinburgh, by Mr. JOHN STEELL, R.S.A., was adopted by the Sub-Committee in February 1838. As already stated at p. 5, it was wisely determined at that time that the Monument should combine Sculpture with Architecture.

The Statue, formed from a block of white Carrara marble, gives successfully an accurate and striking representation of Sir Walter's personal appearance; and it must have been a gratifying commission to the Sculptor to be employed last year in completing a full-sized repetition of this grand Statue, to be cast in Bronze, to be erected at New York, in the United States.

It may be proper here to add, that the preference given to this Statue had no secondary influence in securing the adoption of Kemp's architectural design. Both at least were submitted to fair and open competition, notwithstanding the attempt to employ Sir Francis Chantrey, as an artist of established reputation. Mr. Steell, on the other hand, was a young man, returned from his studies at Rome to his native place a few months previously, and scarcely known even to his fellow-citizens. Had the resolution of the Committee been overturned, instead of the happy conjunction of the two Sister Arts, Edinburgh might have obtained a colossal bronze figure raised on a high pedestal, to keep company in the line of George Street with William Pitt and George the Fourth. Fortunately the subscribers desired neither a monumental design nor a simple figure, whether raised on a pedestal or on a lofty column, but a monument worthy of SIR WALTER SCOTT and of his native City.

It must, however, be matter of some regret that the Committee, in their arrangements with Mr. Steell, stipulated for a figure not less than nine feet high, measured from the pedestal, at the cost of £2000. It cannot be denied that the size is disproportionate to the open space between the lofty pointed arches of the Monument where it is placed. This was chiefly owing to the dimensions of the Monument in height, as first proposed, having been increased nearly one-third. In this way the figure has lost its colossal and imposing appearance. Whether it might be possible to remedy this want of proportion is doubtful, without injuring the architectural character of the structure.

Mr. Steell having, about the end of the year 1849, completed a marble Statuette of the same figure, it was purchased, along with the copyright (for £105), by the *Royal Association for Promotion of the Fine Arts in Scotland.* An arrangement was then made with Mr. W. T. Copeland to furnish One Hundred Copies of it in Statuary Porcelain, for distribution among the prizes to their Annual Subscribers. Others in Parian composition were also obtained for the like purpose at occasional intervals.

The present photograph is taken from a Statuette, in Marble, somewhat larger than that of 1849, also prepared by the Sculptor. It was in the Exhibition of the Royal Scottish Academy for 1865.

While this sheet is at press, it may be noticed that the Trustees of the Scott Monument have commissioned from Mr. Steell another Statuette, to be cast in bronze, to place in the interior room of the Monument now fitting up as a permanent Scott Museum.

VI.

STATUETTE BY SLATER. 1860. (No. 10.)

The exhibition of this Statuette was suggested by the circumstance that the name of Sir Walter Scott, during the last ten years of his life, was intimately connected with the institution and success of a literary and historical association in Edinburgh, known as The Bannatyne Club. The following Note by the Secretary sufficiently explains its history :—

"At the termination of the Bannatyne Club in 1860, of which Sir Walter Scott was the Founder in February 1823, the Members, without my knowledge or desire, subscribed for a Testimonial to be presented to me, having acted as Hon. Secretary during the whole term of its existence. The form that this Testimonial might assume was left to myself; and I could not but desire, in grateful and pleasing recollections, to have the chief portion associated with the name of the Founder. A composition designed and modelled by Mr. Peter Slater was adopted, consisting of a handsome Silver Vase, and of three emblematical figures of History, Poetry, and Music, surmounted with a Statuette of Sir Walter Scott, as Founder of the Club. In a volume of *Adversaria*, which I subsequently presented to the Members from the surplus fund, a lithograph print of these figures was given.[1] —It would be superfluous to say anything of the great interest taken in the proceedings of this literary association by Sir Walter Scott, who continued as President till his death."—D. L.

Peter Slater, Sculptor, the son of John Slater, marble-cutter, Leith Walk (1808-1831), was born at Edinburgh, May 8, 1809. He was educated in Heriot's Hospital, and was employed in the studios of Mr. S. Joseph and of Mr. Henry Westmacott, both of whom were resident in Edinburgh for some years. Slater's name first appears in the Catalogue of the Scottish Academy's Exhibition for 1834. In 1836 he exhibited in the Royal Scottish Academy a sketch in clay of a Statue of Sir Walter Scott, from which the Statuette afterwards was partly taken. In the year 1860 or 1861 he removed to London, where he died, November 27, 1870.

[1] "Before sending this Statuette to the Exhibition, I had a slight alteration made by cutting away an obtrusive hat, and substituting a book in Sir Walter's right hand. Except for the above-mentioned lithograph, this change was not worth noticing."—D. L.

VII.

TWO MINIATURE PORTRAITS. 1777 AND 1797.

(Nos. 46 and 47.)

[A.]

THE Portrait of Scott in his youth, known as the Bath Miniature, was engraved from the supposed original, preserved at Abbotsford. Mr. Lockhart, not aware of the existence of any similar Portrait, says,—

"A very good miniature of Sir Walter, done at Bath, when he was in the fifth or sixth year of his age, was given by him to his daughter Sophia, and is now in my possession—the artist's name unknown. The child appears with long flowing hair, the colour a light chestnut; a deep open collar, and scarlet dress. It is nearly a profile; the outline wonderfully like what it was to the last; the expression of the eyes and mouth very striking, grave, and pensive."

The original Miniature (No. 46) is carefully painted on ivory, without name or date. It was given by the mother of Sir Walter Scott, early in the present century, to Mrs. Captain Watson, in whose family it had since remained. By some accident, the ivory having been partially split, in repairing it there is a discoloration at the joining, scarcely discernible in the accompanying photograph. This accident may not unlikely have led Mrs. Scott to have it copied, and to present the original to Mrs. Watson, whose son, William Stewart Watson, raised himself to some eminence as a Portrait-Painter. (See No. 74.) It now belongs to Mr. D. LAING. Having been acquired only a few days after the opening of the Exhibition, it was not included in the copies of the Catalogue that were first issued.

It may be added that, after the Exhibition had closed, an opportunity occurred accidentally, in the presence of a competent authority, to make an actual comparison of the two Miniatures. This served clearly to confirm the opinion that the one exhibited was the original; and that the other at Abbotsford was a very careful copy, at a later date, apparently the work of a young artist or an amateur.

[B.]

By the kind permission of Mr. Hope Scott, we are enabled for the first time to give a representation of the small Miniature of 1797 (No. 47). Mr. Lockhart somewhat undervalues it, when he remarks, "It is not a good work of art, and I know not who executed it."

It is, however, elaborately finished, and might be assigned to one of the chief Miniature Painters of the time at Edinburgh. Its effect, in the Photograph, is lost, indeed, by not exhibiting the colours of the military dress. But its interest consists in being the second authentic likeness of Scott. He is in military dress, as an officer in the Royal Edinburgh Light Dragoons: a scarlet coat with green facings, and an epaulet of silver on his right shoulder. According to the fashion of the day, his hair is powdered. A lock of light brown hair is fastened, under glass, at the back of the frame.

In Miss Carpenter's letters to Mr. Scott, previous to their marriage, from Carlisle, October 25 (1797), she writes :—

"Indeed, Mr. Scott, I am by no means pleased with all this writing. I have told you how much I dislike it, and yet you still persist in asking me to write, and that by return of post. O, you really are quite out of your senses," etc.

And on the following day :—

"I have only a minute before the post goes, to assure you, my Dear Sir, of the welcome reception of the Stranger (a Miniature of Scott). The very great likeness to a friend of mine will endear him to me; he shall be my constant companion, but I wish he could give me an answer to a thousand questions I have to make, one in particular, what reason have you for so many fears you express," etc.

VIII.

PORTRAIT BY SAXON. 1805. (No. 48.)

THIS Portrait was reckoned to have the merit of giving "an impress of the elasticity and youthful vivacity, which Scott used to complain wore off after he was forty." In his account of Sir Walter's Portraits, Mr. Lockhart says:—

"The first oil-painting, done for Lady Scott in 1805, by Saxon, was, in consequence of repeated applications for the purpose of being engraved, transferred by her to Messrs. Longman & Co., and is now in their house in Paternoster Row. This is a very fine picture, representing, I have no doubt, most faithfully the author of the *Lay of the Last Minstrel*. Length, three-quarters; dress, black; hair, nut-brown; the favourite bull-terrier Camp leaning his head on the knee of his master. The companion portrait of Lady Scott is at Abbotsford."

The loan of the original Portrait was obligingly furnished by William E. Green, Esq., a partner in the great publishing house of Messrs. Longman & Co., Paternoster Row, London. It was first engraved, in an excellent style, by James Heath, and prefixed to the original edition of the *Lady of the Lake*, 1810, 4to.

As the dark colour of the painting would not admit of obtaining a successful copy, the accompanying photograph is taken from an early impression of Heath's engraving.

In the Third Exhibition of the Scottish Artists at Edinburgh, in 1810, Saxon's Portrait of Mrs. Scott appears in the Catalogue. This Portrait is at Abbotsford, and has been engraved for the *Life of Scott*.

JAMES SAXON was an English Artist, born in Manchester: came to Edinburgh in the year 1803. Saxon afterwards went to St. Petersburg, where he practised successfully for several years. On his return he spent a short time in Glasgow; and died in London about the year 1817: See Preface, p. vi., note, in the Bannatyne Club volume of *Etchings*, by John Clerk of Eldin, completed 1855, folio.

NO. VIII.]

IX.

PORTRAIT BY RAEBURN. 1808. (No. 49.)

This full-length Portrait, the earliest of Scott by Raeburn, remains unsurpassed among the numerous Portraits of a later date by the most eminent Artists of his age. Mr. Lockhart thus describes it :—

"The first picture by Raeburn was done in 1808 for Constable, and passed, at the sale of his effects, into the hands of the Duke of Buccleuch. Scott is represented at full length, sitting by a ruined wall, with Camp at his feet—Hermitage Castle and the mountains of Liddisdale in the background. This noble portrait has been repeatedly engraved. Dress, black; Hessian boots. The second full-length by Raeburn (done a year later) is nearly a repetition; but the painter had some new sittings. Two greyhounds (Douglas and Percy) appear in addition to Camp, and the background gives the valley of the Yarrow, marking the period of *Ashestiel* and *Marmion*. This piece is at Abbotsford."

Of the first Portrait, Mr. Lockhart indeed elsewhere says, "The literal fidelity of the portraiture, however, is its principal merit. The expression is serious and contemplative, very unlike the hilarity and vivacity then habitual to his speaking face, but quite true to what it was in the absence of such excitement." This is the very circumstance that adds so much value to it, independently of its importance as a work of art.

As no good Photograph could be taken from the original Painting, it was found necessary to have recourse to an early or proof-impression of the fine engraving, in 1810, by Charles Turner, quite worthy of the original painting.

The repetition by Raeburn of this Portrait is equally fine, and is preserved at Abbotsford. In the passage just quoted, Lockhart is mistaken when he describes it as having two greyhounds. In the picture there happens to be only one greyhound.

The painting of the second Portrait by Raeburn, in 1809, may evidently be ascribed to the quarrel of Scott and Constable & Company. On the 12th of January 1809, Scott wrote a letter expressing his desire that Raeburn's Portrait of 1808 should be considered as done for himself, and at his expense. Mr. Constable, says Lockhart, "declined in very handsome terms to give up the picture. But for the time the breach between them, as author and publishers, was complete."

The death of Charles Duke of Buccleuch in 1819 having prevented Sir Henry Raeburn painting for his Grace another large Portrait of Sir Walter for Bowhill (No. XIII. p. 69), the original one of 1808 belonging to Mr. Constable was sold in 1826 by private bargain to the Duke of Buccleuch, its present noble proprietor, for the sum of Three Hundred and Fifty Guineas.

X.

PORTRAIT BY NICHOLSON. 1815. (No. 50.)

This drawing has the date 1815, and was apparently the earliest of three Portraits, in water-colours, of Scott, by Nicholson. The second, also in the Exhibition (No. 49), was presented, it is believed, by Scott himself to his friend William Erskine of Kinnedder; and the third is at Abbotsford. As the photographic process fails in representing colour, the accompanying copy is given, somewhat reduced, from the spirited etching (No. 139) from this drawing by the artist himself in 1817.

At that time Mr. Nicholson commenced to publish a series of *Portraits of Eminent Scotsmen*, from his own drawings. Two Parts, each containing three of these Etchings (with his initials W. N.) and biographical notices, appeared in 1820. The six were—(1.) Walter Scott, 1817; (2.) Francis Jeffrey, 1817; (3.) Henry Raeburn (from his own painting), 1818; (4.) Professor Playfair, 1819; (5.) William Allan, the Artist, 1819; and (6.) Robert Burns, 1819. Six other Etchings were finished as a continuation, but not published—(7.) James Hogg, 1817; (8.) George Thomson, the correspondent of Burns, 1817; (9.) Professor John Wilson, 1818; (10.) James Watt, 1819; (11.) Rev. Dr. A. Cameron, Roman Catholic Bishop, 1818; and (12.) Rev. Dr. Alexander Carlyle, of Inveresk, 1820.

William Nicholson, a native of Newcastle-on-Tyne, was born in the year 1784. He settled in Edinburgh as a Portrait-Painter, about 1813, and attracted much notice by his drawings of a cabinet size in water-colours. In the present Exhibition, besides the two of Sir Walter Scott, there were Portraits of Mrs. Lockhart (No. 90), of William Erskine of Kinnedder (No. 100), and of Daniel Terry (No. 108). Mr. Nicholson afterwards changed his style to oil, for full-sized Portraits. He was one of the Founders of the Scottish Academy in 1825, and

NO. X.]

continued during life to act as Secretary; nor is it too much to say that its ultimate success was in no small degree owing to his unwearied exertions. He died at Edinburgh, August 16, 1844, in the sixtieth year of his age.

XI.

PORTRAIT BY WATSON (GORDON). 1820. (No. 54.)

THE Committee were indebted to Mark Napier, Esq., Advocate, for calling their attention to this undescribed Portrait, belonging to Lord Napier, and to the courtesy (in his Lordship's absence from this country) of the Dowager Lady Napier in sending it for exhibition. It is signed, "John Watson, 1820," and is the earliest of several Portraits of Scott by the artist, best known as Sir John Watson Gordon, having assumed the name of Gordon in 1825. It seems to have escaped Mr. Lockhart's knowledge, nor has it previously been engraved.

This Picture was painted for the Marchioness of Abercorn, and presented by her sister, Lady Julia Lockwood, to Lord Napier. The interest attached to this portrait is enhanced by the following extracts from two unpublished letters addressed by Sir Walter Scott to the Marchioness of Abercorn.

"EDINBURGH, *1st July* 1820.—The portrait is advancing by the pencil of a clever Artist, and will, I think, be a likeness, and a tolerably good picture. I hope to get it sent up before I leave town ; at any rate, I will have it finished so far as sittings are concerned. If I look a little sleepy, your kindness must excuse it, as I had to make my attendance on the man of colours betwixt six and seven in the morning."

In reply to an inquiry by the Marchioness, he says :—

"ABBOTSFORD, *August 2d*, 1820.—The dog which I am represented as holding in my arms is a Highland terrier from Kintail, of a breed very sensible, very faithful, and very ill-natured. It sometimes tires, or pretends to do so, when I am on horseback, and whines to be taken up ; where it sits before me like a child, without any assistance. I have a very large wolf-greyhound, I think the finest dog I ever saw ; but he has *sate* to so many artists that, whenever he sees brushes and a palette, he gets up and leaves the room, being sufficiently tired of the constraint."

XII.

PORTRAIT BY LAWRENCE. 1820. (No. 55.)

HER GRACIOUS MAJESTY having been pleased to allow this interesting Portrait to be seen in Scotland, the following notices regarding it may not be without interest. It was commenced in 1820, at the time that Sir Walter sat to Chantrey for his first Bust. The usual practice of Sir Thomas Lawrence was, to put in the head of his portrait before deciding the position of his figure, and drawing in coloured chalks the true outline and expression of the face, so that he might transfer the same to canvas in the absence of his sitter.

Mr. Lockhart's account of this Portrait in its unfinished state in 1820, may be quoted :—

"To adorn the walls of the Great Gallery at Windsor Castle, it was the pleasure of George the Fourth that one series should commence with Walter Scott. The portrait was of course begun immediately, and the head was finished before Scott left town. Sir Thomas has caught and fixed with admirable skill one of the loftiest expressions of Scott's countenance at the proudest period of his life ; to the perfect truth of the representation every one who ever surprised him in the act of composition at his desk will bear witness. The expression, however, was one with which many who had seen the man often were not familiar : and it was extremely unfortunate that Sir Thomas filled in the figure from a separate sketch after he had quitted London. When I first saw the head, I thought nothing could be better ; but there was an evident change for the worse when the picture appeared in its finished state ; for the rest of the person had been done on a different scale, and this neglect of proportion takes considerably from the majestic effect which the head itself, and especially the mighty pile of forehead, had in nature. I hope one day to see a good engraving of the head alone, as I first saw it floating on a dark sea of canvas."

As already stated, this Portrait was not finished until 1826, and was first exhibited in the Royal Academy, 1827. In the *Life of Lawrence*, the author, D. E. Williams, says :—

"The artist felt his pride excited in painting the portrait of Sir Walter Scott, and he had been annoyed at reports of Sir Walter's having fallen off in his personal appearance. The pencil and the subject were reciprocally calculated to transmit each other to posterity."—(Lond. 1831. Vol. ii. p. 455.)

NO. XII.]

Sir Thomas, in a letter to a lady, says :—

"RUSSELL SQUARE, *Thursday Evening.*—MY DEAR MADAM,—I shall wait on you with the greatest pleasure. Sir Walter comes over to refute all the past reports about his looks, increased age, etc. I had the happiness of breakfasting with him this morning at Mr. Rogers'; and all the alteration I see is, in his complexion being fresher, his eye brighter, his face smoother, and his hair less grey than it was; for it is now, I acknowledge, of silvery whiteness."—(*Ib.* p. 455.)

Sir Walter, in his Diary, November 12, 1826, says :—

"Went to sit to Sir T. L., to finish the picture for His Majesty, which every one says is a very fine one. I think so myself, and wonder how Sir Thomas has made so much out of an old weather-beaten block. But I believe the hard features of old Dons like myself are more within the compass of the artist's skill than the lovely face and delicate complexion of females."

"This Portrait has," says Allan Cunningham, "also been much praised; it is certainly very like, but wants the manly massive vigour of the heads of the same illustrious poet by Raeburn. When I saw it first, the head alone was finished, all the surrounding ground was dark, and I thought it much more like than when the shoulders and body were added. 'Tell Lawrence,' said an artist of high name, 'to let the portrait of your friend Scott stand as it is; it is full of character and mental vigour, all of which he will diminish if he paints the body.'"—*British Painters*, vol. vi. p. 241.

It is proper to add, that the Photograph, in order to give the portrait to greater advantage, does not represent the entire picture, of which there are excellent engravings, by Robinson, Horsburgh, and others.

The death of Sir Thomas Lawrence, January 7, 1830, prevented his producing a full-length figure of Scott, among other commissions he had to execute for Sir Robert Peel.

XIII.

PORTRAIT BY RAEBURN. 1822. (No. 57.)

THE two full-lengths of Scott, representing him seated, painted by Sir Henry Raeburn in the year 1808, and repeated in 1809, are already described (No. IX.) At a later period, it is matter of regret that he was not employed to paint a third full-length, as intended.

In the extensive additions to Bowhill, Charles fourth Duke of Buccleuch, in his last letter addressed to Scott, when on the eve of embarking at Portsmouth, early in 1819, reminded him of a promise to sit for his portrait by Raeburn, to be hung up in his Grace's large library-room there. The Duke's death at Lisbon, April 20, that year, put a stop to this. Lord Montagu, however, having again put Sir Walter in mind of this old promise in May 1822, he replied, he thought it would be better to wait two or three years longer, and allow the young Duke to judge for himself as to the mode of adorning this favourite residence at Bowhill.

"Acquiescing," says Lockhart, "in the propriety of what Sir Walter had thus said respecting the proposed portrait for Bowhill, Lord Montagu requested him to sit, without delay, for a smaller picture on his own behalf; and the result was that half-length now at Ditton, which possesses a peculiar value and interest, as being the very last work of Raeburn's pencil. The Poet's answer to Lord Montagu's request was as follows:—

"'ABBOTSFORD, *27th March* 1822.—MY DEAR LORD,—I should be very unworthy of so great a proof of your regard did I not immediately assure you of the pleasure with which I will contribute the head you wish to the halls of Ditton. I know no place where the substance has been so happy, and therefore the shadow may be so far well placed. I will not suffer this important affair to languish, so far as I am concerned, but will arrange with Raeburn when I return to Edinburgh in May,'" etc.

The later Portraits by Raeburn are of a head size. The one best known, which remained in the artist's possession, was engraved by W. Walker (No. 162), and has often been copied. The dates are somewhat uncertain. A second was painted by Raeburn for Sir Francis Chantrey.

A third is that represented in the present Photograph. Scott's biographer describes one or other of these heads as "a massive, strong likeness, heavy at first sight, but grows into favour upon better acquaintance."

This third Portrait is now in the possession of the Earl of Home.[1] It was painted, as already mentioned, for Scott's friend, Lord Montagu, in the year 1822, but perhaps not finished till the year following. Sir Henry Raeburn died at Edinburgh, July 8, 1823, in the sixty-eighth year of his age. Lord Montagu, who died October 30, 1845, without male issue, among his testamentary bequests of family portraits and other works of art in the gallery of Ditton Hall (near Windsor),[2] specially mentions this portrait of Scott and three others, which, under some arrangement with Lord Douglas, were to be sent to Scotland. In this way it became the property of the Earl of Home, who married Lord Montagu's eldest daughter.

[1] "On closely examining this picture, the elevation of the head seems to have been tampered with, and from the clumsy and coarse way in which this has been done, it must have been altered by another hand. In a photograph done from it, this comes out more distinctly than in the picture." —(*Note by* J. D.)

Some years ago, a desire was expressed to obtain a copy of this portrait for the High School of Edinburgh, and the Earl of Home, with great courtesy, allowed this to be made from the one in his possession. It was skilfully executed by Francis Cruikshanks, at the expense of some old pupils of the High School.

[2] Ditton Park, Buckinghamshire, is situated in the parish of Datchet, about three miles from Windsor. The old house of Ditton was entirely consumed by fire in April 1812; but was rebuilt as a large modern mansion on the same site. An engraving of the new house is given in Neale's *Views of Seats, etc.*, vol. i. Lond. 1818.

XIV.

PORTRAIT BY WILKIE. 1824. (No. 56.)

GEORGE THE FOURTH, in the view of commemorating his reception by the Scottish Nobility and Gentry at His Majesty's entrance to the Palace of Holyrood, August 15, 1822, gave Wilkie a commission for a painting of this memorable event. In a composition of this kind it was of course out of the question that Sir Walter Scott should be overlooked, although in treating such a difficult subject, crowded with figures, he has no prominent place, appearing in the background in the character of Historian or Bard, with an open collar and furred cloak. This painting, sent, by HER GRACIOUS MAJESTY'S permission, to the present Exhibition (No. 82), was not completed till the year 1830.

Wilkie returned to Scotland in 1824, to finish his studies for the painting. In that year, September 26, when in Edinburgh, he says :—"The likeness of Sir Walter Scott is the only one now wanting to complete my studies for the picture."—October 23, after his visit to Raith, he says, "I must get a sitting of Sir Walter Scott for my picture, this being one of my objects in coming to Scotland."—November 1, "Sir Walter Scott expects me at Abbotsford, and is ready to sit. He has, however, sat so frequently of late to artists, and has had so many people about his house, that I grudge going upon such an errand ; however, it is a matter of duty rather than choice with me, and I must go at all hazards."

Wilkie, on his return to London, writes to Sir Thomas Lawrence, November 20, 1824 :—

"On leaving Scotland, the last person I parted with was Sir Walter Scott ; and one of the last things he said to me was, that I would remember him to Sir Thomas Lawrence. He means, I am happy to say, to be in London next spring ; and to see you, as I learnt, is one object of his visit."

Also, in a letter to Sir George Beaumont, December 28, Wilkie adds :—

"The last place I visited before my journey south was Abbotsford, where Sir Walter Scott has completed a most superb château, much in the Flemish style ; and, though not suited to the country about it, has got within itself so much comfort and magnificence, and his style of entertaining his friends is so truly baronial, that one can scarcely fancy an instance of wealth or honours being more happily bestowed. He purposes being in London next spring, and is at present in excellent health."

Soon after this, Wilkie was laid aside from work, and spent three years on the Continent, partly for the recovery of his health. The present portrait of Scott, the finished study for his Holyrood Picture, had been bespoke by their mutual friend, Sir William Knighton. It does not seem, however, to be mentioned either by Mr. Lockhart or by Wilkie's biographer, Allan Cunningham, whose work has supplied the above extracts. Wilkie, in a letter to Sir William, dated December 1828, or six months after his return to England, says:—"The head of Walter Scott I am proceeding with. It comes better than I expected. I have ordered a frame, and I hope to have it nearly done by the time you see it. Indeed, upon the subject of working, you have in your kindness given me great encouragement."

There is an excellent engraving of it by Edward Smith, in June 1831 (No. 169).

XV.

PORTRAIT BY SMITH. 1828. (No. 62.)

MR. LOCKHART, in his Catalogue of Scott Portraits, has given an erroneous statement in mentioning those painted by Mr. Smith, when he says :—

"13. A half-length, by Mr. Colvin Smith, of Edinburgh, done in January 1828, for the artist's uncle, Lord Gillies. I never admired this picture; but it pleased many, perhaps better judges. Mr. Smith executed no less than fifteen copies for friends of Sir Walter's; among others, the Bishop of Llandaff (Copleston), the Chief-Commissioner Adam, and John Hope, then Lord Justice-Clerk of Scotland."

Now, from the best authority, we know that Mr. Smith *never* painted a half-length of Sir Walter Scott; and that the original was done for the Lord Chief-Commissioner Adam, and is at Blair-Adam. It was No. 60 in the present Exhibition. The circumstance of so many of Sir Walter's friends being desirous to obtain repetitions of the Portrait is certainly in its favour, both as a painting and a faithful and expressive likeness.

On applying to the Artist, he has kindly favoured us with the following list of those he actually painted, he thinks to the number of about twenty, and for seven of these Sir Walter gave him occasional sittings. These repetitions exhibit some variations in attitude or dress, but in general they are quite alike.

"PORTRAITS OF SIR WALTER SCOTT BY MR. COLVIN SMITH.

"1. (Original) Lord Chief-Commissioner Adam; 2. Lord Chief-Baron Shepherd; 3. Lord Gillies; 4. Lord Jeffrey; 5. Rev. Dr. Hughes, Dean [Canon] of St. Paul's; 6. Another copy; 7. Bishop of Llandaff; 8. Lord Justice-Clerk Hope; 9. Andrew Skene, Esq.; 10. Sir Frederick Adam; 11. Mr. Blackburn; 12. Mr. Campbell of Blythswood; 13. Sir George Warrender; 14. Mrs. Laing; 15. Lord Minto; 16. Taylor's Institute, Oxford; 17. Mr. Kay, London; and two or three other copies.—For seven of these, Sir Walter gave me one sitting each.

"C. SMITH."

The accompanying Photograph is from No. 62, the painting retained by Mr. Colvin Smith for himself.

In 1828, the Rev. Dr. Thomas Hughes, Canon Residentiary of St. Paul's, Vicar of Uffington, etc., having seen one of Mr. Smith's Portraits of Sir Walter Scott, purchased it, and gave a commission for a second one, with the intention of presenting it to Dr. Copleston, Bishop of Llandaff. In a letter to the artist, dated January 6, 1829, Dr. Hughes says :—

"The picture arrived only last evening, such has been the state of the weather, and I have just had the Bishop of Llandaff here, who is as much delighted with it as myself. It is the only picture of Sir W. that ever satisfied me—the only *familiar likeness;* for Sir Thomas Lawrence's great picture is work of another character and class. I must now tell you a secret. The copy for the Bishop of Llandaff is a *present* from me. He was private tutor to my son at Oriel, and has been the intimate friend of us both ever since. He is also acquainted with Sir Walter—I believe well acquainted; but certainly as great an admirer of him as any of us. Yet knowing the value of Sir Walter's time, he seems fearful of asking for that *short* sitting which would give the picture so much additional value. Perhaps Sir Walter will concede to the Bishop's *modesty* what he will not venture to ask. It would be no sign of *modesty* in *me* to ask, after the sitting that he has given me."

Dr. Hughes died at his Residentiary House, Amen Corner, St. Paul's, January 6, 1833, aged seventy-seven. He had been private tutor to two of the Royal Family; and was well acquainted with Sir Walter Scott, who was godfather to one of his grandsons. His son, John Hughes, Esq. of Donnington Priory, county Berks, was author of an *Itinerary of Provence and the Rhone*, 1819, mentioned in the preface to *Quentin Durward* as by "a young Oxonian friend of mine, a poet, a draughtsman, and a scholar."

It was published in 1822; and was followed by an interesting series of "Views in the South of France, chiefly on the Rhone," engraved from Drawings by Dewent, as Illustrations of Mr. Hughes's *Itinerary*. Lond. 1825, small folio.

XVI.

PORTRAIT BY GRAHAM GILBERT. 1829. (No. 63.)

SIR WALTER SCOTT was elected President of the Royal Society of Edinburgh, in November 1820. The Society, instituted in 1783, having commenced to form a series of Portraits of the several Presidents, as an ornament to their present hall in the Royal Institution Buildings; this of Scott in 1829 was added to the number. It may perhaps be thought, like that of Lawrence, rather too much dressed up for the occasion: but it is a pleasing likeness and a favourable specimen of the artist. It was engraved in 1834 (No. 184) for Jerdan's *National Portrait Gallery*, vol. iii.

The Artist retained in his own collection a duplicate of this Portrait. It was presented by his widow, in 1867, to the National Portrait Gallery, now removed to South Kensington. In this repetition the head has rather a square look; there is no silver guard-chain round his neck; nor a book in his right hand. In other respects, as to attitude, etc., the the two paintings are alike.

JOHN GRAHAM, who afterwards assumed the name of GILBERT, was the son of a West India merchant resident in Glasgow, where he was born in the year 1794. He was allowed to follow the natural bent of his genius in his devotion to Art. He went to London in 1818, and was enrolled a student of the Royal Academy, where he distinguished himself by gaining the silver medal in 1819, and the gold medal in 1821 for the best historical painting, in oil-colours, of The Prodigal Son. After spending two years in Italy, he commenced portrait-painter in Edinburgh, and raised himself to a high position in that department of Art. His residence in Italy gave him a decided love of the refined and classical style which he imparted to his Portraits. That of Provost Lawson has been much admired; in the words of an Art critic of the time, when the Portrait was exhibited, "Mr. Lawson looks, in his official robes, like a Doge of old Venice, and the notion is sustained by the Venetian sweetness and lucidity of the colouring, etc., as though it belonged to an earlier and a greater school altogether." With no less truth it may be said that his full-length portrait of Sir John Watson Gordon, *P*.R.S.A., would be worthy of Sir Thomas Lawrence. In 1830 he was elected a Member of the Royal Scottish Academy. Upon his marriage, in 1834, with the niece of Mr. Gilbert of Yorkhill, he assumed the name of Gilbert, and took up his residence at Glasgow; but still continued to exhibit in the Royal Scottish Academy. After a short illness, he died there, June 5, 1866.

XVII.

PORTRAIT BY WATSON GORDON. 1830. (No. 65.)

THIS unfinished study was retained by the artist, and no doubt served as a model for other Portraits painted by Sir John Watson Gordon during the later period of Sir Walter's life. We cannot say with any certainty how many such Portraits he actually painted. From his later note-books, we have been favoured by his brother, Henry G. Watson, Esq., with the following list:—

EXCERPTS from the Books of the late SIR J. WATSON GORDON, relative to the PORTRAITS of the late SIR WALTER SCOTT painted by him.

1. Sir Walter Scott, Kit Cat. 1830.
2. Sir Walter Scott for Mr. Cadell, half-length. 1830.
3. Head-size of Sir Walter Scott, purchased by Mr. Cadell. 1830.
4. Head-size of Sir Walter Scott for Mr. Shortreed. 1831.
5. Copy of Sir Walter Scott for the Speculative Society. 1835.
6. Head of Sir Walter Scott. 1851.

Of these later Portraits, the one exhibited as No. 67, painted for Mr. Cadell in 1830, was considered the most important. It was engraved on a small scale by Horsburgh for some of the Editions of Scott's Works. It is by no means a pleasing likeness. A copy of this painting, the full size, was made by Sir John in 1835 for the Speculative Society, and was exhibited (No. 73).

Of head-size Portraits, there are repetitions in the possession of

SIR WILLIAM STIRLING MAXWELL, BART. (No. 70.)
ARCHIBALD CAMPBELL SWINTON, ESQ. And
FRANCIS RICHARDSON, ESQ.

JOHN WATSON, eldest son of Captain James Watson, R N., was born at Edinburgh in 1788. His father designed him for the Engineers, but having the advantage of attending the Trustees' Academy of Drawing under John Graham, he was allowed to complete his studies, and devoted himself to the profession of an Artist. In the first Edinburgh Exhibition, June 1808, he sent an "Historical picture," with this quotation :—

> "He ceased, and loud the boy did cry,
> And stretch'd his little arms on high ;
> Implored for aid each well-known face,
> And strove to seek the Dame's embrace."
>
> *Lay of the Last Minstrel*, Canto iv.

For some years he painted historical or poetical compositions, but his reputation as a portrait-painter increasing, he finally confined himself to that branch of Art. In 1826, partly for distinction sake from other artists of the same name, he assumed that of Watson-Gordon. He was one of the earliest Members of the Scottish Academy, founded in 1823. He was elected a Royal Academician in 1851, having for ten years previously been an Associate.

On the death of Sir William Allan in 1850, he was unanimously chosen PRESIDENT of the Royal Scottish Academy, also Limner to Her Majesty, on which occasion he obtained the honour of knighthood. Sir John Watson Gordon died unmarried, June 1, 1864.

XVIII.

PORTRAIT BY GRANT. 1831. (No. 68.)

"A CABINET PICTURE done at Abbotsford in 1831 by Francis Grant, R.A., who had the advantage of a familiar knowledge of the subject, being an attached friend of the family. This interesting piece, which has armour and stag-hounds, was done for Lady Ruthven."—LOCKHART.

The Artist afterwards repeated this Painting with some alterations for the Engraving by Thomas Hodgetts, in 1835 (No. 196). The following letter from Sir Francis Grant, *P.*R.A., addressed to Sir William Stirling Maxwell, respecting the variations between the original painting and the engraving, cannot fail to interest the reader:—

"THE LODGE, MELTON MOWBRAY, *June* 5, 1872.

"MY DEAR SIR WILLIAM,—The print was made from a copy painted by me of the original picture of Sir Walter Scott belonging to Lady Ruthven. The alterations in the dress, chair, etc., were unwisely made at the suggestion of the engraver (Mr. Hodgetts). It has always been a source of regret to me that the original picture had not been engraved. The copy became the property of the sixth Earl of Chesterfield, and is at Bretby Park, Derbyshire.

"The circumstances of the painting of the original picture (the property of Lady Ruthven) are as follows:—

"Sir Walter had consented to the wish expressed by Lady Ruthven that he should sit to me for a cabinet picture to be painted for herself. I accordingly went to Abbotsford, accompanied by Mrs. Grant, for that purpose. I suggested to Sir Walter that instead of his giving me special sittings, if he would allow me to place my easel in his study I could paint his portrait whilst he was occupied in dictating his novel. He said, 'Can you indeed! that will be a great accommodation to me.' I accordingly, the following morning, placed my easel between Sir Walter and his amanuensis, William Laidlaw, who had formerly occupied land adjoining to Sir Walter's hill-farm. Sir Walter had frequently consulted him on farming matters, and had become very friendly with him. After a time poor Mr. Laidlaw failed, and all his stock and property were sold by auction. Laidlaw was at his wits' end, not knowing what to do, when Scott said to him, 'Willie, do you think you could write my books for me, from dictation? for I am getting old, and have some gout and rheumatism in my hands, which makes it difficult for me to write much.' His answer was, 'I am very willing to try,' and soon after he was regularly established as amanuensis. I had these particulars from Sir Walter himself.

"Whilst I remained at Abbotsford, William Laidlaw arrived every morning at ten o'clock, in the costume of a Lowland hill-farmer, with his broad blue bonnet, a shepherd's plaid thrown across his shoulders, accompanied by his colly dog, which remained all day outside the house, waiting till his master's labours were completed, which generally occurred between one and two o'clock.

"Sir Walter then mounted his pony, as he called him to me 'a laigh sweered beast,' and accompanied by his two deer-hounds, with William Laidlaw and his colly, the group proceeded to the hill-farm. When they arrived, whilst Scott and Laidlaw were discussing farming matters, the colly, followed by Scott's deer-hounds, would hunt about till he started a hare, when the deer-hounds gave chase. Sir Walter used to be highly interested in these chases, though he confessed to me they very rarely succeeded in catching the hare.

"This is my recollection of Scott's daily proceedings, followed by an evening of abundant anecdotes and charming conversation.

"Whilst I was painting the picture, Scott was occupied chiefly in dictating *Count Robert of Paris*, which he occasionally laid aside for a work he was at that time writing on Demonology. The large folio represented in the left hand of the picture was a volume of reference on that subject, which he brought down from the upper shelves of his Library, which I introduced into the picture at the time.

"I was surprised at the extreme fluency with which Sir Walter dictated; he never appeared to hesitate for a moment, unless Laidlaw failed to give him the last word. Laidlaw was much interested in the progress of the picture, and frequently looked over my shoulder to see how it was getting on, and consequently was not always ready to give Scott the last word. This entirely put him out, and seemed to break the thread of his inspiration. On such occasions he would absolutely groan aloud, and exclaim, 'Oh Mr. Laidlaw! Mr. Laidlaw!' He would then require him to read over the last two pages before he was able to resume the story, which he did with much animation, suiting his voice to the nature of the subject. If it was of a melancholy character he would speak in slow and solemn tones. If of a gay and lively nature he would draw himself up and assume a look of animation, and change his voice and manner.

"After I had been four days painting in his study, I was in the afternoon walking with him, when I said, 'I have now been four days in your study, and must have heard many fine passages, but I have been so much engrossed with my picture that I am ashamed to own that I cannot carry away a single sentence,' upon which he stopt his walk, and turning to me, resting on his staff, and with that charming smile that was so peculiar to him, said, 'Well, my good friend, then it appears there was no love lost between us, for I was quite unconscious of your presence.'

"I remember on one occasion, when our sitting was somewhat prolonged, the dog Bran, the one represented standing up in the picture, began to show some symptoms of impatience, and went with his nose poking up Sir Walter's hand, which in the picture is seen holding the pen. Scott, addressing me, said, 'You see, Mr. Grant, Bran begins to think it is time we went to the Hill.' I said, 'May I ask you to wait a few minutes longer to enable me to finish the hand?' Upon which he turned to the dog, and in slow and measured words said, 'Bran—my man—do you see that gentleman (pointing to me); he is painting my picture, and he wants us to bide a wee bit, till he has finished my hand (pointing to his hand); so just lie down for a while and THEN we'll gang to the Hill.'

"The dog had been looking during this address into his face, and seemed perfectly to understand, and retired quietly, and again curled himself up on the rug. Scott then turned to me and said, 'Depend upon it, if people would speak slowly and with emphasis to their dogs, they understand a great deal more than we give them credit for.'

"In Lockhart's *Life of Scott*, I think in the sixth volume, Sir Walter in his diary makes a lengthened allusion to our visit, and especially mentions the picture.

"I have only to add that in Lady Ruthven's picture Sir Walter is represented in the chair he always sat in, and in the dress he daily wore. When I left Abbotsford it had been my intention to complete the background of the picture more carefully at home. But Lady Ruthven, I think with judgment and taste, said, 'You should never touch this picture again.' It was therefore entirely painted as it now exists in the study of Sir Walter Scott.—I am ever yours very truly,

"FRANCIS GRANT."

SIR FRANCIS GRANT, D.C.L., a younger son of Francis Grant of Kilgraston, in Perthshire, was born in 1804. He was educated for the Bar; but taking a strong dislike to the study of the Law, and having a not less strong passion for Art, he resolved to change his profession to that of a Painter. He became a Member of the Scottish Academy in 1830. At first, having been a keen sportsman, he distinguished himself by subjects of field sports and groups of figures in hunting-costume, which were much admired. He afterwards established his reputation as a portrait-painter under the most favourable circumstances, from his social position. Sir Walter Scott, in his diary, March 26, 1831, while referring to his change of life and pursuits, speaks of him in high terms. Mr. Grant was elected an Associate of the Royal Academy of London in 1842, and a Royal Academician in 1851.[1] His successful career as a painter secured his elevation to the high distinction of PRESIDENT OF THE ACADEMY, February 1, 1866.

[1] Sandby's *History of the Royal Academy*, Lond. 1862, vol. ii. p. 294-296.

XIX.

PORTRAIT BY LANDSEER. 1833. (No. 72.)

THIS posthumous Portrait of Sir Walter Scott and his Dogs was painted in 1833.

"Mr. Edwin Landseer, R.A.," says Mr. Lockhart, "has recently painted a full-length portrait, with the scenery of the Rhymer's Glen; and his familiarity with Scott renders this almost as valuable as if he had sat for it. This beautiful picture is in the gallery of Mr. WELLS."

It will be seen by an extract from Leslie's *Autobiography* at p. 93, that the Rhymer's Glen was a favourite haunt of its proprietor.

SIR EDWIN HENRY LANDSEER, R.A.—This very eminent painter was the younger son of John Landseer, the Engraver (1759-1852), one of the early Associates of the Royal Academy.

His son Edwin was born in London in 1802, and received his first lessons in drawing from his father, showing from his early youth a taste for the study of animals. He became a student of the Royal Academy in 1826, and was elected an Associate in 1816, and an Academician in 1831. He was an Honorary Member of the Royal Scottish Academy; and obtained from Her Majesty the honour of knighthood in 1850.

XX.

PORTRAIT OF LOCKHART, BY GRANT. (No. 83.)

The Committee, as an exception to their rule regarding Illustrations, of the three Portraits of Mr. Lockhart exhibited as Nos. 87, 88, and 89, selected that by Sir Francis Grant. It is a very pleasing likeness, painted about the year 1833.

John Gibson Lockhart, son-in-law and biographer of Sir Walter Scott, was born in the Manse of Cambusnethan, July 14, 1794. His father, who was Minister of that parish, in the Presbytery of Hamilton (1786-1796), was translated to one of the City Churches of Glasgow in 1796; and obtained the title of D.D. from Edinburgh in 1803. He died December 6, 1842, in the eighty-second year of his age. His son John was educated at the University of Glasgow, and obtained one of the Snell Exhibition Bursaries in Baliol College, Oxford, in 1809. He graduated B.C.L. in 1817, and was created D.C.L. in 1834. He had previously come to Edinburgh to complete his Law studies, and passed Advocate in 1816. His marriage with Sophia, eldest daughter of Sir Walter Scott, was in April 1820.

Along with his friend Professor Wilson, Lockhart became one of the chief contributors to Blackwood's *Edinburgh Magazine* in October 1817. In this periodical first appeared his much admired Translations of *Spanish Ballads.* He also attained celebrity by his Novels, *Valerius, Adam Blair, Reginald Dalton*, etc.; and was the chief writer of a work known as *Peter's Letters to his Kinsfolk*, under the assumed name of Dr. Peter Morris, as having taken his degree of M.D. at the University of Edinburgh, in 1819. It consists of a series of letters, containing lively spirited sketches of the most noted Edinburgh characters of that time. His Lives of Burns in Constable's Miscellany, and of Napoleon, and other volumes in Murray's Family Library, display no ordinary skill as a biographer; but his great work undoubtedly was his *Life of Sir Walter Scott.*

Mr. Lockhart, on his appointment, in 1825, to be Editor of the *Quarterly Review*, removed to London. He occasionally revisited his friends in Scotland; and at length, with broken health and spirits, he was removed to Abbotsford, where he breathed his last, November 25, 1854. He was interred in Dryburgh Abbey.

ADDITIONAL ILLUSTRATIONS.

XXI.

STATUE BY GREENSHIELDS. 1830.

Mr. Lockhart describes Sir Walter Scott as having accompanied him in a visit to his brother's at Milton-Lockhart, in Clydesdale, in January 1829, where he enjoyed some days of relaxation. "It was there that he first saw the self-educated sculptor, John Greenshields, who greatly interested him from a certain resemblance to Burns, and took his first sitting for a very remarkable statue in freestone, now in Mr. Cadell's possession,—the last work which this worthy man was destined to complete."

This Statue was presented by the Trustees of Robert Cadell, Esq. (who died January 20, 1849), to the Faculty of Advocates, and is now placed in their Under Library. All who personally knew Sir Walter Scott must acknowledge it to be a striking resemblance; and the inscription for Bacon's statue at St. Albans, when carved on the pedestal, Sic Sedebat, was most appropriate. The original Statue, owing to its ponderous weight, could not well be removed to the Exhibition rooms, neither was its present position well fitted for taking a photograph. Mr. M'Glashon however has since succeeded in the accompanying photo-lithograph, for which the permission of the Library Curators had previously been obtained.

John Greenshields, a native of Carluke, in Lanarkshire, died there in April 1835, at the age of 40. (See Lockhart's *Life of Scott*, vol. ix. pp. 280-288.)

SIC SEDEBAT

XXII.

MEDALLION PORTRAIT BY HENNING. 1810.

JOHN HENNING, Sculptor, as already stated (p. 4, No. 11, and p. 45), who was born at Paisley in 1771, exhibited at Edinburgh a Medallion Portrait of Scott, in 1809. The Drawing of which a facsimile is here given belongs to the subsequent year. A cast of a similar Medallion in the present Exhibition (No. 11), was most likely made from this drawing by Henning in 1810. It was recently found by Mr. Drummond, R.S.A., in a volume of Studies acquired not long since by his friend JOHN PENDER, Esq., M.P., who allowed the Volume to be brought to Edinburgh for this purpose. It contains twelve drawings which had remained in the possession of one of Henning's family. They have since been carefully mounted for preservation, and handsomely bound, with this title—

STUDIES FROM LIFE, BY J. HENNING, SCULPTOR.

The contents of this Volume may be enumerated :—

1. Medallion Head of King William the Fourth, in black lead, with the date June 25, 1827, at the Admiralty, done for the Medal struck by William Wyon, on the King's accession.

   *** WILLIAM WYON, R.A., gem-engraver and medallist, was born in 1795. In 1828 he was appointed chief engraver to the Mint. Amongst his numerous works he executed a medal of Sir Walter Scott, the reverse of which was designed by that worthy old man Thomas Stothard, R.A. Wyon, who had been a student of the Royal Academy in 1817, was elected an Associate in 1831, and an Academician in 1838. He died October 29, 1851.—(Sandby's *History*, vol. ii. p. 192.)

2. Portrait of the Princess Charlotte of Wales, drawn 1822.

3. Medallion Head of the Duke of Wellington, March 1827.

4. Ditto of Louis XVIII.

5. "Sketch of my Drawing of Sir H. Davy," 1810.

6. Portrait of Mrs. Siddons.

7. Medallion Portrait of Lord Jeffrey.

8. Ditto of Dr. Adam Fergusson, 1807.

9. Ditto of the Rev. Sir Henry Moncreiff, Bart., minister of St Cuthbert's, Edinburgh, 1806 or 1808.

10. Ditto of SIR WALTER SCOTT, 1810.

11. Ditto of Earl Grey.

12. Ditto of John Cartwright, in outline, 1821.

Of Henning himself, who was an Honorary Member of the R.S.A., and died in 1851, there are two or three characteristic photographs or calotypes in his venerable old age. In one of these, along with Henning, there is a striking likeness of Alexander Handyside Ritchie, Sculptor, A.R.S.A., who died in 1870. His figures for the pediment of the Commercial Bank, and other public buildings in Edinburgh, show that he was no unworthy pupil of Thorwaldsen. The prints have neither names nor date, but were taken by Messrs. D. O. Hill and Robert Adamson, at their "Calotype Studio, Calton Stairs, Edinburgh" (1844-1848).

XXIII.

TWO HEADS, BY GEDDES, 1818, AND SLATER, 1821.

(A.)

THE Portrait of Scott by Geddes, exhibited as No. 52, was one of the studies or sketches made for a large painting of "the Discovery of the Regalia" in February 1818. The present head is taken from an engraving (No. 150), under the Artist's inspection, by F. C. Lewis, in 1824.

The following note by Mr. Geddes, addressed to Abraham Cooper, R.A., proves that the large painting referred to had been completed. This note is contained in a very interesting volume of Autographs and Engravings, which was recently acquired for the British Museum:—

"15 BERNERS STREET, *6th July* 1843.

"MY DEAR SIR,—I fear I cannot name to a certainty the year I painted the study of Sir Walter's head; it was done at the same time I did the heads of the other Commissioners, to be inserted into the large picture I painted of the FINDING OF THE REGALIA OF SCOTLAND.—Yours faithfully, ANDW. GEDDES.

"*To* ABR. COOPER, ESQ."

(B.)

This head represents an excellent Engraving by R. W. Sievier, of an original sketch by Mr. Slater, in the possession of Sir Robert Henry Inglis, Bart., and published by the Artist in 1821 (No. 155).

JOSEPH SLATER was a well-known Portrait-Painter, who was settled in London as a resident, first in Greek Street, Soho, afterwards for many years in Newman Street, Oxford Street. Slater continued to be an exhibitor at the Royal Academy from the year 1806 till 1836. By him are the drawings of all the heads in the first volume, and of four in the second volume, of *Portraits of the Members of Grillion's Club,* 1813-1863 (London, privately printed, 1864, folio), of which there is a copy in the Print Room of the British Museum. This Club commenced, say the Editors (the late Sir Thomas Dyke Acland and Sir James Buller East), "with a few College friends, who lived together in the most cordial intimacy at Christ Church during the years 1805-6-7-8, and most of whom, after leaving Oxford, re-assembled in Edinburgh for attendance on the lectures of Dugald Stewart, Playfair, Hope, and other distinguished Professors of that University." In the winter of 1812-13 was laid the foundation of the present Society. The entire number enrolled from 1812-13 to 1863 was 155, and the living members in the latter year were 80, of whom 55 assembled on the 6th May to celebrate the fiftieth anniversary of the Club, under the Presidency of the late Earl of Derby. The meetings have always taken place at Grillion's Hotel, Albemarle Street, W., whence the name of the Club. The 66 portraits by Slater were engraved by F. C. Lewis, R. J. Lane, and other artists.

The collection took its rise from a commission given to him by Sir T. Dyke Acland in 1819 to execute the portraits of some twenty Christ-Church and other friends. In or about 1824 the Members of the Club whose portraits had thus been taken, agreed each to cause his own to be engraved, and to present it to the rest. Since that time, it has been the rule that each Member who shall present his own engraved portrait to the Club shall be entitled to the complete collection, which is not to be obtained on any other terms. In the rare cases in which copies of the completed volumes have occurred for sale, they have brought very high prices. The portraits in the second volume are 67, five by Slater and 62 by George Richmond, R.A., to whom, on the death of Slater, his commission was transferred, and by whom it was held with universal approval until his resignation in 1864. Mr. Slater died in or about 1836. His "Grillion Portraits," embracing many of the most distinguished men of his day, will probably be the works by which he will be best remembered.

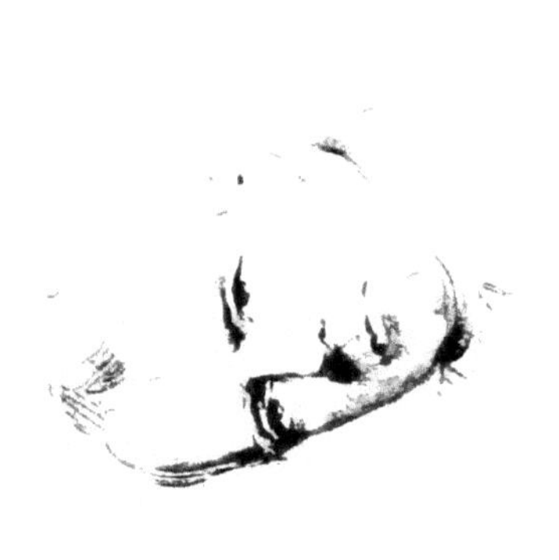

XXIV.

PORTRAIT BY LESLIE. 1824.

"A half-length, painted by C. R. Leslie, R.A., in 1824, for Mr. Ticknor of Boston, New England, is now in that gentleman's possession. I never saw this picture in its finished state, but the beginning promised well, and I am assured it is worthy of the artist's high reputation. It has not been engraved—in this country, I mean—but a reduced copy of it furnished an indifferent print for one of the Annuals."—LOCKHART.

Mr. George Ticknor, the accomplished author of the *History of Spanish Literature*, a native of Boston, Massachusetts, was born August 1, 1791. After spending two or three years on the Continent, he came to Scotland, and was kindly received at Abbotsford, in the year 1819. In a letter, sent through Mr. Constable to Sir Walter Scott, dated at Boston, May 7, 1824, he requested, as a special favour, that Sir Walter would sit for his Portrait, by any artist he chose to employ. Sir Walter having consented, Mr. Constable recommended Mr. Leslie, then a rising artist, who had furnished some admirable designs for *Waverley*. It was finally arranged that Leslie, for this purpose, should visit Abbotsford in July that year.

GEORGE TICKNOR, Esq., was for several years Professor of Modern Languages and Literature in Harvard College. He died in 1871.

As there seemed some doubt respecting Leslie's portrait, Mr. Ticknor's representatives were communicated with on the subject, and in reply Messrs. James R. Osgood and Co. wrote: "We have applied to the family of the late Mr. George Ticknor for permission to make a photograph of Leslie's portrait of Scott, painted for Mr. Ticknor. During Mr. Ticknor's life, several applications were made to him for photographing and engraving this portrait. These applications were uniformly declined, and for this reason the family are reluctant to grant any such permission. They have, however, given their consent to the use of photographs for purposes of this Catalogue only, with the understanding that it shall not be engraved, and that only such number of photographs shall be printed as are needed for the Catalogue."

In acknowledging this letter, Mr. Laing, while expressing the thanks of the Committee to Messrs. Osgood and to Mr. Ticknor's family for this obliging offer, said that ordinary photographs would not suit their purpose for Illustration, besides the want of time, as it was then expected that no delay would occur in completing the Catalogue. He requested, however, to be favoured with a description of the portrait, which was complied with in the following polite note:—

"BOSTON, *July* 12, 1872.

"DEAR SIR,—On behalf of the family of the late George Ticknor, Esq., I beg leave to answer the inquiries contained in your letter of June 29, addressed to Messrs. Osgood and Co.

"The Portrait of Sir Walter Scott, by Leslie, is a half-length, shewing both the hands. The figure is seated. The right hand rests upon a staff, the left lies upon the left thigh. It represents him in a morning dress; the coat is green, the waistcoat drab or yellow, the cravat black, the collar limp and turned over. In the upper left-hand corner are the arms of Scott. The dimensions of the canvas are three feet in height and two feet four inches in width. It is an excellent work of art, and the likeness was pronounced by the late Mr. George Combe to be admirable.—Your obedient servant, G. S. HILLARD.

"TO D. LAING, ESQ."

It was imagined from the words of Sir David Wilkie, September 15, 1824, that it had been a full-length portrait.—"Leslie," he says, "is painting a portrait of Sir Walter Scott as large as life." The above description settles the question that the portrait was a half-length, of which Mr. Leslie may have retained a duplicate, besides painting the one for Mr. Constable, from which there are two or three small engravings, in England.

In a volume in the British Museum, containing the Correspondence of Abraham Cooper, Esq., R.A., the celebrated animal painter, and purchased from his widow, February 13, 1869, there are many letters relating to portraits and other illustrations for Sir Walter Scott's works; among

these is the following note by Leslie, which proves that one of the small engravings was done under his own inspection :—

"41 Portman Square, *Thursday*.

"Dear Cooper,—Do not engage any engraver for the little portrait [of Scott?], as I think I can get Danforth to do it. I shall write to day to Lord Egremont.—Yours most truly,

"C. R. Leslie."

Along with this note there is a proof impression of the small portrait, inscribed "Sir Walter Scott. Painted by C. R. Leslie, R.A. Engraved by M. J. Danforth. Published by Longman, Rees, Orme, and Green. 1828." It was therefore thought desirable to give a lithographic facsimile, somewhat enlarged, of this pleasing portrait.

Charles Robert Leslie, R.A., was born at Clerkenwell, near London, in 1794, of American parents. They left England in 1799, and their son was educated at Philadelphia. In 1811 Leslie returned to London; became a student of the Academy; was admitted an Associate in 1821, and R.A. in 1826. In many English galleries, especially in the South Kensington Museum, there are numerous examples of Leslie's paintings. This eminent artist, who is also favourably known as an author, died at London, May 4th, 1859. In the following year, Mr. Tom Taylor published *Autobiographical Recollections of the late Charles Robert Leslie, R.A.* In this work there is an account of his visit and agreeable reception at Abbotsford.

During his visit Leslie says,—

"When I began the portrait, Scott suggested that for the background I should take "Thomas the Rhymer's Glen," one of his favourite haunts. I went with him and Mr. Rose to see it, and when we came near the spot where Thomas was supposed to have met the Queen of the Fairies, Sir Walter and I dismounted from our ponies, and as the descent into the Glen was steep, I offered to help him; but he declined assistance, saying, he could get along best in his own way, etc. . . . The Glen was beautiful, and as he rested himself in his favourite seat near a little succession of waterfalls, he said, with a strong emphasis of satisfaction on the two last words, 'A poor thing, but *mine own*.' I told him the dimensions of my picture would not admit the scene as a background, as its leading features could not be brought into so small a compass. I might, however, have made a sketch of it with Sir Walter in the spot he loved, and my only excuse for not doing it is that Mr. Rose, who was too infirm to descend into the glen, was waiting for us above."—(Vol. i. p. 89.)

XXV.

PORTRAIT BY NEWTON. 1824. (No. 57.)

THE Original Portrait of Scott by Newton is now at Abbotsford. It is thus described by Mr. Lockhart:—

"A small three-quarters in oil, done at Chiefswood in August 1824, by the late Gilbert Stewart Newton, R.A., and presented by him to Mrs. Lockhart. This pleasing Picture gives Sir Walter in his usual country dress—a green jacket and black neckcloth, with a leathern belt for carrying the forester's axe round the shoulders. It is the best domestic portrait ever done. A duplicate, in Mr. Murray's possession, was engraved for Finden's *Illustrations of Byron.*"

The duplicate Painting mentioned in this extract was in the Exhibition (No. 57), lent by JOHN MURRAY, Esq., London, and is well known from small Engravings by Finden, Ryall, and Bird (Nos. 171, etc.)

Another Original by Newton belongs to JOHN FORSTER, Esq., Palace Gate House, Kensington. It is in excellent preservation, and the accompanying Photograph was obtained by Sir William Stirling Maxwell. Upon comparing this with the Abbotsford painting there are several minute variations; but not necessary to be pointed out, unless it be that the face in the Abbotsford painting is more contemplative, and the mouth more curved, and expressive.

XXVI.

PORTRAIT BY MACLISE. 1825.

In the *Memoir of Daniel Maclise, R.A.*, by W. Justin O'Driscoll, M.R.I.A., Barrister-at-Law (London, 1871), there is the following notice of Sir Walter Scott's visit to Cork, in 1825, which may be quoted in connexion with the interesting chalk or pencil drawing of his head by that late eminent artist, then a youth, of which an exact facsimile is here given.

"In the autumn of 1825, Sir Walter Scott made a hasty tour of Ireland, accompanied by Mr. and Mrs. Lockhart and Miss Edgeworth. Amongst other places he stayed a short time at Cork, and whilst there he visited the establishment of Mr. Bolster, an eminent bookseller. The presence of the illustrious author attracted crowds of literary persons there. Maclise, then a mere boy [he was born January 25, 1811], conceived the idea of making a sketch of Sir Walter, and having placed himself unobserved in a part of the shop which afforded him an admirable opportunity, he made in a few minutes three outline sketches, each in a different position. He brought them home, and having selected that one which he considered the best, worked at it all night, and next morning brought to Bolster a highly finished pen-and-ink drawing, handled with all the elaborate minuteness of a line engraving. Bolster placed it in a conspicuous part of his shop, and Sir Walter with his friends having again called during the day it attracted his attention when he entered. He was struck with the exquisite finish and fidelity of the drawing, and at once inquired the name of the artist who had executed it. Maclise, who was standing in a remote part of the shop, was brought forward and introduced to Sir Walter. The great author took him kindly by the hand, and expressed his astonishment that a mere boy could have achieved such a work, and predicated that he would yet distinguish himself. Sir Walter then asked for a pen, and wrote with his own hand *Walter Scott* at the foot of the sketch. Maclise was advised by Mr. Bolster to have it lithographed. That branch of art was only then in its infancy. There was no lithographic press in Cork, and but one in Dublin. Maclise himself prepared the tracings for transferring the drawing to the slate. Five hundred copies were struck off and were sold as rapidly as they were printed. One of these original sketches, with the study in oils for *The Spirit of Justice*, and some early drawings of the artist, were to be seen in the National Exhibition at Cork in 1852.—This little sketch of Sir Walter Scott created such a sensation amongst art critics and the public, that Maclise, not without great reluctance and diffidence on his part, was induced by his friends to open an *atelier* in Patrick Street. He attained at once full practice for his pencil," etc. (pp. 20-22.)

The present Drawing seems not to be known to the Artist's biographer. It now belongs to John Forster, Esq., and the use of it was obtained by Sir William Stirling Maxwell, Bart.

NO. XXVI.]

XXVII.

THREE FULL-LENGTH SKETCHES OF SCOTT. 1825-1831.

THESE Sketches are brought together, as exhibiting, from different points of view, a whole-length of the Author of *Waverley*, as he used to be seen on the streets of Edinburgh.

(A.)

The first of these Sketches, or the one to the left, is by DANIEL MACLISE, done at Cork in 1825. The quotation from the *Memoir of Maclise*, in No. XXVI., explains the circumstances under which the youthful artist was enabled to take his sketches on the spot, and to attract the notice and approbation of Sir Walter Scott himself.

A few years later, in *Fraser's Magazine*, there appeared a series of clever sketches, as the "GALLERY OF ILLUSTRIOUS LITERARY CHARACTERS," chiefly contributed by Maclise with the signature of *Alfred Croquis*. In No. VI. of this series the accompanying lithograph sketch by Maclise was given in November 1830, with a descriptive account of Scott, from which the following is an extract :—

"On the opposite page is old Sir Peveril! Many a time has he figured on canvas or paper, in stone, bronze, or plaster, in oil or water-colours, lithographed, copperplated, mezzotinted, in all the variety of manner that the art of the sculptor, the founder, the modeller, the painter, the etcher, the engraver, the whole tribe of the imitators of the face divine, could display him. He has hung in the chamber of kings, and decorated the door of the alehouse—has graced the boudoir of beauty, and perambulated the streets borne upon the head of a swarthy Italian pedlar. He has been depicted in all moods and all postures; but we venture to say that the Baronet, as he really looks, was never so exactly put before the public as we now see him.

"There he is, sauntering about his grounds, with his Lowland bonnet in his hand, dressed in his old green shooting-jacket, telling old stories," etc.—(*Fraser's Magazine, November* 1830, p. 412.)

(B.)

The centre figure is reduced from the large (and somewhat unfinished) painting exhibited as No. 71. To the notices of Mr. JAMES HALL, given at pages 15 and 113, it may further be added, that at the time of the great fire in Edinburgh, in November 1824, Mr. Hall made various spirited drawings and sketches of the ruins. Eight of these, some in lithography, others engraved in outline, were published for the benefit of the sufferers—an instance of the liberal-minded spirit which Mr. Hall displayed through life.—See Burgon's *Memoir of Patrick Fraser Tytler*, 1859, p. 171.

(C.)

The third or right-hand figure is from a Drawing by BENJAMIN WILLIAM CROMBIE, a Miniature Painter, Edinburgh, in 1831. He was the son of Mr. Andrew Crombie, Solicitor-at-Law, Edinburgh (*b.* 1761, *d.* Sept. 1847), and was born at Fountainbridge, in the parish of St. Cuthbert's, Edinburgh, July 19, 1803. His name occurs as an Exhibitor at the Scottish Academy in 1829, and in subsequent years, with few exceptions, during the rest of his life. He died at Edinburgh, June 10, 1847.

Crombie will chiefly be remembered by a series of plates, coloured or tinted, which were published in separate parts, each plate having two figures, exhibiting a marked contrast, of the more striking personages in Edinburgh. They were afterwards collected and published in oblong folio, with this title, *Men of Modern Athens; or Portraits of Eminent Personages (existing or supposed to exist) in the Metropolis of Scotland.* Edinburgh, Hugh Paton, 1839-1851. They are cleverly drawn; and the names of the persons are given on a separate leaf, in the complete set of forty-eight plates, or ninety-six full-length figures. The one of *The Author of Waverley* is of an earlier date, and not included in that Volume.

XXVIII.

THE ABBOTSFORD FAMILY, BY WILKIE. 1817. (No. 76.)

The above is an Outline Sketch of the upper portion of a fine Painting by Wilkie, representing (not indeed very happily) Scott and his family in the character of peasants.

This painting, executed in 1817 for Sir Adam Ferguson, whose portrait is the most successful in the group, has been several times engraved (Nos. 141-144). It is thus graphically described by Sir Walter himself, in a letter to his friend Sir Adam Ferguson, dated Abbotsford, 2d August 1827 :—

"The idea which our inimitable Wilkie adopted, was to represent our family group in the garb of south-country peasants, supposed to be concerting a merry-making, for which some of the preparations are seen. The place is the terrace near Kayside, commanding an extensive view towards the Eildon Hills. 1. The sitting figure, in the dress of the miller I believe, represents Sir Walter Scott, author of a few scores of volumes, and proprietor of Abbotsford, in the county of Roxburgh. 2. In front, and presenting, we may suppose, a country wag, somewhat addicted to poaching, stands Sir Adam Ferguson, knight, Keeper of the Regalia of Scotland. 3. In the background is a very handsome old man, upwards of eighty-four years old at the time, painted in his own character of shepherd. He also belonged to the numerous clan of Scott. . . . 4. 5. 6.—4. Of the three female figures, the elder is the late regretted mother of the family represented. 5. The young person most forward in the group is Miss Sophia Charlotte Scott, now Mrs. John Gibson Lockhart, and 6. her younger sister, Miss Ann Scott. Both are represented as ewe-milkers, with their *leglins*, or milk-pails. 7. On the left of the shepherd, the young man holding a fowling-piece, is the eldest son of Sir Walter, now Captain in the King's Hussars. 8. The boy is the youngest of the family, Charles Scott, now of Brazenose College, Oxford. The two dogs were distinguished favourites of the family; the large one was a stag-hound of the old Highland breed, called Maida."

This description of the Picture, to which Wilkie alludes in a letter to his sister, from Madrid, Oct. 30, 1827, had appeared in the newspapers, and is quoted in the prospectus of the Engraving by Robert Graves, A.R.A., when the Engraving was "Nearly Ready," 1837:—

"I have just seen in the papers Sir Walter Scott's letter, giving an account of my little picture of his family. I cannot help admiring it extremely for its cleverness and goodness of heart, and Washington Irving is quite delighted with it."

Sir David Wilkie was born in the manse of the parish of Cults, Fifeshire, November 18, 1785; and was educated as an Artist under John Graham, master of the Trustees' Drawing Academy, Edinburgh. He was admitted a Student of the Royal Academy, London, in 1805; and taking up his residence in London, he was elected an Associate in 1809; and an Academician in 1811. On the death of Sir Henry Raeburn in 1823 Wilkie was appointed Limner to His Majesty for Scotland. In 1830 he became successor to Sir Thomas Lawrence as Portrait Painter in ordinary to the King. In 1836 he received from William IV. the honour of knighthood. He died on his return home from the East on board a steamer, off Gibraltar, June 1, 1841.

XXIX.

GALA DAY AT ABBOTSFORD, BY ALLAN. (No. 80.)

The accompanying Plate is a reduced facsimile of a sketch, in sepia, by Sir William Allan, *P*.R.S.A. A somewhat similar, but unfinished, sketch in oil was also exhibited (No. 79). Neither of these requires any minute description. The Artist, in his visits at Abbotsford in later years, may have intended to paint the subject on a larger scale; but this he never accomplished.

In a very clever painting for William Gott, Esq., Banker, Leeds, in 1823, of "The Ettrick Shepherd's House-heating," Allan introduced a figure of Scott, but not a very successful likeness. A few years later we have a portrait representing "The Author of Waverley in his Study," with this inscription, "W. Allan, A.R.A., *pinx.* R. Goodall, *sculp.* Published October 1, 1828, by John Sharpe, London." It may have been engraved for one of the Annuals.

One of Allan's most finished works was that of "Sir Walter Scott Bart., at Abbotsford," painted in 1831 (No. 66). It was engraved in a superior style by John Burnet (No. 194). In March 1871 it was purchased for the National Portrait Gallery, London, at £367, 10s.

The Painting represents Sir Walter Scott seated in his Study at Abbotsford, reading Queen Mary's Proclamation previous to her marriage with Henry Lord Darnley, "Subscribed with our hand, and gevin vnder our Signet At Halirudhous the xxviij day of Julij, and of our Regnne the xxiij zeir 1565.—Marie R."—It cannot be said that the Artist was fortunate in his design, as the document is so apt to be mistaken for an ordinary newspaper. The original precept is still preserved in the General Register House; it measures 12 inches by 8¾.

Sir William Allan, historical painter, was born at Edinburgh in

1782. He was educated at the Trustees' Drawing Academy. He also had the advantage of being a student of the Royal Academy, of which he became an Associate in 1825. In the following year he was chosen Master of the Trustees' School for Drawing, Edinburgh. In early life he was in Russia, visiting Tartary and Turkey, and returned to his native city in 1814. His "Circassian Captives," and other similar subjects, which he then exhibited in Edinburgh, established his reputation. He was elected R.A. London, in 1835, and President of the Royal Scottish Academy in 1838. On the death of Sir David Wilkie he was appointed Limner to Her Majesty for Scotland, obtaining the honour of knighthood. He died in 1850.

XXX.

SIR WALTER SCOTT AND HIS FRIENDS AT ABBOTSFORD, BY FAED. (No. 78.)

1. Sir Walter Scott.
2. James Hogg.
3. Henry Mackenzie.
4. John Wilson.
5. Rev. George Crabbe.
6. John G. Lockhart.
7. W. Wordsworth.
8. Lord Jeffrey.
9. Sir Adam Ferguson.
10. Thomas Moore.
11. Thomas Campbell.
12. Sir William Allan
13. Sir David Wilkie.
14. Archibald Constable.
15. James Ballantyne.
16. Sir Humphry Davy.
17. Thomas Thomson.

THE above is an outline sketch of the original Painting in the possession of Alexander Dennistoun, Esq., by Thomas Faed, R.A., which was exhibited as No. 78. The object of this sketch was to serve as a Key to the persons represented in an imaginary assemblage at Abbotsford, when the engraving, by the Artist's brother, Mr. James Faed (No. 230), was published by James Keith, January 2, 1854.

It is proper to mention that the original picture was painted by Mr. Faed in 1849, upon a commission for Mr. Keith, an Edinburgh

Publisher, with the view of having it engraved. The engraving proved a very lucrative speculation, from the mode in which the keen and enterprising publisher was enabled to push its sale in the United States as well as in this country: he thought, therefore, that by obtaining a second and smaller painting, and having a distinguished American introduced in some conspicuous position, to be engraved anew, this introduction of a "great Yankee" would insure a still greater success on the other side of the Atlantic. Before this could be accomplished, the publisher died.

The second and smaller Painting was, however, completed, and acquired by the late Mr. Joseph Gillott of Birmingham, at the sale of whose extraordinary collection of paintings at London, April 19, 1872, Mr. Faed's picture fetched the very large sum of 910 guineas. On applying to the Artist, in regard to the difference between this Painting and the one exhibited as No. 78, Mr. Faed, in a note to Mr. James Drummond, R.S.A., says:—

"This picture of Sir Walter and his Literary Friends, sold last Friday at Gillott's Sale, was not Mr. Dennistoun's, but a smaller one, some 1 foot 5 inches by 2 feet—in fact, the size of the engraving from Mr. D.'s; and was painted in 1856, and then, or rather when commenced, intended for publication to suit *the American market*,—I mean by publication, to be engraved. You may remember (no; I don't suppose you do anything of the kind), but I will tell you, that in the large work there was no great Yankee, so in the second venture Washington Irving was introduced, and that introduction made me make others that, to a great extent, changed the whole left of the work—from a picturesque point of view, totally changed it. I have nothing more to say on the matter, except that poor Keith died before the original intention was carried out."

Washington Irving, as Author of *Abbotsford, or Recollections of a Friendly Visit to Sir Walter Scott*, in 1816, published in *Irving's Miscellanies* in 1835, was well entitled to be represented in such a group. For picturesque effect, in consequence of the alteration in grouping the figures, the composition on the left-hand side, as Mr. Faed says, required to be altered; and while Lord Byron and Washington Irving were introduced, the actual number of figures was lessened by the omission of Nos. 12, 14, 15, 16, and 17, who were reckoned, it might be, as persons chiefly of local celebrity.

Third Division.

MANUSCRIPTS AND EARLY EDITIONS OF SCOTT'S WRITINGS.

I.—ORIGINAL MANUSCRIPTS, WITH FACSIMILES.

II.—POETICAL AND PROSE WORKS, IN CHRONOLOGICAL ORDER.

III.—BOOKS EDITED BY SIR WALTER SCOTT.

IV.—ORIGINAL LETTERS AND MISCELLANEOUS PAPERS IN CONNEXION WITH SIR WALTER SCOTT.

N

ORIGINAL MANUSCRIPTS.

The circumstances under which the earlier Waverley Novels were published, contributed to the care that was bestowed in preserving the Original Manuscripts. These Volumes, written by the Author *currente calamo*, having subsequently been widely dispersed at public Sales or by private arrangements, it was of course not possible to obtain the entire Series for the Loan Exhibition. In the present Catalogue, however, it may be well that this division should not be restricted to such MSS. as were actually exhibited: by giving a correct notice of these Sales from the printed Catalogues, it will assist in tracing the subsequent fate of the respective Manuscripts.

The public acknowledgment by Sir Walter Scott of the authorship of the Waverley Novels took place on the 23d of February 1827. This was on occasion of his presiding at a Theatrical Fund dinner in the Assembly Rooms, Edinburgh; and a better opportunity could scarcely have happened for making a public avowal than to such a large assemblage. As one of the survivors of those who had the happiness to be present, the writer of this notice cannot forget the enthusiastic excitement with which his clear, explicit, and unhesitating avowal as the sole Author was received.

Four years previously, Sir Walter had presented the Manuscripts of the Novels to his friend the publisher, Mr. Constable, under the seal of secrecy. Indeed, so decided was he to conceal the authorship during his life, that the instrument, dated in December 1818, conveying to Messrs. Constable and Company the existing copyrights, contained a clause by which they bound themselves never to divulge the name of the Author of Waverley during his life, under a penalty of £2000. The same clause was repeated in a subsequent deed in 1821.

The Manuscripts, it is well known, for the purpose of such concealment of the authorship, were transcribed by one or other persons in strict confidence, under Mr. Ballantyne's direction, to be placed in the compositors' hands.

Subsequent to this transcription and publication, the Original manuscripts were delivered, from time to time, either to Scott himself or to the charge of his friend, Mr. Erskine of Kinnedder. Upon the lamented and unexpected death of the latter, his trustees, in examining his repositories, carefully sealed up and returned all Sir Walter's private correspondence. This we learn from the trustees' minutes, and it sufficiently explains the fact that none of Scott's letters or manuscripts could be discovered at Kinnedder upon a recent and careful search.[1]

In noticing the dispersion of the Waverley Manuscripts, there were three collections which require to be specially described.

I.—THE CONSTABLE MANUSCRIPTS, 1823-1831.

Sir Walter Scott's letter presenting the Waverley Manuscripts to Mr. Constable in 1823, was first published in Lockhart's *Life*, and is as follows :—

"On the morning (says Mr. Lockhart) after that first Bannatyne Club dinner, Scott sent such of the Waverley MSS. as he had in Castle Street to Mr. Constable, with this note :—

"'Edinburgh, 10*th March* 1823.—Dear Constable,—You who have so richly endowed my little collection, cannot refuse me the pleasure of adding to yours. I beg your acceptance of a parcel of MSS., which I know your partialities will give more value to than they deserve ; and only annex the condition that they shall be scrupulously concealed during the Author's life, and only made forthcoming when it may be necessary to assert his right to be accounted the Writer of these Novels.

"'I enclose a note to Mr. Guthrie Wright, who will deliver to you some others of those MSS. which were in poor Lord Kinnedder's possession ; and a few more now at Abbotsford, which I can send in a day or two, will, I think, nearly complete the whole, though there may be some leaves missing.

[1] Extract and information communicated by William Traquair, Esq., W.S.

"'I hope you are not the worse of our very merry party yesterday.—Ever yours truly, WALTER SCOTT.'"

Previously to this gift, Mr. Constable had collected some of the MSS. of Sir Walter's Poems. On the fly-leaf of *Rokeby*, No. 235, we find this notice, dated 1821:—

"This is the Original Manuscript of *Rokeby*, by Sir Walter Scott, Bart., the whole in his own handwriting,—some few of the notes excepted, which appear to have been copied by Henry Weber. I now possess the Originals of

Marmion, ...	One Volume,
Don Roderick, ...	One Volume,
Field of Waterloo, ...	
Lord of the Isles, ...	One Volume,
Life of Swift, ...	One Volume,

and the present Manuscript. The Original MS. of the *Lay of the Last Minstrel* was not preserved, such things not having been thought important till the publication of *Marmion*, when I desired Mr. Ballantyne to preserve the Manuscript for me. The Original of the *Lady of the Lake* is in Mr. John Ballantyne's possession, to whose liberality I am indebted for this valuable addition [of *Rokeby*] to my Collection of the Original MSS. of Sir Walter Scott. ARCHD. CONSTABLE.

"*18th April* 1821."

Among other matters in which Sir Walter was too deeply involved by the misfortunes of his Edinburgh and London publishers, a question arose regarding the public sale of the Waverley Manuscripts. Mr. Constable, to whom they had been presented, died in 1827, and these MSS. were claimed by his creditors. It was finally referred to the arbiter, with matters of still greater importance, as it was maintained that the solemn promise respecting the authorship should not be divulged during his life had not been kept. In a letter to his law-agent (John Gibson, Esq., W.S.), November 1829, Scott says, "I only wish a decision about the Manuscripts to get out of disputes at once." After a long and apparently unnecessary delay, the arbiter (about April 1831) held "that the condition which had been originally attached to the gift was no longer of any avail." It was then proposed that Sir Walter should have a voice as to the mode of disposing of the MSS. by the creditors, on learning which he emphatically wrote, "If they are not mine, I do not wish to interfere in the matter."[1]

[1] *Reminiscences of Sir Walter Scott.* By John Gibson, Writer to the Signet. Edinburgh: Adam and Charles Black. 1871. 12mo, pp. 74.

The trustees accordingly, acting upon this decision, sent the Manuscripts in question to London, to Mr. R. H. Evans, the principal book-auctioneer of the time; and notwithstanding the lateness in the season, the sale took place on Friday, August 19th, 1831. "The salerooms of Mr. Evans (says one literary journal) were crowded by the curious to witness the sale of the original manuscripts of some of the Waverley Novels." In the words of another journalist we read :—

"1831.—*August 20th* (*Saturday*).—The announcement of the sale of these interesting MSS. did not excite so much attention as we had anticipated; however competitors were not wanting yesterday, etc. The manuscripts were all in Sir Walter Scott's handwriting; neat, clean, and in green morocco bindings."

The sale consisted of the following lots, and the prices realized came very far short of what might have reasonably been expected. The vague rumours which were afloat as to the large sums that such Manuscripts would likely fetch, may have actually deterred purchasers from attending the sale or sending commissions :—

	Price.			*Purchaser.*
1. The Monastery, . .	£18	0	0	Mr. THORPE.
*** THE MANUSCRIPT OF THE ABOVE AND OF THE FOLLOWING NOVELS, ROMANCES, AND TALES ARE ALL IN THE HANDWRITING OF SIR WALTER SCOTT, BART. The annals of literature scarcely afford a similar instance of facility of composition. The public will be astonished to perceive the few erasures, alterations, or additions which occur from the first conceptions of the author to their final transmission to the press.				
2. Guy Mannering, . .	27	10	0	Mr. THORPE.
3. Old Mortality, . .	33	0	0	Mr. ROBERTSON.
4. Antiquary, . . .	42	0	0	Captain BASIL HALL.
5. Rob Roy, . . .	50	0	0	Mr. WILKS, M.P.
6. Peveril of the Peak, . .	42	0	0	Mr. COCHRAN.
These were all perfect, or nearly so; the following were not complete :—				
7. Waverley, . . .	18	0	0	Mr. WILKS, M.P.
8. The Abbot, . . .	14	0	0	Messrs. POOLE & EDWARDS.
9. Ivanhoe, . . .	12	0	0	Mr. RUMBOLD, M.P.
10. The Pirate, . . .	12	0	0	Mr. MOLTENO.
11. The Fortunes of Nigel, .	16	16	0	Mr. J. BAIN.
12. Kenilworth, . . .	17	0	0	Mr. WILKS, M.P.
13. The Bride of Lammermoor, .	14	14	0	Captain BASIL HALL.
Total,	£317	0	0	

It will be observed that this Sale in August 1831 was limited to the earlier Manuscripts of the Waverley Novels. A Second Collection of Scott Manuscripts, containing the Poetry, remained in the possession of Mr. Constable's eldest son (DAVID CONSTABLE, Esq., Advocate), and on November 9, 1833, was sold by private bargain to Mr. Cadell. The result of the first London sale had probably its effect in enabling Mr. Cadell to acquire these volumes upon the most moderate terms. Along with a series of Scott's early Letters there were the ORIGINAL MANUSCRIPTS of :—

1. MARMION. 2. DON RODERICK. 3. FIELD OF WATERLOO.
4. ROKEBY. 5. LORD OF THE ISLES.

In referring to these MSS. which Mr. Cadell had thus acquired, he adds :—

"The early Letters of Sir Walter Scott I purchased from Mr. D. Constable, along with the volumes of Poetry already adverted to. A good many I got from time to time from James Ballantyne. I need not say how I got those addressed to myself. They are contained in five quarto volumes, commencing at 2d October 1796, and coming down to 14th April 1832."

The price, we understand, that Mr. Cadell paid for the Letters was £105; and for the Poems, only £60. The number of letters was seventy-one.

II.—THE BALLANTYNE MANUSCRIPTS, 1831-1838.

It is already stated that all Sir Walter Scott's Manuscripts passed through the hands of Mr. James Ballantyne; and having been transcribed by an amanuensis, employed confidentially, were returned by Mr. Ballantyne either to the Author or to his friend Mr. Erskine. We do not find the most distant allusion to any desire on his part to retain them in his own possession. He survived Sir Walter only about four months; and after his death, when his Trustees examined his repositories and drawers or presses in the printing-office, they found various fragmentary portions of the Novels, and numerous proof-sheets with corrections, and perhaps one or other of the Waverley Manuscripts of a later date, which had been overlooked. These fragmentary leaves and proof-sheets remained in the hands of Mr. Ballantyne's trustees, who carried on the printing business till his son came of age. Of these MSS. he presented some to his father's trustees or to particular friends by way of memorial. In a few years, however, the state of the printing concern led to a sequestration; and the following lots which still remained in his hands were sold with his library for behoof of the trust-estate :—

Relics of Sir Walter Scott at Mr. John A. Ballantyne's Sale.

JAMES A. DOWELL, *Auctioneer, Saturday, 6th May* 1848.

	Price.	Purchaser.
403. Original Manuscript of *The Black Dwarf*, in 1 vol. 4to, morocco, elegant, . . .	£28 17 6	Mr. STILLIE.
404. Author's Proofs of Scott's *Life of Napoleon*, 9 vols. 8vo, full-bound in russia, extra, . .	47 5 0	Mr. TAYLOR.
405. Waverley Novels: Author's Proofs, containing *Woodstock*, *Fortunes of Nigel*, *Quentin Durward*, *Tales of the Crusaders*, *Ivanhoe*, *Peveril of the Peak*, *The Pirate*, in all 12 vols. 8vo, full-bound russia, extra, . . .	43 1 0	Mr. TAYLOR.
406. Scott's *Letters on Demonology and Witchcraft*, interleaved copy, with Notes and Additions in the handwriting of the author, .	2 10 0	Messrs. BLACKWOOD.

III.—THE CADELL MANUSCRIPTS, 1831-1868.

MR. ROBERT CADELL, a partner in the firm of A. Constable & Company, became latterly the sole publisher of Scott's Works, and also acquired one-half of the copyrights, which, under his management, proved a very lucrative concern. In this way he felt an honourable desire to collect and preserve the Original Manuscripts; and Nos. 3, 8, and 10 were purchased for him (by commission) at the Sale of 1831. We have been favoured by the Rev. Dr. Stevenson, of St. George's, Edinburgh (one of his sons-in-law), with the use of a list, written by Mr. Cadell himself in 1846, from which it appears that he had succeeded in acquiring eight volumes of Scott's Poetical Works, twelve volumes of the Novels and Tales, besides fragments of others, with an extensive collection of Original Letters of Sir Walter Scott, arranged and bound in five volumes, the correspondence extending from October 2, 1796 to April 14, 1832.

IV.—"MEMORANDUM OF MANUSCRIPTS OF SIR WALTER SCOTT IN THE POSSESSION OF ROBERT CADELL.

"RATHO HOUSE, 28*th July* 1846.

"The Contents of the oak cabinet in dining-room are as follows:—

"The Original MSS. of the Waverley Novels are comprised in twelve quarto volumes, with the addition of Vol. i. of the Fragments. Of course the series is not complete; the auction list at the commencement of vol. i. (OLD MORTALITY) shows the destination of all those sold by auction on 19th August 1831. The volumes of this series may be considered as the *prima cura* of the respective tales. I have attached to each a memorandum stating how I became possessed of it. Only a part of COUNT ROBERT OF PARIS is in Sir Walter Scott's handwriting. All CASTLE DANGEROUS is in that of William Laidlaw, [with] some alterations by the Author.

VOL. I.	contains	OLD MORTALITY.	VOL. VII.	contains	TALES OF THE CRUSADERS.
II.	"	THE ABBOT.	VIII.	"	WOODSTOCK.
III.	"	THE PIRATE.	IX.	"	CHRONICLES OF THE CANONGATE.
IV.	"	QUENTIN DURWARD.	X.	"	ANNE OF GEIERSTEIN.
V.	"	ST. RONAN'S WELL.	XI.	"	COUNT ROBERT OF PARIS.
VI.	"	REDGAUNTLET.	XII.	"	CASTLE DANGEROUS.

[In a subsequent note, March 27, 1847, Mr. Cadell refers to the purchase of ROB ROY. See No. 248.]

"The Original Manuscripts of the Poetry comprise eight volumes, folio and quarto. They have almost all come into my possession by purchase; MARMION, DON RODERICK and FIELD OF WATERLOO, ROKEBY and LORD OF THE ISLES from Mr. David Constable; THE LADY OF THE LAKE from Mr. John Ballantyne. I doubt the authenticity of MOTHER AND SON.

"These MS. volumes are not the *prima cura*, but all are in the hand of Sir Walter Scott, and as they went to the printer:—

VOL. I.	contains	MARMION.	VOL. VI.	contains	INTRODUCTION TO BALLAD POETRY. HALIDON HILL, and DOOM OF DEVORGOIL.
II.	"	LADY OF THE LAKE.			
III.	"	DON RODERICK, and FIELD OF WATERLOO.			
IV.	"	ROKEBY.	VII.	"	AUCHINDRANE.
V.	"	LORD OF THE ISLES.	VIII.	"	MOTHER AND SON.

"The fragments are curious, that part (a small one) of WAVERLEY with the water-mark of 1810, I got from Mr. James Hall, being part of the MS. of WAVERLEY purchased by him on the forementioned 19th August 1831; the portion of IVANHOE I purchased from Mrs.

Terry; it had been sent to her husband during its progress that he might consider how it could be dramatized.

VOL. I. contains Part of WAVERLEY, IVANHOE, etc.
II. „ Part of TALES OF A GRANDFATHER.

"I may here remark that Sir Walter Scott did not write the whole of IVANHOE with his own hand. I think it probable that all he did so write is contained in vol. i. of Fragments. John Ballantyne acted as amanuensis for a considerable part of that noble romance, the author having recently recovered from a very severe illness."

Mr. Cadell's success enabled him to purchase the estate of Ratho, near Edinburgh. He died at Ratho House, January 20, 1849, leaving a family of daughters, who inherited the Scott Manuscripts as a joint property. It was reported that these MSS. had been offered for private sale at £2000. If it was so, this offer having been declined, the following portion was selected and sent to Messrs. Christie, Manson, & Woods, London, in July 1867.

SALE of the ORIGINAL AUTOGRAPH MANUSCRIPTS of SIR WALTER SCOTT'S celebrated Poems, and of several of his Novels and Prose Works, by Messrs. Christie, Manson, & Woods, at their Great Rooms, 8 King Street, London, on Saturday, July 6, 1867.

	Price.	*Purchaser.*
1. Marmion, 4to, . .	191 Guineas,	Mr. HARVEY.
2. The Lady of the Lake, 4to, .	264 „	Mr. F. RICHARDSON.
3. The Vision of Don Roderick, 4to,	37 „	Mr. F. RICHARDSON.
4. Rokeby, folio, . .	130 „	Mr. HOPE SCOTT.
5. The Lord of the Isles, .	101 „	Mr. HOPE SCOTT.
6. Introductory Essay on Popular Poetry, 4to, . .	54 „	Mr. F. RICHARDSON.
7. Auchindrane, folio, . .	27 „	Messrs. NIXON & RHODES.
8. Anne of Geierstein, 4to, .	121 „	Mr. HOPE SCOTT.
9. Waverley and Ivanhoe, 4to, .	130 „	Mr. HOPE SCOTT.
10. Tales of a Grandfather, folio, .	145 „	Mr. F. RICHARDSON.
11. Castle Dangerous, 4to, .	32 „	Mr. F. RICHARDSON.
12. Count Robert of Paris, 4to, .	23 „	Mr. MASSEY.
Total amount of the Sale,	1255 Guineas.	

The remaining portion (a few excepted) of the Cadell Manuscripts were sent to a second sale at London next year: the five volumes of Correspondence were of course excepted, as by his settlement Mr. Cadell expressly enjoined that these should not pass out of the hands of his family. The result of the sale was as follows :—

SALE of the ORIGINAL AUTOGRAPH MANUSCRIPTS of several of SIR WALTER SCOTT'S Novels and Poems, at Messrs. Christie, Manson, & Woods, Thursday, July 9, 1868.

	Price.	*Purchaser.*
1. Quentin Durward, russia, extra, uncut, .	£142 0 0	Mr. TOOVEY.
2. The Abbot, 4to, russia, extra, uncut, . .	50 0 0	Mr. J. MURRAY.
3. Chronicles of the Canongate, 1st and 2d Series, russia, extra, uncut, ...	51 0 0	Mr. MELVILLE.
4. Woodstock, 4to, russia, extra, uncut, . .	120 0 0	Mr. THORPE.
5. The Betrothed, 4to, ...	77 0 0	Mr. LAUDER.
6. The Talisman, 4to, ...	70 0 0	Mr. LAUDER.
7. St. Ronan's Well, 4to, russia, uncut, . .	120 0 0	Mr. LAUDER.
8. The Vision of Don Roderick, . . .	57 0 0	Mr. A. W. ELRICK.

The following minute description may be added from the London Sale Catalogue, 1868, of the Author's Works in the form of Proof-sheets of the Original editions, containing his MS. Corrections and Additions which were then sold :—

	Price.	*Purchaser.*
9. The Life of Napoleon Buonaparte, 9 vols. 8vo. The Proof-Sheets, with MS. Notes by Sir Walter Scott's friend and printer, Mr. James Ballantyne, and the margins covered with Corrections and Additions in the autograph of the Author, bound in russia extra, uncut, ...	£69 0 0	Mr. BEET.
In these interesting Volumes is inserted Sir Walter Scott's correspondence with Mr. James Ballantyne during the progress of the work, comprising fifty-seven autograph letters.		
10. Woodstock, 3 vols. in 2, 8vo. The Proof-Sheets of the First Edition, with numerous MS. Notes by Mr. James Ballantyne, and very extensive Corrections and Additions in the autograph of the Author, russia, extra, uncut, . . .	79 0 0	Messrs. BOONE.
Inserted are fourteen autograph letters written to Mr. James Ballantyne during the progress of the work.		
11. Tales of the Crusaders; The Betrothed; and The Talisman, 4 vols. in 2, 8vo. The Proof-Sheets of the First Edition, with MS. Notes by Mr. James Ballantyne, and numerous Corrections and Additions in the autograph of the Author, russia, extra, uncut, ...	40 0 0	Mr. BEET.
Inserted are eight autograph letters written to Mr. James Ballantyne during the progress of the work.		

	Price.	*Purchaser.*
12. Fortunes of Nigel and Quentin Durward, 6 vols. in 3, 8vo. The Proof-Sheets of the First Edition, with MS. Notes by Mr. James Ballantyne, and numerous Corrections and Additions in the autograph of the Author, russia, extra, uncut, .	£45 0 0	Mr. TOOVEY.
13. Peveril of the Peak, 4 vols. in 2, 8vo. The Proof-Sheets of the First Edition, with MS. Notes by Mr. James Ballantyne, and numerous Corrections and Additions in the autograph of the Author, russia, extra, uncut, ...	26 0 0	Mr. H. STEVENS.
14. The Pirate, 4 vols. in 2, 8vo. The Proof-Sheets of the First Edition, with MS. Notes by Mr. James Ballantyne, and numerous Corrections and Additions in the autograph of the Author, russia, extra, uncut, ...	27 0 0	Messrs. BOONE.
15. Ivanhoe, Bride of Lammermoor, Legend of Montrose, 8vo, fragments of the Proof-Sheets, with MS. Notes by Mr. James Ballantyne, and numerous Corrections and Additions in the autograph of the Author,	21 0 0	Mr. TOOVEY.

Mr. Ballantyne's MS. Notes are very interesting, as they contain the Corrections which he suggested during the printing of these works, as well as occasional criticisms and remarks. Sir Walter Scott appears generally to have adopted the advice of his friend, but sometimes they did not agree, and some of his notes in reply are very characteristic, of which the following (from *Woodstock*) may be taken as a specimen :—"'Completing' wants a nominative."—*MS. Note by J. Ballantyne.* "You certainly have had the toothache. Why, it puts me in mind of the epigram, when Pitt and Dundas came drunk into the House of Commons,—

'I cannot see the Speaker, Hal, can you?'
'Not see the Speaker! d—n me, I see *two!*'"
MS. Note by Scott.

16. Tales of a Grandfather, being Stories from the History of Scotland, 6 vols. 12mo, interleaved, with numerous Corrections and Additions by the author half-bound russia, extra, uncut. Edinburgh, 1828, ...	100 0 0	Mr. BEET.
	£1074 0 0	

*** The names given above from the Sale Books obviously do not indicate the actual purchasers, as most of the Volumes were bought upon commission. D. L.

p. 233]

The Lady of the Lake

Harp of the North! that mouldering long hast hung
On the witch-elm that ~~shades~~ shades Saint Fillans spring,
And ~~on~~ down the fitful breeze thy numbers flung,
Till envious ivy did around thee cling,
Muffling with ~~her~~ verdant ringlet every
string,—
O ~~wizzard~~ minstrel harp, still must thine accents sleep,
Mid rustling leaves & fountain's murmuring,
Still must thy sweeter sounds their silence keep,
Nor bid a warrior smile, nor teach a maid to weep?

Not thus, in ancient days of Caledon,
Was thy voice mute amid the festal crowd,
When lay of hopeless love, or glory won,
Aroused the fearful, or subdued the proud.
At each according pause, thou spokest aloud &
Thine ardent ~~sympathy~~ symphony sublime & high,
Fair dames & crested chiefs attention bowd;
For still the burthen of thy minstrel lay
Was knighthoods dauntless deed, & beauty's matchless ey

O wake once more! how rude so e'er the hand
That ventures ~~in~~ o'er thy magic maze to stray;
O wake once more! ~~al~~though ~~to~~ scarce ~~bid~~ my skill command
Some feeble echoing of thine earlier lay:
Though harsh & faint, & soon to die away
And all unworthy of thy nobler strain,
Yet if one heart throb higher at ~~its~~ ~~the~~ its sw
The wizzard note has not been touched in va
Then silent be no more! Enchantress, wake again

ORIGINAL MANUSCRIPTS OF SIR WALTER SCOTT'S WORKS.

I.—POETRY.

1805.

231. THE LAY OF THE LAST MINSTREL.

The Original MS. is not known to be preserved. (See Mr. Constable's note to *Rokeby*, No. 235.)

A COPY of the Original Edition of *The Lay of the Last Minstrel*, 1805, 4to, from the Royal Library, Windsor, was sent for this Exhibition. It contained MS. corrections by the Author, for the Second Edition. See No. 290. This interesting Volume was presented to HER MAJESTY by the late Mr. JOHN A. BALLANTYNE, in 1842.

1808.

232. MARMION: A TALE OF FLODDEN FIELD.

"THE Original Autograph Manuscript contained many curious and interesting variations from the printed text. 4to.

"This is the Original Manuscript of *Marmion*, which I requested the printer might preserve; it is nearly perfect, there being only wanting, in Canto II., Stanzas 5, 6, 7, 8, and part of 4 and 9; in Canto III., Stanzas 2, 3, 32, and 33. Some of the Stanzas in the three last Cantos are numbered differently in print, as will be seen by the pencil-marks in the MS. In the Poem as printed, there are occasional slight variations from the copy, which probably occurred to the Author during the correction of the proof-sheets. This collation refers of course to the first edition, published in 1807.—ARCHIBALD CONSTABLE."—At the *London Sale*, 1867, No. 1, this MS. fetched £200, 11s. Mr. Cadell purchased it from Mr. D. Constable in 1833. (See p. 103.)

1810.

233. THE LADY OF THE LAKE.

Lent by
FRANCIS RICHARDSON, ESQ.

A Facsimile of the first page is given on the opposite leaf.

"*The Lady of the Lake:* the Original Autograph Manuscript, containing many interesting variations from the printed text. 4to.

"This is the Original Manuscript of *The Lady of the Lake*, written in the Author's own hand, and precisely in the state in which it was sent to the press of Ballantyne and Co., from which it was carefully preserved by me. The notes, which are written in a lady's hand, are the MS. of Mrs. Scott; the others those of Mr. Scott's amanuensis, Mr. Weber, and of Robert Jamieson, Esq., who is alluded to by Mr. Scott in the course of these Notes. The directions to the printer are in the handwriting of James Ballantyne.—JOHN BALLANTYNE."

At the *London Sale*, 1867, No. 2, £277, 4s.—This is the highest price any of Scott's MSS. has realized. It no doubt is a volume of peculiar interest.

1811.

234. THE VISION OF DON RODERICK.

"*The Vision of Don Roderick;* Romance of Dunois, from the French; The Dance of Death; The Field of Waterloo; Farewell to Mackenzie, High Chief of Kintail, from the Gaelic; War-Song of Lachlan, High Chief of Maclean, from the Gaelic; Saint Cloud. The Original Autograph Manuscripts. 4to.

"Stanzas 19 to 54 in *Don Roderick* are deficient."—*London Sale*, 1867, No. 3, £38, 17s.

"*The Vision of Don Roderick;* Romance of Dunois, from the French; The Dance of Death; The Field of Waterloo; Farewell to Mackenzie, High Chief of Kintail, from the Gaelic; War-Song of Lachlan, High Chief of Maclean, from the Gaelic; Saint Cloud. The Original Autograph Manuscripts, 4to.

"Stanzas 19 to 54 in *Don Roderick* are deficient."—*London Sale*, 1868, No. 8, £57.

1813.

235. ROKEBY. A Poem in Six Cantos.

Lent by
JAMES R. HOPE SCOTT, ESQ., Q.C.

~~A Facsimile page of this MS. is here given.~~

"*Rokeby:* the Original Autograph Manuscript, containing curious variations from the printed text, with many interesting letters to his friend and printer, Mr. Ballantyne, written while the Poem was being printed. Folio.

"This is the Original Manuscript of *Rokeby*. The whole in Sir Walter Scott's handwriting, some few of the Notes excepted, which appear to have been written by H. Weber. The Original Manuscript of *The Lay of the Last Minstrel* was not preserved, such things not having been thought important till the publication of *Marmion*, when I desired Mr. Ballantyne to preserve the Manuscript for me. The Original of *The Lady of the Lake* is in Mr. J. Ballantyne's possession, to whose liberality I am indebted for this valuable addition [of *Rokeby*] to my Collection of the Original MSS. of Sir Walter Scott.—ARCHIBALD CONSTABLE, 1813."—*London Sale*, 1867, No. 4, £136, 10s.

The Original Manuscript, on mixed quarto and folio paper. The chief portion of Cantos I.-III. had been transmitted in single sheets by the Post-Office, addressed Mr. James Ballantyne, Printer, Hanover Street, Edinburgh, with the stamps Melrose, Gallashiels. It contains various notes and letters of instructions, etc., from the Author to Mr. Ballantyne. 1813.

At the end of Canto I. is the following note, addressed "Mr. James Ballantyne, Printer, Hanover Street, Edinr.":—

No 237]

When turning from the battle-field
~~What said the noble stag~~
What answer made the Chief? he kneeled
Durst not look up but muttered low
Some mingled sounds ~~of joy and awe~~ that none might know
And greeted him twixt joy and fear
As being of superior sphere &

XXXVII

Now upon Bannocks bloody plain
Heapd ~~high~~ then with thousands of the slain
~~Amid~~ Mid victor monarchs musings high
Mirth laughd in good King Roberts eye
And bore he such angelic air?
Such noble front, such waving hair?
Hath Ronald kneeld to him? he said
Then must we call the church to aid—
Our will be to the Abbot known
Ere these ~~high~~ strange news are wider blown
To Cambuskenneth straight he pass
And deck the church for solemn mass
That priests & choir with morning beams
Prepare with reverence as beseems
To pay for high deliverance given
A nations thanks to gracious heaven
Let him ~~[struck]~~ array besides such state &M
As should on princes ~~[struck]~~ nuptials wait.
Ourself the cause, through fortunes might
That once broke short that spousal rite
Ourself will ~~so~~ grace with early morn
The bridal of the Maid of Lorn

"DEAR JAMES,—I send you the whole of the Canto. I wish Erskine and you would look it over together, and consider whether upon the whole matter it is likely to make an impression. If it does really come to good, I think there are no limits to the interest of that style of composition, for the varieties of life and character are boundless.—Yours truly, W. S.

"ABBOTSFORD, *Monday*.

"I don't know whether to give Matilda a mother or not. Decency requires she could (*sic*) have one, but she is as likely to be in my way as the gudeman's mother, according to the protocol, is always in that of the goodwife."

1813.

236. THE BRIDAL OF TRIERMAIN. (Anon.)

A portion of the Original MS. is at Abbotsford, in a Vol. of Fragments. See note to No. 253.

1815.

237. THE LORD OF THE ISLES.

Lent by

JAMES R. HOPE SCOTT, ESQ., Q.C.

A Facsimile of the concluding page of this MS. is here given.

The Original Manuscript, with the Printers' Marks, and some portions written upon a larger-sized paper, with extracts for the Notes mostly in a different hand.

On the reverse of the last page is this note to Mr. Ballantyne, but there is no post-mark or date:—

"DEAR SIR,—You have now the whole affair excepting two or three concluding stanzas. As your taste for brides'-cake may incline you to desire to know more of the wedding, I will save you some criticism by saying, I have settled to stop short as above. Witness my hand,—W. S."—*London Sale*, 1867, No. 5, £106, 1s.

1815.

238. THE FIELD OF WATERLOO. In Vol. with Don Roderick (No. 234.)

1822.

239. HALIDON HILL: A DRAMATIC SKETCH FROM SCOTTISH HISTORY.

London Sale, 1867, No. 7, £56, 14s., contained in a volume in the possession of FRANCIS RICHARDSON, Esq.

*** Mr. Richardson, in reply to a query, says:—"You are quite right about the Scott Manuscripts. I have one other volume which contains, all in Sir Walter's hand,

HALIDON HILL.

THE FORTUNES [DOOM] OF DEVORGOIL.

INTRODUCTORY ESSAY ON POPULAR POETRY, and ESSAY ON IMITATION OF POPULAR BALLADS, with Dedicatory Letter of Poetical Works to the Duke of Buccleuch.

PREFACES TO MARMION, ROKEBY, AND LORD OF THE ISLES."

1830.

240. The Doom of Devorgoil: a Melo-Drama.

In Vol. with Halidon Hill. *London Sale*, 1867. See No. 239.

1831.

241. Auchindrane; or, The Ayrshire Tragedy.

The Autograph Manuscript. Folio. *London Sale*, 1867, No. 7, £28, 7s.

II.—THE WAVERLEY NOVELS.

1805-1814.

242. Waverley, commenced in 1805, and completed in 1814.

Lent by

The Faculty of Advocates.

A Facsimile of the first page (or Chap. V.) of the Original MS. is given on the opposite leaf.

"My early recollections," says Sir Walter Scott, "of the Highland scenery and customs made so favourable an impression in the poem called The Lady of the Lake, that I was induced to think of attempting something of the same kind in prose. . . .

"It was with some idea of this kind that about the year 1805 I threw together about one-third part of the first volume of Waverley. It was advertised to be published by the late Mr. John Ballantyne, bookseller in Edinburgh, under the name of *Waverley: or, 'Tis Fifty Years Since*, a title afterwards altered to *'Tis Sixty Years Since*, that the actual date of publication might be made to correspond with the period in which the scene was laid."

"Waverley, 3 Vols. The Autograph Manuscript. Imperfect. Vol. I.—From the beginning of Chapter I. to the end of Chapter XI. Vol. II.—From the middle of Chapter VI. to the end; imperfect. Vol. III.—From Chapter XIII. to the end, with the exception of Chapter XXIII., which is wanting."—*London Sale*, 1831, No. 7, £18.

This Volume, at the London Sale, 1831, was bought by Mr. Wilks. Within a few days, it was purchased from him by Mr. James Hall for £42. At a later date, Mr. Cadell states, that he obtained a small portion of this MS. from Mr. Hall, contained in Vol. I. of "Fragments" (see No. 253). The volume of Fragments was bought by Mr. Hope Scott, at the London Sale, 1867, No. 9: the leaves of Waverley formed the opening chapters of the Novel, and are now at Abbotsford.

Chapter V.

Choice of a profession

From the minuteness with which I have traced Waverley's pursuits and the bias which they unavoidably communicated to his imagination, the reader may perhaps anticipate in the following tale an imitation of the romance of Cervantes. But he will do my prudence injustice in the supposition. My intention is not to follow the steps of that inimitable author in describing such total perversion of intellect as misconstrues the objects actually presented to the senses but that more common aberration from sound judgment which apprehends occurrences indeed in their reality but communicates to them a tincture of its own romantic tone & colouring. So far was Edward Waverley from expecting general sympathy with his own feelings or concluding that the present state of things was calculated to exhibit the reality of those visions in which he loved to indulge, that he dreaded nothing more than the detection of those sentiments as were dictated by his musings. He neither had nor wished to have a confident with whom to communicate his reveries and so sensible was he of the ridicule attached to them that had he been to chuse between any punishment short of ignominy and the necessity of giving a cold and composed account of the ideal world in which he lived the better part of his day I think he would not have hesitated to chuse the former infliction. This secrecy became doubly precious as he felt in advancing life the influence of the awakening passions. Female forms of exquisite grace & beauty began to mingle in his mental adventures, nor was he long without looking abroad to compare the creatures of his own imagination with the females of actual life. The list of the beauties who displayd their hebdomadal finery at the parish Church of Waverley was neither numerous nor select. By far the most passable was Miss Sisly (or as

she

*** As the Original MS. of *Waverley* is of peculiar interest, some further particulars may be subjoined. Opposite the first folio of the MS. Mr. Hall has written the following description :—

"This Manuscript of *Waverley* was purchased at London in August 1831, unbound; and in 1833 was bound in imitation of most of the other MSS., but with blank paper inserted, corresponding with the gaps of the MS. when compared with the printed work. Rather more than half of the entire MS. is here preserved.

"The total number of leaves in this manuscript is 210."

Then follows a detailed note of the number of pages in each series of the volume, and Mr. Hall continues :—

"Compared with the print of First Edition (1814), this MS. contains what corresponds nearly to 579 pages of print; and has lost what nearly corresponds to pp. 515 of print, so that what corresponds to about 64 pages of print, more than the half is preserved.

"The first or quarto portion of the paper of this MS. is water-marked 1805. The folio part is water-marked 1813.

"At pages xi. and xvii. of the 'General Preface' of edition 1830 of the Waverley Novels are some interesting details respecting this MS. of *Waverley*.

"At the end of p. 2 of the Postscript, the words 'our Scottish Addison' are erased: being required in the lapidary dedication that followed. J. H.

"LONDON, *Sept.* 1850."

Mr. Hall has preserved the following letters in the volume :—

"FINSBURY SQUARE, *Aug.* 25, 1831.

"Mr. JOHN WILKS presents compliments to Mr. Hall, and apprises him that as he will continue to possess two MS. of Sir Walter Scott if he should part with the MS. of *Waverley*, he should not object to gratify the wishes expressed by Mr. Hall; and he will only add that he may be found at home any morning between half-past ten and twelve o'clock. There, after that hour, an interview would be uncertain.

"J. WILKS."

Addressed "JAS. HALL, Esq.,
75 Pall Mall."

"SUSSEX PLACE, R. P., *May 17th*, 1850.

"MY DEAR HALL,—No Sadducee can dare to question the authenticity of your autograph of *Waverley*. I am fortunate enough to possess the *Rob Roy*, and even between these two the hand had changed a good deal. In your MS. it is exactly as in that of *Marmion*.—Ever yours, J. G. LOCKHART."

"40 BREWER STREET, GOLDEN SQUARE, LONDON,
16 *September* 1850.

"MY DEAR MR. DEAN OF FACULTY,—Soon after becoming possessed of the Manuscript of *Waverley*, I made up my mind to leave it as a legacy to the Advocates' Library.

"It now occurs to me as more satisfactory if I send you the Manuscript at once, and beg of you to offer it for acceptance to the body of which I am so unworthy a member, but to which I continue to be attached by many enduring and grateful associations.

"With due precautions for its safe custody, I should desire the Manuscript to remain in its present shape; and to be always accessible to visitors who may feel interest in such a relic.—Believe me, my dear Mr. Dean, yours most respectfully and sincerely, JAMES HALL, *Advocate*.

"DUNCAN M'NEILL, Esq., M.P., *Dean of Faculty*."

243. WAVERLEY, a Fragment of the early portion of the MS. (See Nos. 242 and 253.)

1815.

244. GUY MANNERING.

"GUY MANNERING, 3 Vols. Wants a folio at the end of Vol. II. The Autograph Manuscript, green morocco.

"The alterations in this Manuscript are more numerous than the preceding."—*London Sale*, 1831, No. 2, £27, 10s.

*** This volume was bought on commission for Mr. HEBER. Resold in Heber's Sale, by Evans, February 1836, Part XI. No. 1420, for £63, and was bought (it was supposed) for the DUKE OF DEVONSHIRE.

1816.

245. THE ANTIQUARY.

"THE ANTIQUARY, 3 Vols. quarto. The Autograph Manuscript. Perfect, green morocco."—*London Sale*, 1831, No. 4, £42, bought by CAPTAIN BASIL HALL.

In the Third series of *Fragments of Travels*, vol. iii., by Captain Basil Hall, R.N., 1833, he has given a detailed account of his friendly intercourse with Sir Walter Scott, when the vessel was detained for some days at Portsmouth in the autumn of 1831. He there mentions that having sent for this MS. to London, the Author, at his earnest request, wrote him a letter on the subject, of which a facsimile is given in the above work, dated Portsmouth, 27th October 1831.

1816.

TALES OF MY LANDLORD. FIRST SERIES.

246. (1.) THE BLACK DWARF.

At the *Edinburgh Sale*, 1848, £28, 17s. 6d. It was bought upon commission for SIR WILLIAM TITE, M.P.

247. (2.) OLD MORTALITY.

Lent by

FRANCIS RICHARDSON, ESQ.

"OLD MORTALITY, 3 Vols. quarto. The Autograph Manuscript. Perfect, green morocco."—*London Sale*, 1831, No. 3, £33, bought for Mr. CADELL. After his death it was acquired by Mr. RICHARDSON.

1817.

248. ROB ROY.

Lent by

JAMES R. HOPE SCOTT, ESQ.

A Facsimile Page of the MS. is here given.

"ROB ROY, 3 Vols. quarto. The Autograph Manuscript, complete. The second volume is wrong paged, the numbers passing from 39 to 50 instead of 40, and

Rob. Roy
Vol. 3.

Far as the eye could reach no tree was seen
Earth clad in russet scorned the lively green
No birds ~~ex~~ except as birds of passage flew
No bee was known to hum no dove to coo
No streams as amber smooth as amber clear
Were seen to glide or heard to warble here

Prophecy of Famine

It was in the balmy atmosphere of a delightful harvest morning that I met by appointment Fairservice with the horse at the door of the inn which was but little space distant from Mrs Flyter's hotel. The first matter which caught my attention was that whatever were the deficiencies of the pony which Mr Fairservice's legal adviser Clerk Touthope generously bestowed upon him in exchange for Thorncliffe's mare he had contrived to part with it & procure in its stead an animal with so curious and complete a lameness ~~[illegible]~~ that it seemed only to make use of three legs for the purpose of progression while the fourth was only meant to be flourished in the air by way of accompaniment. "What do ye mean by bringing such an ~~animal~~ creature as that here Sir? and where is the pony you rode to Glasgow upon?" were my very natural & impatient enquiries. "I sell't it Sir. It was a slink beast and wad hae eaten its head aff standing at Luckie Flyter's at livery. ~~but~~ And I hae bought this ane on your honours account — its a grand bargain cost but a pound sterling the foot — that's four a'thegither — the string-halt will gae aff when its gaen a mile. Its a weel-kend ganger — they ca' it Souple Tam." "On my soul Sir" said I "you will never rest till my supple-jack & your shoulders become acquainted. If you do not go instantly & procure the other brute you shall pay the penalty of your ingenuity." Andrew notwithstanding my threats continued to battle the point as he said it would cost him a guinea of rue-bargain to the man who had bought his pony ere he could get it back again. Like a true Englishman though sensible I was duped by the rascal I was about to pay his exaction rather than lose time when forth sallied Mr Jarvie cloaked mantled hooded and booted as if for a Siberian winter while two apprentices under the immediate direction of Mattie led forth the douce ambling steed which had the honour on such occasions to support the person of the Glasgow magistrate. Ere he "clombe to the saddle" an expression more descriptive of the Bailie's ~~his~~ mode of mounting than that of the knights-errant to whom Spenser applies it he enquired the cause of the dispute betwixt my servant & me. Having learned the nature of ~~An~~ honest Andrew's manoeuvre he instantly cut short all debate by pronouncing that if Fairservice did not forthwith return the three-legged palfrey and produce the more useful quadruped which he had ~~[illegible]~~ discarded he would send him to prison and amerce him in half his wages.

To the Best of patrons

A pleased and indulgent Reader

Jedediah Cleishbotham

wishes health and increase and contentment

Courteous Reader

so foul a stain

If ingratitude comprehendeth every other vice surely ~~so~~ worst of all beseemeth him whose life has been devoted to instructing youth in virtue and in humane letters Therefore have I chosen in this prolegomena to unload my burthen of thanks at thy feet for the favour with which thou hast kindly entertained the Tales of my Landlord. Certes if thou hast chuckled over their facetious and festivous descriptions or hast had thy mind filled with pleasure at the strange and pleasing turns of fortune which they record verily I have also simpered when I beheld a second story with Atticks ~~which~~ that has arisen on the basis of my small domicile at Gandercleugh Nor has it been without delectation that I have indued a new coat (snuff-brown and with metal buttons) having all other garments corresponding thereto. We do therefore lie in respect of each other under a reciprocation of benefits whereof those received by me being the most solid in respect that a new house and a new coat are better than a new ~~old~~ tale or an old song it is meet that my gratitude should be expressed with the louder voice and more preponderating vehemence. And how should it be expressed? certainly not in words only but in act and deed. It is with this sole purpose and disclaiming all intention of purchasing that pendicle or poffle of land called the Carlinescroft lying adjacent to my garden & measuring seven acres three roods & four perches that I have committed to the eyes of those who thought well of the former tomes these four additional volumes of the Tales of my Landlord. Not the less if Peter Prayfort be minded to sell

Deacon Barrow to be capable of enduring such elevation

the mistake is continued to the end of the volume."—*London Sale*, 1831, No. 5, £50, bought by Mr. Wilks. After his death, it was resold March 22, 1847, for £82, and acquired by Mr. Cadell, who wrote as follows on the fly-leaf:—

"This, the Original Manuscript (*prima cura* of the Author) of the Novel of *Rob Roy*, was one of the volumes of MSS. presented by Sir Walter Scott to Mr. Constable in 1822 on the death of Lord Kinneder, and was sold by auction by Mr. Constable's Trustees on 19th August 1831: and it was purchased by Mr. Wilks, M.P., and resold by auction on 22d March 1847, when it fell into the possession of Mr. R. Cadell of Edinburgh, by whom it is this day presented, with kind regards, to J. G. LOCKHART, Esq.

"RATHO, 15*th August* 1848."

The MS. is written on two sizes of quarto paper, the first half smaller. As numbered by Sir Walter Scott, Vol. I. ends on fol. 102; Vol. II. on fol. 102; and Vol. III. on fol. 95.

There is inserted the following note to "Mr. James Ballantyne, St. John Street:"—

"DEAR JAMES,

With Great Joy
I send you Roy.
'Twas a tough job,
But we're dune wi' Rob.

I forgot if I mentioned Terry in my list of friends. Pray send me two or three copies so soon as you can. And we must not forget Sir William Forbes.—Yours ever. W. S."

1818.

TALES OF MY LANDLORD. SECOND SERIES.

249. THE HEART OF MIDLOTHIAN.

Lent by

JOHN COWAN, ESQ.

A Facsimile page of the MS. is here given.

The leaves in the volume, as numbered by the Author, are Vol. I. fol. 1 to 90, besides 4 additional of Introduction, dated Gandercleuch, the 1st of April 1818; Vol. II. fol. 1 to 77; Vol. III. fol. 8 to 70; and Vol. IV. fol. 1 to 78—in all, 315 leaves.

*** This, the original MS., was presented by Mr. John A. Ballantyne to Alexander Cowan, Esq., one of his father's trustees.

1819.

TALES OF MY LANDLORD. THIRD SERIES.

250. (1.) THE BRIDE OF LAMMERMOOR. A Fragment.

Lent by

CHRISTOPHER DOUGLAS, ESQ.

*** This portion of the MS. was presented by Mr. John A. Ballantyne to Alexander Douglas, Esq., W.S., one of his father's trustees.

Containing Chapters I.-VII. of Vol. I. and Chapters IV. to the beginning of Chapter XII., Vol. II. In 1 Volume.

251. (1.) THE BRIDE OF LAMMERMOOR. Another Portion.

Lent by
SIR JAMES HALL OF DUNGLASS.

"THE BRIDE OF LAMMERMOOR. The Autograph Manuscript. 61 pages of Manuscript."—*London Sale*, 1831, £14, 14s. Bought by CAPTAIN BASIL HALL, R.N., for his brother, MR. JAMES HALL, "and given to his nephew, James Hall, jun., Esq. of Dunglas."

252. (2.) THE LEGEND OF MONTROSE. A Fragment.

Lent by
DAVID LAING, ESQ.

A Facsimile page of the MS. is here given.

This fragment of the Original Manuscript, of which not more has been discovered, is numbered folios 15 to 33 (or Chapter III., *The gallant Rittmaster*, etc., to near the close of Chapter VI., *Nevertheless, friend Ranald*, etc.) These Chapters, in the Centenary and other editions, are numbered XI.-XIV. The present fragment was presented to Mr. D. Laing by Mr. John Alexander Ballantyne, along with a similar portion of *Kenilworth*, numbered by the Author folios 3 to 13. See No. 256*.

1819.

253. IVANHOE.

"IVANHOE. Quarto. The Autograph Manuscript. Imperfect. The latter part of Vol. II.; Vol. III., from folio 1 to 29, and from 50 to 57. *Cætera desunt.*"—*London Sale*, 1831, No. 9, £12.

It seems doubtful if this portion is the same as what appeared in the Sale of 1867, which consists of about sixty leaves:—

"WAVERLEY and IVANHOE. Fragments of the Original Manuscripts in the autograph of the Author:—*The Bridal of Triermain*, a portion of the Original autograph MS.; *Carle, now the King's come*, Part I.; and Two Papers written for the *Edinburgh Observer* and *Scots Magazine*. 4to.

"The fragment of *Ivanhoe* contained in this volume is believed to be the only portion which exists in the autograph of the author, the remaining part having been written by Mr. J. Ballantyne, Sir Walter Scott having only recently recovered from a severe illness. It was purchased of Mrs. Terry by the late Mr. Cadell, Sir Walter Scott having sent it to her husband during its progress, that he might consider how it could be dramatized."—*London Sale*, 1867, No. 9, £136, 10.

_ This volume was bought by J. R. HOPE SCOTT, Esq., Q.C.

1820.

254. THE MONASTERY.

"THE MONASTERY. 3 Vols. in 1, quarto. The Autograph Manuscript. Perfect, green morocco."—*London Sale*, 1831, No. 1, £18, bought on commission for Mr. HEBER. In the sale of his library, Part XI. No. 1421, February 1836, it some one comes to relieve him. If he ordered us a late dinner Ranald he is like to be the [illegible]." To examine Ranald's chain was the next occupation. It was under [illegible] [illegible] of the keys which hung behind the private door probably deposited there that the [illegible] [illegible] of, he pleased to [illegible] a prisoner or remove him elsewhere without the necessity of summoning the warder. The [illegible] which had his benumbed arms and [illegible] from the floor of the dungeon [illegible] the ecstasy of recovered freedom. "Take the ivory [illegible] of that noble present" said Captain Dalgetty "and put it on and follow close at my heels." The outlaw obeyed and they ascended the private stair, having first secured the door behind them and safely reached the apartment of the Marquis.

Chapter. VI.

"Look out for the private way through the chapel Ranald" said the Captain "while I give a hasty regard to these matters." Thus speaking he seized with one hand a bundle of Argyles most private papers and with the other a purse of gold both of which lay in a drawer of a rich cabinet which stood invitingly open. "Intelligence and booty" said the [illegible] as he pocketed the spoils each [illegible] with [illegible] should look to the one on his general's behalf and the other on his own? Soldadoes are not to be endangered and endangered [illegible] [illegible] my good Lord of Argyle. But soft, soft Ranald, we [illegible] of the [illegible] whither are these bound?" It was indeed full time to stop MacEagh's proceedings for not finding the private passage [illegible] and impatient at would [illegible] of further delay he had [illegible] down a sword and target and was about to enter the great gallery with the purpose doubtless of fighting his way through all opposition. "Hold wait [illegible] live" whispered Dalgetty angrily "hold on him. We must be [illegible] if possible. To bar in [illegible] door that it may be thought MacCallum More [illegible] to private. And now let [illegible] [illegible] reconnoitre [illegible] for the private passage." By looking behind the [illegible] in various places the Captain at length discovered a winding passage [illegible] by an other door which [illegible] entered the chapel. But what was his [illegible] to have on the other side of the door the sonorous voice of a divine in the act of preaching. "[illegible]" said the [illegible] "he said a [illegible] that to us is a private passage. I have [illegible] to return and ask his [illegible]." He then opened very gently the door which opened into the gallery used by the Marquis himself the [illegible] of which were drawn perhaps with the purpose of having it supposed that he was engaged in attendance upon divine worship when in fact he was absent upon his secular affairs. There was no other person in the seat for the family of the Marquis such was the high state maintained in these days [illegible] several [illegible] other gallery placed somewhat lower than that of the great man himself. This being the case Capt. Dalgetty ventured to ensconce himself in the gallery of which he carefully secured the door. N.B. Never (although the comparison be a bold one) was a sermon listened to with more impatience [illegible] of [illegible] on the part of one at least of the audience. The Captain heard [illegible] [illegible] thirdly — and to conclude with a sort of feeling [illegible] protracted [illegible]. But no man [illegible] (for this sermon was called a lecture) [illegible] and the discourse was at length closed the clergyman [illegible] to make a profound bow towards the latticed gallery little suspecting whom he honoured by that reverence. To judge from the [illegible] with which they [illegible] dispersed the domestics of the Marquis were scarcely more pleased with their late occupation than the anxious Captain Dalgetty — [illegible] many of them being highlandmen had the excuse of not understanding a single word which the clergyman spoke although they gave their attendance on his doctrine & would have done so had he been a Turkish Imaum by the special order of MacCallum More. But although the congregation dispersed thus rapidly the divine [illegible] and [illegible] in the chapel and walking up & down its Gothic precincts seemed either to be meditating on what he had just been delivering or preparing a fresh discourse for the next opportunity. Bold as he was Dalgetty [illegible] what he ought to do. Time however passed and every moment increased the chance of their escape being discovered by the [illegible] visiting the dungeon and discovering the exchange which had been made there. At length [illegible] Ranald who watched all his motions to follow him and preserve his countenance Captain Dalgetty with a very composed air descended a flight of steps which led from the gallery into the body of the chapel.

fetched £45. 3s., bought on commission for SIR THOMAS PHILLIPS, Bart., Middlehill, Worcestershire.

1820.

255. THE ABBOT.

"THE ABBOT. 3 Vols. quarto. The Autograph Manuscript. Imperfect. Vol. I.—Wants folio 7; hiatus from folio 30 to 54. Vol. II.—Hiatus from 5 to 11, and from 28 to 32. Vol. III.—Imperfect, ends at folio 44."—*London Sale*, 1831, No. 8, £14. It was bought for Mr. R. CADELL.

"THE ABBOT. The Original Autograph Manuscript, quarto, russia extra, uncut. Pp. 31-53 in Vol. I., and 29-31 in Vol. II. are deficient."—*London Sale*, 1868, No. 2, £50. Bought by JOHN MURRAY, Esq.

1821.

256. KENILWORTH.

"KENILWORTH. The Autograph Manuscript. Vol. I.—Imperfect; begins at folio 16, wants folio 38, 39, 40, 59, and 60. Vol. II.—Wants folio 15 to 18. Vol. III.—Begins at folio 4; the rest perfect."—*London Sale*, 1831, No. 12, £17, bought by Mr. WILKS, M.P.

At the sale of Mr. Wilks's autographs, etc., in 1847, the purchaser was Mr. PETER CUNNINGHAM, at £16. After his death, it was resold in his collection of autograph letters, etc., in February 1855, and bought by commission for the BRITISH MUSEUM. The three volumes are now bound in one, forming the Egerton MS., No. 1661.

256*. KENILWORTH. A Fragment of the earlier portion. See No. 252.

1821.

257. THE PIRATE.

Lent by

REV. DR. R. H. STEVENSON.

"THE PIRATE. The Autograph Manuscript, Vol. I., pages 25 and 26 repeated by mistake. Imperfect, ending at fol. 42. Vol. II. wanting. Vol. III. contains only from folio 46 to the end."—*London Sale*, 1831, No. 10, £12. It was bought for Mr. R. CADELL.

258. THE PIRATE. A Fragment.

Lent by

MARK NAPIER, Esq.

*** The concluding leaves of the Original Manuscript, Vol. I. Presented to Mr. Mark Napier, by Mr. John A. Ballantyne. This remnant, says Mr. N., "is specially valuable, as it comprehends Sir Walter Scott's corrected draft of the beautiful verses with which the First Volume of the *Pirate* concludes—the 'Farewell to Northmaven.' . . . Mr. Ballantyne took occasion one day in his own office, to present me with this valuable and interesting Autograph, which he told me was the last fragment he possessed of Sir Walter Scott's copy for the printer."

1822.

259. THE FORTUNES OF NIGEL.

"THE FORTUNES OF NIGEL. The Autograph Manuscript. Vol. I. and II. perfect. Vol. III. ends at folio 60."—*London Sale*, 1831, No. 11, £16, 16s.

1823.

260. PEVERIL OF THE PEAK.

"PEVERIL OF THE PEAK. 4 Vols. in 2. Quarto. The Autograph Manuscript. Complete, green morocco."—*London Sale*, 1831, No. 6, £42.

*** This MS. was bought on commission for E. V. UTTERSON, Esq. When the sale of his valuable Library took place in 1851, it was bought for the present proprietor, SIR WILLIAM TITE, M.P., who has obligingly favoured us, upon application, with a description of this and of Nos. 246 and 266.

1823.

261. QUENTIN DURWARD.

"QUENTIN DURWARD. The Original Autograph Manuscript, russia, extra, uncut."—*London Sale*, 1868, No. 1, £142.

1823.

262. ST. RONAN'S WELL.

Lent by

A. SKENE, ESQ.

"ST. RONAN'S WELL. The Original Autograph Manuscript. 4to. Russia, extra, uncut."—*London Sale*, 1868, No. 7, £119.

The following note by the Author is preserved in the original MS. Mr. Skene, the proprietor of the MS., in sending a copy of it to a newspaper, truly says, it is "a characteristic note, without date, to James Ballantyne, in connexion with *St. Ronan's Well*, written evidently about July 1823, when the novel was commenced; and of touching interest as showing the bent of Sir Walter's mind towards the tale, at the time he had but reached the third chapter."

"DEAR JAMES,—I will be delighted to see you to-morrow with scrip and scrippage at breakfast-time. The resemblance between Lovil and Tyrrel is only that of situation. I have thoughts of making the tale tragic, having 'a humour to be cruel.' It may go off, however. If not, it will be a pitiful tragedy, filled with most lamentable mirth. I find I must have a moment's peep at the revise of sheet C; or, stay, insert the following addition and corrections:—

"*Del.* the alteration, line 2, p. 65, and *stet* as before, I *wadna*, etc.

"P. 66, line 2, add—And Nanny,[1] ye may tell them he has an illustrated poem —illustrated— mind the word, Nanny—that is to be stuck as fou o' the likes o' that as ever turkey was larded wi' dabs o' bacon.—Yours truly, W. S."

[1] "In authorized editions of Scott's works the name is printed 'Nelly.'"

1824.

263. REDGAUNTLET.

Lent by

DOWAGER LADY LISTON FOULIS.

REDGAUNTLET. The Original Manuscript. 4to. In Mr. Cadell's List. No. 6. This MS. was not sent to the London Sale.

1825.

TALES OF THE CRUSADERS.

264. (1.) THE BETROTHED.

"THE BETROTHED. The Original Autograph Manuscript, 4to."—*London Sale*, 1868. No. 5, £77.

265. (2.) THE TALISMAN.

"THE TALISMAN. The Original Autograph Manuscript, 4to."—*London Sale*, 1868. No. 6, £70.

1826.

266. WOODSTOCK.

"WOODSTOCK. The Original Autograph Manuscript, 4to, russia extra, uncut."—*London Sale*, 1868, No. 4, £120.

*** This MS. was bought on commission for SIR WILLIAM TITE, M.P. It contains the following note on the first page:—"This, the Original Manuscript of *Woodstock*, I received as a gift from Sir Walter Scott, at Abbotsford, on 9th April 1831.—ROBERT CADELL, 1834."

1827.

267. CHRONICLES OF THE CANONGATE. FIRST SERIES.

Lent by

DR. JAMES D. GILLESPIE. (Now the Property of JAMES T. GIBSON CRAIG, Esq.)

The above title in the Manuscript is scored out, and the Author has substituted as follows:—

"THE CANONGATE MISCELLANY; OR, TRADITIONS OF THE SANCTUARY. By Michael Croftangry, Esq., of Little Croftangry. First Series.

1. THE TWO DROVERS.
2. THE HIGHLAND WIDOW, folios 1 to 24; and separate leaves, folios 1 to 8, and 1 to 35.
3. THE SURGEON'S DAUGHTER. The beginning is wanting, numbered folios 11 to 68 (or Chapter I.), and part of Chapter II., page 34 of the original edition, Vol. II., and breaks off about the middle of Chapter XI. Vol. II. p. 72.

268. CHRONICLES OF THE CANONGATE. SECOND SERIES.

(*Bound in the same volume with the First Series.*)

THE FAIR MAID OF PERTH.

"The Author's original title was ST. VALENTINE'S DAY. This portion of the volume is not quite perfect. Vol. I. contains folios 10 to 68. Vol. II. contains folios 1 to 66 (excepting folio 57). Vol. III. contains folio 1 to 47 (excepting folios 10 to 15), and breaks off after the middle of Chapter IX. (or Chapter XXXII. in the Centenary Edition).

On the fly-leaf is written, "This, the Original Manuscript of *Chronicles of the Canongate*, First and Second Series, I received as a gift from Sir Walter Scott, at Abbotsford, on 9th April 1831.—ROBERT CADELL, 1834."

London Sale, 1868, No. 3 (the First and Second Series, in one volume). £51.

This MS. is entirely in Sir Walter Scott's hand, and had not, as usual, been transcribed for the printer, as the folds of the paper and the marginal marks clearly indicate that it was sent direct to the press. This may account perhaps for the loss of leaves, owing to greater carelessness in preserving the MS.

A Facsimile page of the MS. is here given.

The Original MS. was recently bought by Mr. Gibson Craig for £105.

1829.

269. Anne of Geierstein.

Lent by

J. R. Hope Scott, Esq., Q.C.

"Anne of Geierstein. The Original Autograph Manuscript, 4to.

"This, the Original Manuscript of *Anne of Geierstein*, I received as a gift from Sir Walter Scott, at Abbotsford, April 9, 1831.—Robert Cadell."—*London Sale*, 1867, No. 8, £127, 1s.

1831.

Tales of My Landlord. Fourth Series.

270. (1.) Castle Dangerous.

Lent by

Francis Richardson, Esq.

"Castle Dangerous. The Original Manuscript, in the handwriting of William Laidlaw, with corrections and additions by Sir Walter Scott. 4to."—*London Sale*, 1867, No. 16, £33, 12s.

271. (1.) Count Robert of Paris.

"Count Robert of Paris. A fragment of the Original Manuscript; a small portion in the autograph of Sir Walter Scott, and the remaining portion in the handwriting of Mr. W. Laidlaw, his friend and amanuensis." 4to.—*London Sale*, 1867, No. 12, £24, 3s.

1828.

272. (2.) Tales of a Grandfather. First Series.

Lent by

George Hogarth, Esq.

Memorandum regarding MS. of "Tales of a Grandfather." First Series.

"The MS. was presented to me by John Alexander Ballantyne, the printer's son: and is contained in one folio volume, and is paged, but with several errors, according to the three vols. of the original printed edition. It is not entirely complete. Vol. I. is contained in 66 pages of MS., although it is marked as ending at p. 59, an additional chapter having apparently been added. This part wants the first two chapters, and in paging it leaps from 46 to 57, and several pagings are twice repeated or passed over, the story however being continuous.

19 exclaimed Simon — My daughter Catharine to my [illegible] apprentice!" "Alas," said Clement, "how do these unworldly [illegible] cling to the world and consent to separation — Look not so angrily upon me good Simon — it is true — The [illegible] of [illegible] [illegible] [illegible] to the daughter of the Perth burgess and [illegible] demand in doing so — But to use thy [illegible] Catharine is dearer to thee than life here and heaven hereafter — to him at least who [illegible]." "There be many of the [illegible]," said Simon Glover, "for the [illegible] burgess of Perth and I would not break my word to make my daughter bride to the Prince of Scotland." "I thought it would be your answer," [illegible] "[illegible] your [illegible] spiritual concerns [illegible] as that [illegible] and [illegible] you [illegible] your temporal affairs." "Hush thee — hush, father Clement!" answered the glover, "when [illegible] in that [illegible] of argument thy words [illegible] of [illegible]. Poor Catharine! I must manage as [illegible] I can [illegible] as not to [illegible] the young [illegible] dignity but well [illegible] for me that this is far beyond her reach." "The mind then be distant indeed," said the Carmelite, "and now brother Simon since you think it perilous to own me among your [illegible] I must walk alone with my own doctrines and the dangers they draw on me. But should your eye less blinded than it now is by worldly hopes and fears ever turn a glance back on him who soon may be snatched from amongst you, remember that by nought save a deep sense of the truth of the doctrine which he taught could Clement Blair have learned to [illegible] the [illegible] of the powerful and [illegible] to alarm the fears of the jealous and timid, to walk in the world as he [illegible] not in it and to be accused [illegible] that he [illegible] of [illegible] to God — Heaven be my witness that I would comply in all lawful things to conciliate the love and sympathy of my fellow creatures. It is no light thing to be shunned by the worthy as an infected patient, to be persecuted by the Pharisees of the Church as an unbelieving heretic, to be regarded with horror and contempt by the multitude who consider me as a madman who may be expected to turn mischievous — But were all these evils multiplied an hundred fold the fire within would not be stifled, the voice which says within me Speak must receive obedience — Woe unto me if I preach not the Gospel even though I at length preach it from amidst the pile of flames." So spoke this bold witness, one of those whom Heaven raises up from time to time to preserve amidst the most ignorant ages to carry on a manifestation of undoubted Christianity from the time of the apostles down to the age when favoured by the invention of printing the Reformation broke out in full splendour. The selfish policy of the Glover was exposed in his own eyes and he felt contemptible in his own eyes as he saw the Carmelite turn from him. He even felt a momentary inclination to follow the example of the preacher's philanthropy and disinterested zeal but it gleamed like a flash of lightning through a dark vault where there is nothing to catch the fire; and he slowly descended the hill in a direction different from that of the Carthusian, forgetting him and his doctrines and buried in anxious thoughts about his child's fate and his own.

Chapter.

The funeral obsequies were over the [illegible] which had [illegible] in solemn and [illegible] and [illegible] the same preparations [illegible] deeper [illegible] and every demonstration of [illegible] for [illegible] to celebrate festivities when the [illegible] was so nearly approached. It had been agreed that the funeral feast should be blended with that usually given at the inauguration of the young Chief. Some objections were made to this arrangement as containing an ill omen. But on the other hand it had a species of recommendation from the habits and feelings of the Highlanders who to this day are wont to mingle a species of solemn mirth with their mourning and something resembling melancholy with their mirth. The aversion to speak or think of those who have been loved and lost is less known to this grave and enthusiastic race than it is to others. You hear not merely the young mention (as is everywhere usual) the merits and the character of parents who had in the course of nature predeceased them but the widowed partner [illegible] in ordinary conversation of the lost spouse and what is still stranger the parent

"Vol. II. consists of 53 pages, and is complete: some little errors in paging.

"Vol. III. has 69 pages, but wants first eight pages, and from pages 18 to 23 and 26 to 35. GEORGE HOGARTH.

"CUPAR, 23 *Augt.* 1871."

1828.

273. TALES OF A GRANDFATHER.

Lent by

FRANCIS RICHARDSON, ESQ.

"TALES OF A GRANDFATHER. A portion of the Original Autograph Manuscript, folio.

"The fragments of the Original Manuscript of the *Tales of a Grandfather*, which are contained in this volume, I received as a gift from Sir Walter Scott, at Abbotsford, on April 9, 1831.—R. CADELL."—*London Sale*, 1867, No. 10, £152, 5s.

First portion, 4to, early part; second portion, 4to, to the end of sixteenth century: third portion, folio. Third Series.

1829.

274. SCOTT (SIR WALTER). "THE DEATH OF THE LAIRD'S JOCK; and A HIGHLAND ANECDOTE. By the Author of *Waverley*. Folio, 1829."

Sale of Dawson Turner's MSS., Lot 428, June 6, 1859, £10, 10s., Messrs. BOONE.

275. SCOTT (SIR WALTER). "THE TAPESTRIED CHAMBER; or, The Lady in the Sacque. By the Author of *Waverley*. Half-morocco, folio, pp. 10, 1829."

Sale of Dawson Turner's MSS., Lot 429, June 6, 1859, £4, 15s., Messrs. BOONE.

1820.

276. PREFATORY MEMOIRS TO LIVES OF THE NOVELISTS. The Original Manuscript. 4to.

Lent by

CHRISTOPHER DOUGLAS, ESQ.

These Memoirs are—1. Laurence Sterne (folios 3 to 7), 5 leaves. 2. Oliver Goldsmith, 8 leaves. 3. Dr. Samuel Johnson, 6 leaves. In one volume (in all 19 leaves). 4to.

277. INTRODUCTORY ESSAY ON POPULAR POETRY, etc.

Lent by

FRANCIS RICHARDSON, ESQ.

Acquired at *London Sale*, 1867, No. 6 (see No. 239), £54

1823.

278. THE ARTICLE ROMANCE, contributed to the Supplement of the *Encyclopædia Britannica*, in 1823. Scott's Original Manuscript. Presented by the Editor, Professor Macvey Napier, to James T. Gibson Craig, Esq. 4to.

Lent by

J. T. GIBSON CRAIG, ESQ.

A Facsimile of the MS. is here given.

1828.

279. PREFATORY MEMOIR OF MOLIÈRE. 26 pages.

Lent by

HENRY G. BOHN, ESQ.

In the same volume the following original letters of Sir Walter Scott are inserted :—

1. Letter, undated, from Sir Walter Scott, alluding to his purchase of Abbotsford, apparently to Lockhart, and before 1820.
2. Letters to R. P. Gillies, respecting the *Foreign Quarterly*, June 1826.
3. Letter to R. P. Gillies, promising contributions to the *Foreign Quarterly*, June 1826.
4. Letter, December 8, 1827, to R. P. Gillies, in reply to one from him respecting the *Foreign Quarterly*, and promising an article on Molière.
5. Letter, March 12, 1828, to R. P. Gillies, referring to his struggles to extricate his affairs from the consequences of the two great bankruptcies.

1828.

280. MEMOIR OF GEORGE BANNATYNE, by Sir Walter Scott. The Original Manuscript. Eight leaves, 4to. Also the proof-sheets, with the Author's corrections, and some additions.

Lent by

DAVID LAING, ESQ.

This Memoir forms the first portion of *Memorials of George Bannatyne*, 1545-1608, printed for the Club in 1829 (See No. 373). The MS. was accompanied with a letter, which begins :—

[ABBOTSFORD, *September* 2, 1828.]

"DEAR AND LEARNED MR. SECRETARY,—I have incontinent complied with your request, and finished the sketch of George Bannatyne's life. I am so blind that I sometimes mistake dates, so my sketch may be faulty in that particular. Are there no notices of George's decease? You will see I propose to throw Sir William Macleod Bannatyne's note, which I do not quite understand, into Appendix; also Bannatyne's own verses, which are sad trash; also Allan Ramsay's Verses—although mentioning Hardyknute, etc., they are rather to be considered as applying to the Evergreen than the Bannatyne Manuscripts. The next thing would be to have an account of the Editors who have filled their buckets at Banni's fountain, and the general contents of the Manuscripts yet unpublished, if any there be. . . .

"No more at present, but health and fraternity.—Yours truly,

"*Quoth* THE ABBOT OF THE FORD."

Romance

Definition & origin of the word Romance

Dr. Johnson has defined Romance in its primary sense to be "A military fable of the Middle Ages: a tale of wild adventures in war and chivalry."[1] But although this definition expresses correctly the ordinary idea of the word it is not sufficiently comprehensive to answer our present purpose. A composition may be a legitimate Romance yet neither refer to Love nor Chivalry to war nor to the Middle Ages. The "wild adventures" is almost the only absolutely essential ingredient in Johnson's definition. We would be rather inclined to describe a Romance as "A fictitious narrative in prose or verse the interest of which turns upon marvellous and uncommon incidents" being thus opposed to the kindred term Novel which Johnson has described as "a small tale generally of love" but which we would rather define as "A fictitious narrative differing from the Romance because accommodated to the ordinary train of human events and the modern state of society." Assuming these definitions it is evident from the nature of the distinction that there may exist compositions which it may be difficult to assign precisely or exclusively to the one class or the other and which in fact partake of the nature of both. But the distinction will be found broad enough to answer all general and useful purposes.

The word Romance in its original meaning was far from conveying the definition now assigned. On the contrary it signified merely one or other of the popular dialects of Europe founded (as almost all these dialects were) upon the Roman tongue that is upon the Latin. The name of Romance was indiscriminately given to the Italian to the Spanish even (in one remarkable instance at least) to the English language. But it was especially applied to the compound language of France in which the Gothic dialect of the Franks the Celtic of the ancient Gauls and the classical Latin formed the ingredients. At a period so early as 1150 it plainly appears that the Romance language was distinguished from the Latin and that translations were made from the one into the other.[2] The most ancient Romances of the middle ages were usually composed in the French language which was in a peculiar degree the language of love and chivalry and those which are written in English always affect to refer to some French original which usually at least if not in all instances must be supposed to have a real existence. Hence the frequent recurrence of the phrase

As in Romance we read

or

Right as the Romaunt us tells

and equivalent phrases well known to all who have at any time perused such compositions. Thus very naturally though undoubtedly by slow degrees the very name of Romaunt or Romance came to be transferred

1792.

281. MANUSCRIPT VOLUME, written by Sir Walter Scott, with the title "LEGENDARY FRAGMENTS," and his signature, "WALTER SCOTT, 1792." 4to. 64 leaves, containing probably some original pieces.

Lent from

THE ABBOTSFORD LIBRARY.

282. A SIMILAR VOLUME, with the title "SCOTTISH SONGS." It might rather be styled a *Poetical Commonplace-book*, and had probably served as the foundation of *The Border Minstrelsy*, several leaves having apparently been cut out for the printer. Various handwritings occur towards the end of the volume. 4to.

Lent from

THE ABBOTSFORD LIBRARY.

1798.

283. THE LAMENTATION OF THE FAITHFUL WIFE OF ASAN AGA, from the Morlachian Language. The Original Manuscript, 4to.

Lent by

MESSRS. A. & C. BLACK.—(The MS. has since been presented to MR. D. LAING.)

In twenty-seven stanzas, beginning—

"What yonder glimmers so white on the mountain,
Glimmers so white where yon sycamores grow?
Is it wild swans around Vaga's fair fountain?
Or is it a wreath of the wintry snow?"

This spirited translation from the German Ballad by Goethe has probably never been printed. The handwriting is about 1798, and the translation was well known to some of Sir Walter's early friends.

Goethe's German version is entitled *Klaggesang von der edlen Frau des Asan-Aga*. Morlachisch.

"Was ist Weisses dort am grünen Walde?
Ist es Schnee wohl, oder sind es Schwäne?" etc.

It was first published by Herder in his well-known collection, *Volkslieder*. A more literal version by Professor Aytoun, called *The Doleful Lay of the Wife of Asa Aga*, is contained in the volume of Poems and Ballads of Goethe. Translated by W. E. Aytoun and Theodore Martin. 1859.

In a volume entitled *Selim and Zaïda, with other Poems*, published at Edinburgh. 1800, 12mo, there is (pp. 89-95), a different version, entitled, "A Morlachian Funeral Song, on the death of the illustrious wife of Asan Aga. From the German of Goethe.

"What shines so white in yonder verdant forest?"

The anonymous Author of this volume, John Boyd Greenshields, Esq., was the son of Mr. John Greenshields, merchant, Glasgow. He passed as Advocate in 1793, and distinguished himself at the Scottish Bar. He died in 1845.

"This translation (it is said in the Notes) was made originally from the German of Goethe; but I have since met with another translation by the Abate Fortis, in his Travels in Dalmatia. Goethe's performance, as we might expect, is in general superior to the Abate's; but, in some instances, the latter seems to me preferable, and I have therefore followed those passages in which he appears to have excelled his fellow-translator."

In the *Viaggio in Dalmazia, dell' Abate Alberto Fortis* (Venezia, 1774, vol. i. pp. 98-105), the original ballad is given, along with an Italian translation, in connexion with the division "De' Costumi de' Morlacchi," addressed to "My Lord Giovanni Stuart, Conte di Bute," etc. The ballad in the original has the title, "Xalostna Pjesanza plemenite Asan Aghinize;" and in the Italian version, "Canzone Dolente della nobile Sposa d'Asan Aga." In the English translation of the Travels, 1778, no mention is made of the Ballad.

From Scott's *Life* by Lockhart (second edition, vol. i. pp. 339, 340) we learn that besides his translation of *The Chase*, Scott intended to have published a volume by Manners & Miller, in 1796, of Dramas from the German, all in prose like the originals; but he also versified, at the same time, some lyrical fragments of Goethe, as, for example, the Morlachian Ballad,

"What yonder glimmers so white on the mountain?"

and the Song from *Claudina von Villa Bella.*

1808.

284. Scott's Autobiography, known as The Ashestiel Manuscript. The Original Manuscript.

Lent by

James R. Hope Scott, Esq., Q.C.

A Facsimile of the first two pages of this very interesting MS. is given on the opposite leaf.

*** The Ashestiel Manuscript forms the commencement of Mr. Lockhart's *Life of Sir Walter Scott.* In a Volume, "collected and bound by me, in December 1848, J. G. L." (John G. Lockhart).

The Original MS. of Sir Walter Scott's Autobiography. 50 leaves. There is added in this Volume :—1. The Petition of Walter Scott for admission as an Advocate, 1791. (Exhibited as No. 362.) 2. Certificate of Sir Walter's Marriage in the Parish Church of St. Mary, Carlisle, 23d December 1797. 3. Commission, Walter Scott, Esq., to Mr. Charles Erskine, Sheriff-substitute of Selkirkshire, 14th March 1800. 4. Commission by Lord Napier, Lord-Lieutenant of the County of Selkirk, in favour of Walter Scott, Esq., appointing him a Deputy-Lieutenant of said County, 1800. 5. Burgess Ticket for the Burgh of Kirkwall, 1814. 6. Burgess Ticket for the Burgh of Dunfermline.

Memoirs

Ashestiel 26th April 1808

The present age has discovered a ~~thirst~~ desire, or rather a rage for literary anecdote and private history that may be well permitted to alarm ~~any~~ one who has engaged in a certain degree the attention of the Public That I have had more than my own share of popularity my contemporaries will be as ready to admit as I am to confess that its measure has exceeded not only my hopes but my merits and even wishes. I may be therefore permitted without an extraordinary degree of vanity to take the precaution of recording a few leading circumstances (they do not merit the name of events) of a very quiet and uniform life that should my literary reputation survive my temporal existence the public may know from good authority

all

all that they are entitled to know of an indivi=dual who has contributed to their amusement. From the lives of some poets a most important moral lesson may doubtless be derived & few sermons can be read with so much profit as the Memoirs of Burns of Chatterton or of Savage ~~Both of these wrote [illegible]~~ Were I conscious of any thing peculiar in my own moral character which could render such developement ne=cessary or useful I would as readily consent to it as I would bequeath my body to dissection if the operation could tend to point out the ~~seat~~ nature and the means of curing any peculiar malady. But as my habits of thinking & acting as well as my rank in society were fixed long before I had ~~[illegible]~~ attained or even pretended to any poetical reputation and as ~~therefore~~ it produced when acquired no remarkable change upon either it ~~was~~ is hardly to be expected that much information can be derived from minutely investigating frailties follies or vices not very different in number or degree from ~~those~~ of other ~~young~~ men in ~~the same~~ my situation. As I have not been blessed with the talents of Burns or Chatterton I have been happily exempted from the influence of their violent passions exasp=erated by the struggle of ~~minds~~ feelings which rose up against the unjust decrees of fortune. Yet although I can=not tell of difficulties vanquished ~~by~~ and distance of rank annihilated by the strength of genius those who ~~may~~ shall hereafter read this little memoir may find in it some hints to be improved for the regu=lation of their own minds or the training those of others.

Every

II.—THE WORKS OF SIR WALTER SCOTT.

(I.)—*THE EARLIEST EDITIONS OF THE POEMS, ETC.*

285. The Chase, and William and Helen: Two Ballads from the German of Gottfried Augustus Bürger.

Edinburgh: Printed by Mundell and Son, R. Bank Close, for Manners and Miller, Parliament Square; and sold by T. Cadell, Jun. and W. Davies (successors to Mr. Cadell), in the Strand, London. 1796. 4to, title, pp. v. 41.

286. Goetz of Berlichingen, with the Iron Hand: A Tragedy translated from the German of Goethé, Author of the *Sorrows of Werter*, etc. By Walter Scott, Esq., Advocate, Edinburgh.

London: Printed for J. Bell, No. 148 Oxford Street, opposite New Bond Street. 1799. 8vo, pp. xvi. 202.

286*. The Eve of Saint John. A Border Ballad. By Walter Scott. Esq., Advocate.

Kelso: Printed by James Ballantyne, at the *Kelso Mail* Printing Office. 1800. 4to. Titles 2 leaves, and pp. 11. A copy in the British Museum is marked 11,642 g.

*** On comparing this with the *Minstrelsy of the Scottish Border*, Vol. II., and with the republication of "Ballads, etc.," in 1806, there are several verbal corrections or alterations subsequently made by the Author.

287. Minstrelsy of the Scottish Border: Consisting of Historical and Romantic Ballads, collected in the Southern Counties of Scotland: with a few of modern date, founded upon Local Tradition.

Kelso: Printed by James Ballantyne, for T. Cadell, Jun., and W. Davies, Strand, London; and sold by Manners and Miller, and A. Constable, Edinburgh. 1802. 2 vols. 8vo.

*** The copy exhibited by Mr. Gibson Craig, along with Vol. III., added in 1803 when the Work was republished as a Second Edition, had the view of Hermitage Castle, Williams, *del.*, Walker, *sculpt.*, only inserted in the fine-paper copies.

In all the copies Vol. III. is called "the Second Edition." Edinburgh: Printed by James Ballantyne for Longman and Rees, Paternoster Row, London: and sold by Manners and Miller, and A. Constable, Edinburgh. 1803. 8vo.

288. THE MINSTRELSY OF THE SCOTTISH BORDER. In Three Volumes. Second Edition.

Edinburgh: Printed by James Ballantyne for Longman and Rees, Paternoster Row, London; and sold by Manners and Miller, and A. Constable, Edinburgh. 1803. 3 vols. 8vo. Thick paper copy.

289. THE LAY OF THE LAST MINSTREL: A Poem. By Walter Scott, Esq.

London: Printed for Longman, Hurst, Rees, and Orme, Paternoster Row; and A. Constable and Co., Edinburgh, by James Ballantyne, Edinburgh. 1805. 4to.

*** On the fly-leaf of the copy exhibited, lent from the Abbotsford Library, is written, "Mrs. Scott, from her affectionate Son, the Author."

290. ANOTHER COPY of the same Edition, with Manuscript Corrections and Additions by the Author. (See No. 231.)

Lent by

HER MAJESTY THE QUEEN.

*** On the fly-leaf Sir Walter has written:—

"This copy was prepared for the Second Edition, upon the principle of abbreviating the Notes recommended by the *Edinburgh Review* in their notice of the Poem. But my friend Mr. Constable would not hear of the proposed Abridgment, and so the antiquarian matter was retained.—W. S.—15*th June* 1821."

291. THE SAME, Third Edition. Edinburgh. 1806. 8vo.

*** A Presentation Copy, lent by D. MILNE HOME of Wedderburn, Esq., with a Letter prefixed from the Author to George Home, Esq.

292. BALLADS AND LYRICAL PIECES. By Walter Scott, Esq.

Edinburgh: Printed by James Ballantyne and Co., for Longman, Hurst, Rees, and Orme, London; and Archibald Constable and Co., Edinburgh. 1806. 8vo.

"ADVERTISEMENT.—These Ballads have been already published in different collections, some in *The Minstrelsy of the Scottish Border*, others in *The Tales of Wonder*, and some in both these Miscellanies. They are now first collected into one Volume. The Songs have been written at different times for the Musical Collections of Mr. George Thomson and Mr. White."

The Tales of Wonder, written and collected by M. G. Lewis, Esq., M.P., appeared at London, 1801, in 2 vols. royal 8vo.

293. MARMION: A TALE OF FLODDEN FIELD. By Walter Scott, Esq.

"Alas! that Scottish Maid should sing
The combat where her lover fell!
That Scottish Bard should wake the string,
The triumph of our foes to tell."—LEYDEN.

Edinburgh: Printed by J. Ballantyne and Co. for Archibald Constable and Company, Edinburgh; and William Miller and John Murray, London. 1808. 4to.

294. THE LADY OF THE LAKE: A Poem. By Walter Scott, Esq.

Edinburgh: Printed for John Ballantyne and Co., Edinburgh; and Longman, Hurst, Rees, and Orme, and William Miller, London. By James Ballantyne and Co., Edinburgh. 1810. 4to.

*** Lent by Mr. Erskine of Kinnedder. On the fly-leaf is the Author's inscription: "William Erskine from Walter Scott."

295. THE VISION OF DON RODERICK: A Poem. By Walter Scott, Esq.

"Quid dignum memorare tuis, Hispania, terris,
Vox humana valet." CLAUDIAN.

Edinburgh: Printed by James Ballantyne and Co., for John Ballantyne and Co., Hanover Street, Edinburgh; and Longman, Hurst, Rees, Orme, and Brown, London. 1811. 4to.

296. ROKEBY: A Poem. By Walter Scott, Esq.

Edinburgh: Printed for John Ballantyne and Co., Edinburgh; and Longman, Hurst, Rees, Orme, and Brown, London. By James Ballantyne and Co. Edinburgh. 1813. 4to.

*** Copy on Large Paper, lent by Mr. Erskine of Kinnedder, with the inscription. "William Erskine, Esq., from his affectionate friend, the Author."

297. THE BRIDAL OF TRIERMAIN; OR, THE VALE OF ST. JOHN. In Three Cantos. (Anon.)

"An elf-quene wol I love ywis,
For in this world no woman is
Worthy to be my make in toun;
All other women I forsake,
And to an elf-quene I me take,
By dale and eke by doun."—*Rime of Sir Thopas.*

Edinburgh: Printed by James Ballantyne and Co. for John Ballantyne and Co., Hanover Street; and for Longman, Hurst, Rees, Orme, and Brown; and Gale, Curtis, and Fenner, London. 1813. 12mo.

298. THE FIELD OF WATERLOO; A Poem. By Walter Scott, Esq.

"Though Valois braved young Edward's gentle hand,
And Albret rush'd on Henry's way worn band,
With Europe's chosen sons in arms renown'd,
Yet not on Vere's bold archers long they look'd,
Nor Audley's squires nor Mowbray's yeomen brook'd,—
They saw their standard fall, and left their monarch bound."—AKENSIDE.

Edinburgh: Printed by James Ballantyne and Co. for Archibald Constable and Co., Edinburgh; and Longman, Hurst, Rees, Orme, and Brown, and John Murray, London. 1815. 8vo.

299. THE LORD OF THE ISLES: A Poem. By Walter Scott, Esq.

Edinburgh: Printed for Archibald Constable and Co., Edinburgh; and Longman, Hurst, Rees, Orme, and Brown, London. By James Ballantyne and Co., Edinburgh. 1815. 4to.

300. THE ETTRICKE GARLAND, being two excellent New Songs on the Lifting of the Banner of the House of Buccleuch, at the great Foot-Ball Match on Carterhaugh, Dec. 4, 1815.

Edinburgh: Printed by James Ballantyne and Co. 1815. Royal 8vo. Four leaves.

*** Of these songs, "*The Lifting of the Banner*" is signed, "Quoth the Sheriff of the Forest." The second, "*To the Ancient Banner*," etc., "Quoth the Ettrick Shepherd."

301. HAROLD THE DAUNTLESS: A Poem in Six Cantos. By the Author of "*The Bridal of Triermain.*"

Edinburgh: Printed by James Ballantyne and Co. for Longman, Hurst, Rees, Orme, and Brown, London; and Archibald Constable and Co., Edinburgh. 1817. 12mo.

302. HALIDON HILL; A Dramatic Sketch, from Scottish History. By Sir Walter Scott, Bart.

"Knights, squires, and steeds shall enter on the stage."—*Essay on Criticism.*

Edinburgh: Printed for Archibald Constable and Co., Edinburgh; and Hurst, Robinson, and Co., London. 1822. 8vo.

303. THE DOOM OF DEVORGOIL: A Melo-Drama. AUCHINDRANE; OR, THE AYRSHIRE TRAGEDY. By Sir Walter Scott, Bart.

Printed for Cadell and Company, Edinburgh; and Simpkin and Marshall, London. 1830. 8vo.

---

304. PAUL'S LETTERS TO HIS KINSFOLK.

Edinburgh: Printed by James Ballantyne and Co. for Archibald Constable and Company, Edinburgh; and Longman, Hurst, Rees, Orme, and Brown, and John Murray, London. 1816. 8vo.

305. DESCRIPTION OF THE REGALIA OF SCOTLAND.

"The steep and iron-belted rock,
Where trusted lie the Monarchy's last gems,
The Sceptre, Sword, and Crown, that graced the brows,
Since Father Fergus, of an hundred Kings."—*Albania, a Poem.*

Edinburgh: Printed by James Ballantyne and Company. 1819. 12mo, pp. 34.

*** This Account of the REGALIA OF SCOTLAND, with Illustrations, forms part of the Provincial Antiquities, No. 306.

306. THE PROVINCIAL ANTIQUITIES AND PICTURESQUE SCENERY OF SCOTLAND. With Descriptive Illustrations. By Walter Scott, Esq.

London: Printed for Rodwell and Martin; and sold by J. and A. Arch, Cornhill, London; and William Blackwood, Edinburgh. Printed by James Ballantyne and Co. 1819. 2 vols. 4to.

This splendid work was published in Ten Parts, between 1819 and 1826; and forms two Volumes.

*** It may be mentioned, that as the Work proceeded, the publishers, Messrs Rodwell and Martin, presented the ORIGINAL DRAWINGS to Sir Walter Scott. They are framed and exhibited at Abbotsford.

307. ANOTHER LARGE PAPER COPY, with Proof Impressions and Duplicate Etchings of the Plates, after Turner, E. Blore, Rev. J. Thomson, A. Geddes, H. W. Williams, A. W. Calcott, A. Nasmyth, and J. Schetky. Engraved by George Cooke, Finden, Le Keux, W. Miller, Goodall, etc. Imperial 4to. 2 vols. London. 1826.

Lent from
THE SIGNET LIBRARY.

308. THOUGHTS ON THE PROPOSED CHANGE OF CURRENCY, and other late Alterations, as they affect or are intended to affect the Kingdom of Scotland: (Three Letters to the Editor of the *Edinburgh Weekly Journal* from Malachi Malagrowther, Esq.)

"Ergo, Caledonia, nomen inane, Vale!"

Edinburgh: Printed by James Ballantyne and Company for William Blackwood, Edinburgh. 1826. 8vo.

309. THE LIFE OF NAPOLEON BUONAPARTE, Emperor of the French. With a Preliminary View of the French Revolution. By the Author of *Waverley*, etc. In Nine Volumes.

Edinburgh: Printed by Ballantyne and Co. for Longman, Rees, Orme, Brown, and Green, London; and Cadell and Co., Edinburgh. 1827. 9 vols. post 8vo.

310. RELIGIOUS DISCOURSES. By a Layman. [Written by Sir Walter for his Amanuensis, George Huntly Gordon, then a Probationer.]

I. THE CHRISTIAN AND THE JEWISH DISPENSATIONS COMPARED.

II. THE BLESSEDNESS OF THE RIGHTEOUS.

London: Henry Colburn, New Burlington Street. 1828. 8vo.

311. THE HISTORY OF SCOTLAND. By Sir Walter Scott, Bart. In Two Volumes.

London: Printed for Longman, Rees, Orme, Brown, and Green, Paternoster Row; and John Taylor, Upper Gower Street. 1829, 1830. 2 vols. 12mo. (In Lardner's *Cyclopædia*.)

312. LETTERS ON DEMONOLOGY AND WITCHCRAFT, addressed to J. G. Lockhart, Esq. By Sir Walter Scott, Bart.

London: John Murray, Albemarle Street. 1830. 12mo. (In Murray's Family Library.)

(II.)—THE WAVERLEY NOVELS.

313. THE WAVERLEY NOVELS. Author's Annotated Edition. (Volumes selected as specimens of the Copyright text, containing the Manuscript Introductions and Annotations by SIR WALTER SCOTT.) 1829-1832. 41 Vols. Large 8vo.

Lent by

MESSRS. A. & C. BLACK.

Mr. CADELL, in his "Memorandum of Sir Walter Scott's Original MSS.," says:—

"The Annotated Edition of the Waverley Novels in 41 volumes octavo, which is not only curious but valuable; the additions in Sir Walter Scott's hand carry down the copyright (so far as these alterations go) to a period of forty-two years from the appearance of each volume of the duodecimo, commencing in 1829 and reaching to 1833."

This important copy came into the possession of Messrs. A. & C. BLACK when they purchased the copyright of the Novels; and by their kind permission a selection of the Volumes was made for the Scott Exhibition. A list of the entire series may be subjoined. It may be noticed that in the first volume of *Waverley* are bound up the following original autographs:—

Sir Walter Scott's dedication of this edition to "To the King's Most Gracious Majesty," and the "ADVERTISEMENT.—New Edition of the Novels by the Author of *Waverley*. Revised and Corrected, with a Preface, and Notes Historical and Illustrative, by the Author."

"Fragment of a Romance which was to have been entitled THOMAS THE RHYMER," Chapter I., 13 leaves, the three last pages marked P. A. (of a later date).

Also THE LORD OF ENNERDALE, and some other MS. fragments, printed in the Appendix, annexed to *Waverley*.

		Series of Novels and Tales.	
VOL. I.	Waverley,	1822.	VOL. I.
II.	Waverley,	,,	II.
	Guy Mannering,	,,	III.
III.	Guy Mannering,		
IV.	The Antiquary,	,,	IV.
V.	The Antiquary,	,,	V.
	Rob Roy,		
VI.	Rob Roy,	,,	VI.
VII.	The Black Dwarf,	,,	VII.
	Old Mortality,		
VIII.	Old Mortality,	,,	VIII.
IX.	Heart of Midlothian,	,,	IX.
X.	Heart of Midlothian,	,,	X.
XI.	Bride of Lammermoor,	,,	XI.
XII.	Bride of Lammermoor,	,,	XII.
	Legend of Montrose,		

To the Kings Most Gracious Majesty

Sire

May it please your Majesty

The Author of this Collection of works of Fiction would never have presumed to solicit for them Your Majesty's august Patronage were it not that ~~[illegible]~~ the perusal of them has in any degree succeeded in amusing hours of relaxation or relieving those of languor pain ~~[illegible]~~ or anxiety they must in a trifling degree have aided the warmest wish of Your Majesty's heart by contributing to the Happiness of Your People.

They are ~~[illegible]~~ therefore humbly dedicated to your Majesty agreeably to your Gracious Permission ~~by your Majesty's~~ by Your Majesty's ~~dutiful~~ Subject

Walter Scott

1st January ~~1828~~
Abbotsford 1829

Advertisement

New edition of the Novels by the Author of Waverley Revised and corrected with a preface Introductions and Notes historical and illustrative by the Author

It has been the occasional occupation of the Author of Waverley for several years past to revise and correct that voluminous and numerous class which passes under the name in order that if they should ever appear as his avowed productions they might be in some degree deserving of a continuance of the public favour with which they had been honoured upon first publication. For a long period it seemed likely that the improved edition which he meditated would be a posthumous publication. But the course of events which occasioned the disclosure of the authors name having in a great measure restored to him the property of these copyrights he is naturally induced to give them to the press in a corrected and improved form while life and health permit the task of correcting and illustrating them. Such being his purpose it is necessary to say a few words on the plan of the proposed Edition.

In stating it to be revised and corrected" it is not to be expected that any attempt is made to alter the tenor of the stories or the character of the actors or the spirit of the dialogue. There is indeed ample room for emendation in these respects But where the tree falls it must lie. Any attempt to obviate criticism however just by altering a work already in the hands of the public is generally unsuccessful. In the most improbable fiction the reader still desires some air of vraisemblance and does not relish that it should be altered to suit the taste of critics or the caprice of the author himself. The same natural principle of feeling may be observed in children who cannot endure that a nursery story should be repeated to them in a different manner from the manner in which it is first told.

But without altering in the slightest either the story or the mode of telling the Author has taken this opportunity to correct errors of the press and slips of the pen. That such should exist cannot be wondered at if it is considered that the Publishers found it for their to throw of ten or twelve thousand copies in the first editions of the various novels and that of course neither Author nor printer had an opportunity of correcting errors in subsequent editions as is usually the case. It is hoped that the present edition will be found free from errors of this accidental kind.

But there have been other emendations which without being such apparent deviations from the original as to shock the reader's

		Series of Historical Romances.	
VOL. XIII.	Ivanhoe,	1822.	VOL. I.
XIV.	Ivanhoe, The Monastery,	"	II.
XV.	The Monastery,	"	III.
XVI.	The Abbot,	"	IV.
XVII.	The Abbot, Kenilworth,	"	V.
XVIII.	Kenilworth,	"	VI.
		Series of Novels and Romances.	
XIX.	The Pirate,	1824.	VOL. I.
XX.	The Pirate, The Fortunes of Nigel,	"	II.
XXI.	The Fortunes of Nigel,	"	III.
XXII.	Peveril of the Peak,	"	IV.
XXIII.	Peveril of the Peak,	"	V.
XXIV.	Peveril of the Peak, Quentin Durward,	"	VI.
XXV.	Quentin Durward,	"	VII.
		Series of Tales and Romances.	
XXVI.	St. Ronan's Well,	1827.	VOL. I.
XXVII.	St. Ronan's Well, Redgauntlet,	"	II.
XXVIII.	Redgauntlet,	"	III.
XXIX.	Tales of the Crusaders—I. Betrothed,	"	IV.
XXX.	Do. I. Betrothed. Do. II. The Talisman,	"	V.
XXXI.	Do. II. The Talisman, Woodstock,	"	VI.
XXXII.	Woodstock,	"	VII.
XXXIII.	Chronicles of the Canongate— (*First Series*)—Highland Widow, My Aunt Margaret's Mirror, Tapestried Chamber, Death of the Laird's Jock, (*Second Series*)—The Fair Maid of Perth,	1833.	VIII.
XXXIV.	Fair Maid of Perth,	"	IX.
XXXV.	Fair Maid of Perth, Anne of Geierstein,	"	X.
XXXVI.	Anne of Geierstein,	"	XI.
XXXVII.	Anne of Geierstein, Count Robert of Paris,	"	XII.
XXXVIII.	Count Robert of Paris, Castle Dangerous,	"	XIII.
XXXIX.	Castle Dangerous, Surgeon's Daughter,	"	XIV.
XL.	Introductions, Notes, and Illustrations to the Novels, Tales, and Romances of the Author of Waverley—Waverley to Abbot,	1833.	I.
XLI.	Do. do., Kenilworth to Castle Dangerous,		II.

(III.)—FIRST EDITIONS OF THE WAVERLEY NOVELS, THE TALES OF A GRANDFATHER, ETC.

314. WAVERLEY; OR, 'TIS SIXTY YEARS SINCE.

"Under which King, Bezonian? speak or die!"—*Henry IV.* Part II.

In Three Volumes.

Edinburgh: Printed by James Ballantyne and Co. for Archibald Constable and Co., Edinburgh; and Longman, Hurst, Rees, Orme, and Brown, London. 1814. 3 vols. 12mo.

315. GUY MANNERING; OR, THE ASTROLOGER. By the Author of *Waverley.*

"'Tis said that words and signs have power
O'er sprites in planetary hour;
But scarce I praise their venturous part
Who tamper with such dangerous art."—*Lay of the Last Minstrel.*

In Three Volumes.

Edinburgh: Printed by James Ballantyne and Co. for Longman, Hurst, Rees, Orme, and Brown, London; and Archibald Constable and Co., Edinburgh. 1815. 3 vols. 12mo.

316. THE ANTIQUARY. By the Author of *Waverley* and *Guy Mannering.*

"I knew Anselmo. He was shrewd and prudent,
Wisdom and cunning had their shares of him;
But he was shrewish as a wayward child,
And pleased again by toys which childhood please;
As—book of fables graced with print of wood,
Or else the jingling of a rusty medal,
Or the rare melody of some old ditty
That first was sung to please King Pepin's cradle."

In Three Volumes.

Edinburgh: Printed by James Ballantyne and Co. for Archibald Constable and Co., Edinburgh; and Longman, Hurst, Rees, Orme, and Brown, London. 1816. 3 vols. 12mo.

317. TALES OF MY LANDLORD, Collected and Arranged by Jedediah Cleishbotham, Schoolmaster of Gandercleugh.

"Hear, Land o' Cakes and brither Scots,
Frae Maidenkirk to Johnny Groat's;
If there's a hole in a' your coats,
I rede ye tent it;
A chiel's amang you takin' notes,
An' faith he'll prent it."—BURNS.

In Four Volumes.

Vols. I.-II.—THE BLACK DWARF.
Vols. II.-IV.—OLD MORTALITY.

Edinburgh: Printed for William Blackwood, Princes Street; and John Murray, Albemarle Street, London. 1816. (At the end)—Edinburgh: Printed by James Ballantyne and Co. 12mo. 4 vols.

318. TALES OF MY LANDLORD. Second Series. Collected and Arranged by Jedediah Cleishbotham, Schoolmaster and Parish-Clerk of Gandercleugh.

"Hear, Land o' Cakes," etc.—BURNS.

In Four Volumes.

Vols. I.-IV.—THE HEART OF MIDLOTHIAN.

Edinburgh: Printed for Archibald Constable and Co. (At the end)—Edinburgh: Printed by James Ballantyne and Co. 1818. 4 vols. 12mo.

319. ROB ROY. By the Author of *Waverley*, *Guy Mannering*, and *The Antiquary*.

"For why? Because the good old rule
Sufficeth them; the simple plan,
That they should take, who have the power,
And they should keep who can."

Rob Roy's Grave.—WORDSWORTH.

In Three Volumes.

Edinburgh: Printed by James Ballantyne and Co. for Archibald Constable and Co., Edinburgh; and Longman, Hurst, Rees, Orme, and Brown, London. 1818. 3 vols. 12mo.

320. TALES OF MY LANDLORD. Third Series. Collected and Arranged by Jedediah Cleishbotham, Schoolmaster and Parish-Clerk of Gandercleugh.

"Hear, Land o' Cakes," etc.—BURNS.

In Four Volumes.

Vols. I.-III.—THE BRIDE OF LAMMERMOOR.
III.-IV.—THE LEGEND OF MONTROSE.

Edinburgh: Printed for Archibald Constable and Co., Edinburgh; Longman, Hurst, Rees, Orme, and Brown, Paternoster Row; and Hurst, Robinson, and Co., 90 Cheapside, London. 1819. 4 vols. 12mo.

321. IVANHOE. A Romance. By the Author of *Waverley*, etc.

"Now fitted the halter, now traversed the cart,
And often took leave,—but seem'd loth to depart!"—PRIOR.

In Three Volumes.

Edinburgh: Printed for Archibald Constable and Co., Edinburgh; and Hurst, Robinson, and Co., 90 Cheapside, London. 1820. 3 vols. post 8vo.

322. THE MONASTERY. A Romance. By the Author of *Waverley*.

In Three Volumes.

Edinburgh: Printed for Longman, Hurst, Rees, Orme, and Brown, London; and for Archibald Constable and Co., and John Ballantyne, Bookseller to the King, Edinburgh. 1820. (At the end)—Printed by James Ballantyne and Co., Edinburgh. 3 vols. 12mo.

323. THE ABBOT. By the Author of *Waverley*. In Three Volumes.
Edinburgh: Printed for Longman, Hurst, Rees, Orme, and Brown, London; and for Archibald Constable and Company, and John Ballantyne, Edinburgh. 1820. (At the end)—Edinburgh: Printed by James Ballantyne and Co. 3 vols. 12mo.

324. KENILWORTH. A Romance. By the Author of *Waverley*, *Ivanhoe*, etc.

"No scandal about Queen Elizabeth, I hope?"—*The Critic*.

In Three Volumes.

Edinburgh: Printed for Archibald Constable and Co., and John Ballantyne, Edinburgh; and Hurst, Robinson, and Co., London. 1821. (At the end)—Edinburgh: Printed by James Ballantyne & Co. 3 vols. post 8vo.

325. THE PIRATE. By the Author of *Waverley*, *Kenilworth*, etc.

—— "Nothing in him
But doth suffer a sea-change."—*Tempest*.

In Three Volumes.

Edinburgh: Printed for Archibald Constable and Co.; and Hurst, Robinson, and Co., London. 1822. (At the end)—Edinburgh: Printed by James Ballantyne and Co. 3 vols. post 8vo.

326. PEVERIL OF THE PEAK. By the Author of *Waverley*, *Kenilworth*, etc.

"If my readers should at any time remark that I am particularly dull, they may be assured there is a design under it."—*British Essayist*.

In Four Volumes.

Edinburgh: Printed for Archibald Constable and Co., Edinburgh; and Hurst, Robinson, and Co., London. 1822. (At the end)—Edinburgh: Printed by James Ballantyne and Co. 4 vols. post 8vo.

327. QUENTIN DURWARD. By the Author of *Waverley*, *Peveril of the Peak*, etc.

"La guerre est ma patrie,
Mon harnois ma maison,
Et en toute saison,
Combattre c'est ma vie."

In Three Volumes.

Edinburgh: for Archibald Constable and Co., Edinburgh; and Hurst, Robinson, and Co., London. 1823. (At the end)—Edinburgh: Printed by James Ballantyne and Co. 3 vols. post 8vo.

328. REDGAUNTLET: A TALE OF THE EIGHTEENTH CENTURY. By the Author of *Waverley*.

"Master, go on; and I will follow thee
To the last gasp, with truth and loyalty."—*As You Like It*.

In Three Volumes.

Edinburgh: Printed for Archibald Constable and Co., Edinburgh; and Hurst, Robinson, and Co., London. 1824. (At the end)—Edinburgh: Printed by James Ballantyne and Co. 3 vols. post 8vo.

329. St. Ronan's Well. By the Author of *Waverley, Quentin Durward*, &c.

"A merry place, 'tis said, in days of yore;
But something ails it now—the place is cursed."—Wordsworth

In Three Volumes.

Edinburgh: Printed for Archibald Constable and Co., Edinburgh; and Hurst, Robinson, and Co., London. 1824. (At the end)—Edinburgh: Printed by James Ballantyne and Co. 3 vols. post 8vo.

330. The Fortunes of Nigel. By the Author of *Waverley, Kenilworth*, etc.

"*Knifegrinder.*—Story? Lord bless you! I have none to tell, sir."
Poetry of the Anti-Jacobin.

In Three Volumes.

Edinburgh: Printed for Archibald Constable and Co., Edinburgh; and Hurst, Robinson, and Co., London. 1822. (At the end)—Edinburgh: Printed by James Ballantyne and Co. 3 vols. post 8vo.

331. Tales of the Crusaders. By the Author of *Waverley, Quentin Durward*, etc.

In Four Volumes.

Vols. I. and II.—The Betrothed.

Vols. III. and IV.—The Talisman.

Edinburgh: Printed for Archibald Constable and Co., Edinburgh; and Hurst, Robinson, and Co., London. 1825. (At the end)—Edinburgh: Printed by James Ballantyne and Co. 4 vols. post 8vo.

332. Woodstock; or, The Cavalier. A Tale of the Year Sixteen Hundred and Fifty-one. By the Author of *Waverley, Tales of the Crusaders*, etc.

"He was a very perfect, gentle Knight."—Chaucer.

In Three Volumes.

Edinburgh: Printed for Archibald Constable and Co., Edinburgh; and Longman, Rees, Orme, Brown, and Green, London. 1826. (At the end)—Edinburgh: Printed by James Ballantyne and Co. 3 vols. post 8vo.

333. Chronicles of the Canongate. (First Series.) By the Author of *Waverley*, etc.

"Sic itur ad astra."—*Motto of the Canongate Arms.*

In Two Volumes.

The Two Drovers.
The Highland Widow.
The Surgeon's Daughter.

Edinburgh: Printed for Cadell and Co., Edinburgh; and Simpkin and Marshall, London. 1827. (At the end)—Edinburgh: Printed by Ballantyne and Co. 2 vols. post 8vo.

334. CHRONICLES OF THE CANONGATE. Second Series. By the Author of *Waverley*, etc.

"SIC ITUR AD ASTRA."—*Motto of the Canongate Arms.*

In Three Volumes.

(ST. VALENTINE'S DAY; OR, THE FAIR MAID OF PERTH.)

Edinburgh: Printed for Cadell and Co., Edinburgh; and Simpkin and Marshall, London. 1828. (At the end)—Edinburgh: Printed by Ballantyne and Co 3 vols. post 8vo.

335. ANNE OF GEIERSTEIN; OR, THE MAIDEN OF THE MIST. By the Author of *Waverley*, etc.

"What! will the aspiring blood of Lancaster
Sink in the ground?"—SHAKSPEARE.

In Three Volumes.

Edinburgh: Printed for Cadell and Co., Edinburgh; and Simpkin and Marshall, London. 1829. (At the end)—Edinburgh: Printed by Ballantyne and Company, Paul's Work, Canongate. 3 vols. post 8vo.

336. TALES OF MY LANDLORD. Fourth and Last Series. Collected and Arranged by Jedediah Cleishbotham, Schoolmaster and Parish-Clerk of Gandercleugh.

"The European with the Asian shore—
Sophia's cupola with golden gleam—
The cypress groves—Olympus high and hoar—
The twelve isles, and the more than I could dream,
Far less describe, present the very view
That charm'd the charming Mary Montagu."—*Don Juan.*

In Four Volumes.

Vols. I.-II.—COUNT ROBERT OF PARIS.
III.-IV.—CASTLE DANGEROUS.

Printed for Robert Cadell, Edinburgh; and Whittaker and Co., London. 1832. (At the end)—Edinburgh: Printed by Ballantyne and Company, Paul's Work, Canongate. 4 vols. post 8vo.

337. TALES OF A GRANDFATHER, being Stories taken from Scottish History. Humbly inscribed to Hugh Littlejohn, Esq. In Three Volumes.

Printed for Cadell and Co., Edinburgh; Simpkin and Marshall, London; and John Cumming, Dublin. 1828. 3 vols. 12mo.—The same imprint to the Second and Third Series.

338. TALES OF A GRANDFATHER, etc. Second Series. In Three Volumes. 1829. 3 vols. 12mo.

339. TALES OF A GRANDFATHER, etc. Third Series. In Three Volumes. 1830. 3 vols. 12mo.

340. TALES OF A GRANDFATHER (Fourth Series), being Stories taken from the History of France. Inscribed to Master John Hugh Lockhart. In Three Volumes.

Printed for Robert Cadell, Edinburgh; Whittaker and Co., London; and John Cumming, Dublin. 1831. 3 vols. 12mo.

341. THE LIFE OF JOHN DRYDEN. By Walter Scott, Esq.

London: Printed for William Miller, Albemarle Street, by James Ballantyne and Co., Edinburgh. 1808. Royal 4to.

*** This Biography forms the first volume of the Collected Edition of Dryden's Works, Edited by Scott. See No. 348. Opposite the title of these Large-paper copies is this note:—

"Fifty copies only of the *Life of Dryden* are printed in quarto.

J. BALLANTYNE & CO."

One of these copies is in the British Museum, marked 841, m. 8. Prefixed is the Portrait of Dryden, on India paper, engraved by James Fittler, A.R.A.

---

342. DISPUTATIO JURIDICA, ad Tit. xxiv. Lib. xlviii. Pand., de Cadaveribus Damnatorum, quam etc. . . Pro Advocati Munere consequendo, Publicae Disquisitioni subjecit GUALTERUS SCOTT, Auct. et Resp. Ad diem 10. Julii, hor. loc. sol.

Edinburgi, apud Balfour et Smellie, Facultatis Juridicae Typographos. 1792. 4to.

Lent by
MR. D. LAING.

343. CASE FOR THE REV. MR. M'NAUGHT, Minister of the Gospel at Girthan, to be heard at the Bar of the Venerable Assembly, May 1793, signed "WALTER SCOTT;" and other Papers relating to the same Case. In one vol. 4to.

Lent by
MR. CAMPBELL SWINTON.

To the preceding Catalogue of Sir Walter Scott's Works, it will not be out of place to add a List of the various Collected Editions that have appeared since 1829. This List was obligingly furnished by the Publishers, in compliance with a request made by the Editor.

DATES OF THE VARIOUS EDITIONS OF SCOTT'S WORKS.

AFTER FINAL REVISION BY THE AUTHOR, AND WITH THE ADDITION OF HIS NOTES AND NEW INTRODUCTIONS.

WAVERLEY NOVELS.

1829-33. Author's Favourite Edition, in 48 vols. fcap. 8vo. Plates.

1841-43. Cabinet Edition, in 25 vols. fcap. 8vo. With Vignettes.

1842-47. Abbotsford Edition, 12 vols. super royal 8vo, illustrated with 1811 Woodcuts and 120 Plates.

1842-48. People's Edition, 5 vols. royal 8vo. Double columns.

1852 53. Library Edition, 25 vols. demy 8vo. Plates.

1854-60. Railway Edition, 25 vols. fcap. 8vo.

1859-61. Illustrated Roxburghe Edition, 48 vols. fcap. 8vo. Plates and Woodcuts.

1862-64. Shilling Edition, 25 vols. 12mo.

1866-68. Sixpenny Edition, 25 vols. demy 8vo.

1870-71. Centenary Edition, with additional Notes, 25 vols. crown 8vo.

POETICAL WORKS.

1833-34. Author's Favourite Edition (in continuation of the Novels), 12 vols. fcap. 8vo: and many smaller editions thereafter.

1834-36. MISCELLANEOUS PROSE WORKS, 28 vols. fcap. 8vo.

1837-38. LOCKHART'S LIFE OF SCOTT, 7 vols. post 8vo.

1845-46. Do. Do. 1 vol. royal 8vo, People's Edition.

1847-48. Do. Do. 10 vols. fcap. 8vo.

1848. Do. Abridgment, 2 vols. post 8vo.

1871. Do. Do. New Edition, by J. R. Hope Scott, 1 vol. crown 8vo.

1871. The entire Works in 100 vols. fcap. 8vo. Plates.

III.—BOOKS EDITED BY SIR WALTER SCOTT.

344. SIR TRISTREM; A Metrical Romance of the Thirteenth Century, by THOMAS OF ERCILDOUNE, called The Rhymer. Edited from the Auchinleck MS. by Walter Scott, Esq., Advocate.

> "Now, hold your mouth, pour charitie,
> Both Knight and Lady fre,
> And herkneth to my spell;
> Of battaille and of chivalrie,
> Of Ladies' love and druerie,
> Anon I wol you tel."—CHAUCER.

Edinburgh: Printed by James Ballantyne, for Archibald Constable and Co., Edinburgh; and Longman and Rees, London. 1804. Royal 8vo.

345. ORIGINAL MEMOIRS, written during the Great Civil War; being the Life of Sir Henry Slingsby, and Memoirs of Captain Hodgson, with Notes, etc.

Edinburgh: Printed by James Ballantyne and Co. for Archibald Constable and Co., Edinburgh; and John Murray, 32 Fleet Street, London. 1806. Large paper copy, royal 8vo.

346. MEMOIRS OF ROBERT CARY, EARL OF MONMOUTH, written by Himself. And FRAGMENTA REGALIA; being a History of Queen Elizabeth's Favourites. By Sir Robert Naunton. With Explanatory Annotations.

Edinburgh: Printed by James Ballantyne and Co. for Archibald Constable and Co., Edinburgh; and John Murray, London. 1808. Large Paper, Royal 8vo.

347. QUEENHOO-HALL, a Romance; and ANCIENT TIMES, a Drama. By the late Joseph Strutt, Author of *Rural Sports and Pastimes of the People of England*, etc. In Four Volumes.

Edinburgh: Printed by James Ballantyne and Co. for John Murray, Fleet Street, London; and Archibald Constable and Co., Edinburgh. 1808. 4 vols. 12mo.

*** "The romance entitled *Queenhoo-Hall* was acquired by the Editor in an imperfect state; and although the tale is brought, by a literary friend, to a hasty conclusion, yet, from the materials which remain, there is reason to believe that Mr. Strutt intended it should neither be so abruptly nor so inartificially terminated."

348. The Works of John Dryden, now first Collected in Eighteen Volumes. Illustrated with Notes, Historical, Critical, and Explanatory; and a Life of the Author, by Walter Scott, Esq.

London: Printed for William Miller, Albemarle Street, by James Ballantyne and Co., Edinburgh. 1808. 18 Vols. Large paper copy, royal 8vo.

349. Memoirs of Captain George Carleton, an English Officer; including Anecdotes of the War in Spain under the Earl of Peterborough, and many interesting particulars relating to the Manners of the Spaniards in the beginning of the last Century. Written by Himself.

Edinburgh: Printed by James Ballantyne and Co., for Archibald Constable and Co., Edinburgh; and J. Murray, London. 1808. Large paper copy. Royal 8vo.

350. The State Papers and Letters of Sir Ralph Sadler, Knight-Banneret. Edited by Arthur Clifford, Esq. In Two Volumes. To which is added a Memoir of the Life of Sir Ralph Sadler, with Historical Notes by Walter Scott, Esq.

Edinburgh: Printed for Archibald Constable and Co., Edinburgh; and for T. Cadell and W. Davies, William Miller, and John Murray, London. 1809. 2 vols. 4to.

351. The same Work, in Three Volumes.

These large paper copies have the same imprint of 1809, the pages being altered and the Work divided into Three Vols. Large 4to.

352. A Collection of Scarce and Valuable Tracts, on the most Interesting and Entertaining Subjects; but chiefly such as relate to the History and Constitution of these Kingdoms. Selected from an infinite number in Print and Manuscript, in the Royal, Cotton, Sion, and other Public, as well as Private, Libraries; particularly that of the late Lord Somers. The Second Edition, Revised, Augmented, and Arranged by Walter Scott, Esq. Thirteen Volumes.

London: Printed for T. Cadell and W. Davies, Strand; W. Miller, Albemarle Street; R. H. Evans, Pall Mall; J. White and J. Murray, Fleet Street; and J. Harding, St. James's Street. 1809-1815. 13 Vols. Large 4to.

353. The Poetical Works of Anna Seward, with Extracts from her Literary Correspondence. Edited by Walter Scott, Esq. In Three Volumes.

Edinburgh: Printed by James Ballantyne and Co. for John Ballantyne and Co., Edinburgh; and Longman, Hurst, Rees, and Orme, Paternoster Row, London. 1810. 3 Vols. post 8vo.

353‡. LETTERS OF ANNA SEWARD, written between the years 1784 and 1807. In Six Volumes.

Edinburgh: Printed by George Ramsay and Company, for Archibald Constable and Company, Edinburgh; and Longman, Hurst, Rees, Orme, and Brown, William Miller, and John Murray, London. 1811. 6 Vols. post 8vo.

⁎ These Volumes form a companion to the preceding Number. Sir Walter Scott, however, was not Editor of the Letters.

354. SECRET HISTORY OF THE COURT OF JAMES THE FIRST, containing—1. Osborne's Traditional Memoirs; 2. Sir Anthony Weldon's Court and Character of King James; 3. Aulicus Coquinariæ; 4. Sir Edward Peyton's Divine Catastrophe of the House of Stuarts. With Notes and Introductory Remarks. In Two Volumes.

Edinburgh: Printed by James Ballantyne and Co. for John Ballantyne and Co., Edinburgh; and Longman, Hurst, Rees, Orme, and Brown, London. 1811. 2 vols. Large paper copy, royal 8vo.

355. MEMOIRS OF THE REIGN OF KING CHARLES THE FIRST. By Sir Philip Warwick, Knight.

Edinburgh: Printed by John Ballantyne and Co., Edinburgh; and Longman, Hurst, Rees, Orme, and Brown, London. 1813. Large paper copy, royal 8vo.

356. THE BORDER ANTIQUITIES OF ENGLAND AND SCOTLAND, comprising Specimens of Architecture and Sculpture, and other Vestiges of Former Ages, accompanied by Descriptions. Together with Illustrations of remarkable Incidents in Border History and Tradition, and Original Poetry. By Walter Scott, Esq.

London: Printed for Longman, Hurst, Rees, Orme, and Brown, Paternoster Row; J. Murray, Albemarle Street; John Greig, Upper Street, Islington; and Constable and Co., Edinburgh. 1814, 1817. 2 vols. Large paper copy, royal 4to.

357. ILLUSTRATIONS OF NORTHERN ANTIQUITIES, from the earlier Teutonic and Scandinavian Romances; being an Abstract of the Book of Heroes, and Nibelungen Lay, with Translations of Metrical Tales from the old German, Danish, Swedish, and Icelandic Languages, with Notes and Dissertations. (By Henry Weber, Robert Jamieson, and Walter Scott.)

Edinburgh: Printed by James Ballantyne and Co. for Longman, Hurst, Rees, Orme, and Brown, London; and John Ballantyne and Co., Edinburgh. 1814. 4to.

358. THE WORKS OF JONATHAN SWIFT, D.D., Dean of St. Patrick's, Dublin; containing Additional Letters, Tracts, and Poems, not hitherto Published; with Notes, and a Life of the Author, by Walter Scott, Esq. (In Nineteen Volumes.)

Edinburgh: Printed for Archibald Constable and Co., Edinburgh; White, Cochrane, and Co., and Gale, Curtis, and Fenner, London; and John Cumming, Dublin. 1814. 19 Vols. Large paper copy, royal 8vo.

359. MEMORIE OF THE SOMERVILLES; being a History of the Baronial House of Somerville, by James, eleventh Lord Somerville. In Two Volumes.

Edinburgh: Printed by James Ballantyne and Co. for Archibald Constable and Company, Edinburgh; and Longman, Hurst, Rees, Orme, and Brown, London. 1815. 2 vols. Large paper copy, royal 8vo.

360. THE LETTING OF HUMOURS BLOOD IN THE HEAD VAINE, etc., by S. Rowlands.

Edinburgh: Reprinted by James Ballantyne and Co. for William Laing and William Blackwood. 1815. Square 8vo.

_ A Collection of Satires by a voluminous English writer, Reprinted from the edition Lond. 1611. Small 8vo. With a Preface and Notes by Sir Walter Scott. Some copies were first issued with W. Blackwood's Name as the publisher.

361. THE SALE-ROOM. No. 1. Saturday, January 4, 1817.

_ This Periodical Paper, published weekly at No. 4 Hanover Street, Edinburgh, was carried on to Saturday, July 12, 1817, when it terminated with No. xxviii. (No Title.) 4to, pp. 228.

362. TRIVIAL POEMS AND TRIOLETS. Written in obedience to Mrs. Tomkin's Commands. By Patrick Carey. 20th August 1651.

London: John Murray, Albemarle Street. 1820. 4to.

_ See extract from the Editor's letter regarding the Author, No. 363.

363. MEMORIALS OF THE HALIBURTONS.

Edinburgh: Printed by James Ballantyne and Company, at the Border Press. 1820. 4to, pp. iv. 63.

_ Thirty copies only printed for Private Circulation. The Preliminary Notice is dated Abbotsford, March 1820. Engraved etching of the Haliburton Burial Aisle in Dryburgh Abbey (from a Drawing by James Skene, Esq.)

On the fly-leaf of the copy exhibited is an inscription, "For Mr. David Laing, etc., (signed) WALTER SCOTT."

In the letter that accompanied the above, Sir Walter says:—

"I have had the good fortune to recover the last copy, as I believe, of the Haliburton Memorials, which I enclose for your acceptance. Please to return the imperfect copy with your convenience.

"I send also a copy of CAREY'S Poems (rather scarce) which came through my hands. [See No. 362.] I have since detected the Author, a Catholic priest and younger brother to the celebrated Lucius Lord Carey.—Yours truly, W. SCOTT.

"CASTLE STREET, *Wednesday* [*January* 1823]."

364. A REPRINT of the same Volume. 1824. 4to.

*** Before sending Mr. Laing the copy of No. 363, Sir Walter Scott had given directions to reprint Thirty additional copies of the Memorials. They are printed on paper slightly larger than the former. The preliminary Notice in these Copies has the date, November 1824.

365. NORTHERN MEMOIRS, Calculated for the Meridian of Scotland; to which is added the Contemplative and Practical Angler. Writ in the year 1658. By Richard Franck, Philanthropus. New Edition, with Preface and Notes.

"*Plures necat Gula quam Gladius.*"

Edinburgh: Printed for Archibald Constable and Co., Edinburgh: and Hurst, Robinson, and Co., London. 1821. 8vo.

*** Originally published at London, 1694. 8vo.

366. CHRONOLOGICAL NOTES OF SCOTTISH AFFAIRS from 1680 till 1701; being chiefly taken from the Diary of Lord Fountainhall.

Edinburgh: Printed for Archibald Constable and Co., Edinburgh; and Hurst, Robinson, and Co., London. 1822. 4to.

367. MILITARY MEMOIRS OF THE GREAT CIVIL WAR, being the Military Memoirs of John Gwynne; and an Account of the Earl of Glencairn's Expedition as General of His Majesty's Forces in the Highlands of Scotland, in the years 1653 and 1654. By a Person who was Eye and Ear Witness to every Transaction. With an Appendix.

Edinburgh: Printed for Hurst, Robinson, and Co., London; and Archibald Constable and Co., Edinburgh. 1822. Large 4to.

368. LAYS OF THE LINDSAYS, being Poems by the Ladies of the House of Balcarras.

Edinburgh: Printed by James Ballantyne and Company. 1824. 4to. Pp. 123.

The collection is divided into three portions:—

1. Poems by Lady Anne Barnard, p. 1-72.
2. Poems of the Lady Elizabeth Scott Lindsay, p. 73-83.
3. Poems and Translations, by the Lady Margaret Lindsay Fordyce, p. 85-95.

*** This volume was originally designed by Sir Walter Scott as a contribution to the Members of THE BANNATYNE CLUB.

After the printing had been completed, the Volume was suppressed. In a letter to the Secretary of the Club, Sir Walter writes:—

"The Lays of the Lindsays *have been recalled and cancelled*, Lady Hardwicke having taken fright at the idea of appearing in a printed though unpublished shape. We are, however, to have *Auld Robin* by himself, and I wish you would speak to Mr. Lizars about engraving on my account the enclosed frontispiece, drawn by Mr. Kirkpatrick Sharpe, and let me know the damage when you write again.—I am always, dear Mr. David, yours assuredly,

"WALTER SCOTT.

"ABBOTSFORD, 3*d October* [1824]."

"ABBOTSFORD, *Thursday*.

"DEAR MR. DAVID,—I send by this same opportunity the copy for Ballantyne, to begin setting up AULD ROBIN GRAY. The etching is very cleverly done, and I hope it will make a neat little Bannatinian volume.—Yours truly,

"W. SCOTT."

369. AULD ROBIN GRAY; a Ballad. By the Right Honourable Lady Anne Barnard, born Lady Anne Lindsay, of Balcarras.

Edinburgh: Printed by James Ballantyne and Company. 1825. 4to. Title, etc., and pp. 61, with engraved Frontispiece, "C. Kirkpatrick Sharpe, *delin.*, W. H. Lizars, *sculpt.*"

"Presented as a Contribution to the BANNATYNE CLUB, by Sir Walter Scott, Bart., President of the Club."

*** LADY ANNE BARNARD was the eldest daughter of Alexander sixth Earl of Balcarras; and married, in 1793, Andrew, son of Thomas Barnard, Bishop of Limerick. She died at London in 1825.

"It is worth while saying that this motto ("*Nae langer she wept*," etc.), and the ascription of the beautiful ballad from which it is taken to the Right Honourable Lady Anne Lindsay, occasioned the ingenious authoress's acknowledgment of the Ballad; of which the Editor, on her permission, published a small impression, inscribed to the Bannatyne Club."—*Waverley Novels* (THE PIRATE), vol. xxv. p. 98. Centenary edit., vol. xxii. p. 287.

370. MEMOIRS OF THE MARCHIONESS DE LA ROCHEJAQUELEIN. Translated from the French.

Edinburgh: Printed for Constable and Company. 1827. 12mo. (Constable's Miscellany of Original and Selected Publications in the various departments of Literature, Science, and the Arts.)

371. THE BANNATYNE MISCELLANY; containing Original Papers and Tracts, chiefly relating to the History and Literature of Scotland. Volume I.

Printed at Edinburgh. 1827. 4to. (At the end)—Edinburgh: Printed by Ballantyne and Co.

*** Printed under the joint superintendence of the PRESIDENT and SECRETARY.

372. PROCEEDINGS IN THE COURT-MARTIAL HELD UPON JOHN, MASTER OF SINCLAIR, Captain-Lieutenant in Preston's Regiment, for the Murder of Ensign Schaw of the same Regiment, and Captain Schaw, of the Royals, 17th October 1708, with Correspondence respecting that Transaction.

Edinburgh: Printed by Ballantyne and Company. 1828. 4to. Title, Dedication, pp. xv. and 41.

Dedication:—"To the Members of the ROXBURGHE CLUB, these Documents, containing the account of a singular and Tragical occurrence during Marlborough's Wars, from an Original and Authentic Manuscript in the Editor's possession, are Inscribed and Presented by their most obedient and respectful servant,

WALTER SCOTT.

"ABBOTSFORD, *1st December* 1828."

373. MEMORIALS OF GEORGE BANNATYNE. M.D.XLV.-M.DC.VIII.

Printed at Edinburgh. 1829. 4to. (At the end)—Edinburgh: Printed for the Members of the Bannatyne Club by Ballantyne and Company. 1829.

*** The Volume itself contains:—

1. Memoir of George Bannatyne, by Sir Walter Scott, Bart.
2. Extracts from the "Memoriall Buik of George Bannatyne."
3. Account of the Contents of George Bannatyne's MS., 1568, by Mr. David Laing.

There is also an Appendix, including Poems by George Bannatyne, from his MS., 1568, and Notes respecting Bannatyne and his family.

374. PAPERS RELATIVE TO THE REGALIA OF SCOTLAND.

Printed at Edinburgh. 1829. 4to.

Presented to the Members of the Bannatyne Club by William Bell, Esq., Writer to the Signet.

375. TRIAL OF DUNCAN TERIG *alias* CLERK, AND ALEXANDER BANE MACDONALD, for the Murder of Arthur Davis, Sergeant in General Guise's Regiment of Foot. June, A.D. 1754.

Edinburgh: Printed by Ballantyne and Company. 1831. 4to.

"To the Members of the BANNATYNE CLUB, this copy of a Trial, involving a curious point of evidence, is presented, by Walter Scott. February 1831."

376. TWO BANNATYNE GARLANDS FROM ABBOTSFORD. 8vo. 13 leaves.

*** Of this tract about forty copies only were printed, and presented by the Secretary to those Members of the Bannatyne Club who dined together on Thursday, 23d February 1848, to celebrate THE TWENTY-FIFTH ANNIVERSARY of the Club, of which Sir Walter was the Founder and President.

Of these Ballads, the one "The Reever's Penance," written by Robert Surtees of Mainsforth, Durham, had been printed for Sir Walter Scott, but never circulated. Sir Walter added, "Quod ane gude Squyer of Northumberland.—R. S. of M."

The other, "Captain Ward and the Rainbow," was sent from Abbotsford to the Secretary, 16th September 1831, by Sir Walter, and is partly written in his own hand, not long before his setting out on his last journey.—*See facsimile of his Note, in Facsimile Signatures*, p. 164.

377. SKETCH OF THE LIFE AND CHARACTER OF THE LATE LORD KINNEDDER.

Edinburgh: Printed by James Ballantyne and Co. 1822. 4to, title and pp. 18.

*** A postscript on the last page says:—

"It is affecting to remark, that this Notice was chiefly drawn up by the late Mr. HAY DONALDSON, Writer to the Signet, the intimate friend of Lord Kinnedder, who followed him to the grave within a few weeks. The short intervals of exertion which his mortal disorder permitted, were occupied in recording the virtues of his deceased friend. It was also a singular coincidence in the death of these two excellent men, that each had succeeded but recently to a situation of which he had been ambitious, as the goal of his professional career, and which neither was permitted long to enjoy."

WILLIAM ERSKINE, Lord Kinnedder, according to this Sketch, was born in 1769. He was the eldest son of the Rev. William Erskine, an Episcopal minister at Muthill, Perthshire. He studied at the University of Glasgow, and was called to the Scottish Bar, July 3, 1790. He became Sheriff-Depute of Orkney and Shetland in June 1809; and was raised to the Bench as Lord Kinnedder, January 29, 1822. This promotion, as stated in the above extract, he did not long enjoy, having died within eight months, on August 14, that year. He was a most amiable man; and it is sad to think his death, at the early age of fifty-three, was hastened by a malicious and unfounded calumny preying upon a very sensitive mind.

With his friend Scott's assistance Erskine was the editor of—

"ENGLISH MINSTRELSY, being a selection of Fugitive Poetry from the best English Authors; with some Original Pieces hitherto unpublished. In two volumes.

—— Such forms as glitter in the Muses' ray
With orient hues. GRAY.

Edinburgh: Printed for John Ballantyne and Co. Manners and Miller, and Brown and Crombie, Edinburgh; and John Murray, London. 1810. 2 Vols. 12mo.

Mr. Hay Donaldson passed as Writer to the Signet in the year 1802. The allusion in the above extract was to his appointment as Law-Agent for the Buccleuch Estates upon the death of Hugh Warrender, Esq. Mr. Donaldson died at Sunnybank, Haddington, September 30, 1822.

There can be little doubt that the "Sketch" was prepared for the press by Sir Walter Scott. Only a few copies were printed for private circulation. Erskine was one of his most confidential friends, and was intrusted to act on behalf of "the Author of Waverley" in the publication of *The Tales of My Landlord, etc.*

378. THE POETRY contained in the Novels, Tales, and Romances of the Author of *Waverley*.

Edinburgh: Printed for Archibald Constable and Co.; and Hurst, Robinson, and Co., London. 1822. 12mo.

379. THE WAVERLEY DRAMAS.

Vol. I.—Containing *George Heriot, Ivanhoe, The Battle of Bothwell Bridge, The Pirate*, and *Peveril of the Peak*.

Vol. II.—Containing *Montrose, Waverley, Redgauntlet, Mary Queen of Scots*, and *The Talisman*.

Two Vols. John Anderson, Jun., Edinburgh; and Simpkin and Marshall, London, 1823, 1828. 12mo.

380. AN ACCOUNT OF THE FIRST EDINBURGH THEATRICAL FUND DINNER, held at Edinburgh, on Friday, 23d February 1827.

Edinburgh: John Anderson, Jun. 1827. 8vo, pp. 24.

---

381. AN APOLOGY FOR TALES OF TERROR.

"A thing of shreds and patches."

Kelso: Printed at the *Mail* Office. 1799. 4to. Pp. 76, with the autograph on the title, "WALTER SCOTT," and opposite, this note:—"This was the first book printed by Ballantyne of Kelso—only twelve copies were thrown off, and none for sale."

Lent from

THE ABBOTSFORD LIBRARY.

The Contents of the *Apology* may be added:—

⁂ Pp. 1-3—*The Erl-King*, from the German of Goethe, eight verses of four lines, beginning—

"O! who rides by night thro' woodlands so wild?
It is the fond father embracing his child," etc.

Pp. 4-9—*The Water-King*: a Danish Ballad, twenty verses of four lines, beginning—

"With gentle murmur flow'd the tide,
While by the fragrant flow'ry side," etc.

Pp. 10-18—*Lord William*, thirty-five verses, four lines, beginning—

> "No eye beheld when William plung'd
> Young Edmund in the stream," etc.

Pp. 19-26—*Poor Mary, the Maid of the Inn*, by Mr. Southey, twenty-one stanzas of five lines, beginning—

> "Who is she, the poor maniac, whose wildly-fix'd eyes
> Seem a heart overcharg'd to express?" etc.

Pp. 27-40—*The Chase*, fifty-one verses of four lines, beginning—

> "Earl Walter winds his bugle horn,
> To horse, to horse, halloo, halloo," etc.

Pp. 41-57—*William and Helen*, sixty-six verses of four lines, beginning—

> "From heavy dreams fair Helen rose
> And ey'd the dawning red," etc.

Pp. 58-63—*Alonzo the Brave and Fair Imogine*, seventeen stanzas of five lines, beginning—

> "A warrior so bold, and a virgin so bright,
> Convers'd as they sat on the green," etc.

Pp. 64-72—*Arthur and Matilda*, thirty-five verses of four lines, beginning—

> "Bright shone the stars, the moon was sunk,
> And gently blew the breeze," etc.

Pp. 73-79—*The Erl-King's Daughter*, thirteen verses of four lines, beginning—

> "O'er hills and through forests Sir Olaf he wends,
> To bid to his wedding relations and friends," etc.

⁂ In this Volume is a copy of "The Rape of the Lock," Canto First. Respectfully offered as a specimen of the Typography of the Kelso Press. Kelso: Printed by James Ballantyne, at the Kelso Mail Printing Office. 1801. Pp. 8. Royal 8vo.

---

382. THE HISTORY OF THE BALLANTYNE PRESS, AND ITS CONNECTION WITH SIR WALTER SCOTT.

Edinburgh: Ballantyne and Co. 1871. 4to.

383. CATALOGUE OF THE LIBRARY AT ABBOTSFORD. [Prepared by John G. Cochrane]. Edinburgh, 1838. 4to.

Copies of this Catalogue were presented by Major SIR WALTER SCOTT, Bart., "to the BANNATYNE CLUB, as a slight return for their liberality and kindness in agreeing to continue to that Library the various valuable works printed under their superintendence." Copies were also provided for the MAITLAND CLUB, as the similar contribution of JOHN G. LOCKHART, Esq., one of the Members.

At Edinburgh the twenty fifth day of April One thousand seven hundred and fifty eight years It is Contracted Agreed and Matrimonially Ended Betwixt the parties following Towit Mr. Walter Scott Writer to the Signet Eldest lawfull Son of Mr Robert Scott in Sandiknow with consent of the said Mr Robert Scott his Father And the said Mr Robert Scott for himself his own right and interest On the one part And Mrs Anne Rutherfurd Eldest Daughter of Doctor John Rutherfurd Professor of Medicine in the Colledge of Edinburgh procreate betwixt him and the deceast Mrs Jean Swinton his first Spouse, Daughter of the deceast Sir John Swinton of that Ilk with advice and consent of the said Doctor John Rutherfurd her father And the said Doctor John Rutherfurd for himself his own right and interest with consent of the said Mrs Anne Rutherfurd his Daughter And they both with one advice consent and assent On the other part in manner following That is to say the said Walter Scott and Mrs Anne Rutherfurd have accepted and by these presents accept each of them others for their lawfull Spouses

. . . .

to be interponed hereto And for that Effect they Con stitute

their procurators In witness whereof these presents consisting of this and the ten preceding pages all wrote upon Stampt paper by Alexander Keith Writer in Edinbu Are Subscribed by both Parties Place day month and Year of God foresaid Before these witnesses the Reverend Mr John Cranstoun minister of the Gospel at Ancrum Mr John Coutts merchant in Edinburgh Mr Thomas Scott Son of the said Mr Robert Scott The said Mr Alex Keith of Ravelston the said Mr John Swinton Son of the deceast Mr Robert Swinton merchant in North Berwick And the said Alexander Keith Writer hereof

Walter Scott

Ann Rutherford

Robert Scott

Jo Rutherfoord

[illegible] Cranstoun witness

John Coutts witness

Thomas Scott witness

Alex. Keith witness

John Swinton witness

Alexr. Keith Witness

IV.—MANUSCRIPT PAPERS AND LETTERS

WRITTEN BY OR HAVING REFERENCE TO SIR WALTER SCOTT.

384. CONTRACT OF MARRIAGE betwixt Mr. Walter Scott, Writer to the Signet, eldest lawfull son of Mr. Robert Scott in Sandieknow, and Mrs. Anne Rutherford, eldest daughter of Doctor John Rutherford, Professor of Medicine in the Colledge of Edinburgh, and the deceast Mrs. Jean Swinton, his first spouse, daughter of the deceast Sir John Swinton of that Ilk, etc.

(*Subscribed*) WALTER SCOTT.
ANN RUTHERFORD.

ROBERT SCOTT.
JO. RUTHERFOORD (*witnesses*).

25th April 1758.

Six leaves, written on stamped paper.

See Facsimile of the Signatures on the annexed leaf.

Lent by
DR. DANIEL RUTHERFORD HALDANE, Edinburgh.

385. CONTRACT between James Brown, Architect in Edinburgh, and Walter Scott, Writer to the Signet, to feu and build a Dwelling-house, with Cellars, Coach-house, etc., on the West Row of the great square called George Square [No. 25], at the annual feu of £5, 14s., the first payment to commence at Whitsunday 1773.

Six pages, each signed WALTER SCOTT.

Lent by
MR. D. LAING. Also No. 386.

386. LETTER OF DR. JOHN RUTHERFOORD (*ob.* 1776), without any address or date, evidently relating to his grandchild's illness. It begins,—

"D. SIR,—Mr. Scot has been with me just now, and given me an account of his Son's illness, and what you had done for them very properly. But as the Disease seems to be increasing, I think you should immediately apply a Blister across the forepart of his neck, etc. . . . Meantime keep the room quiet tho' not too closs or warm. I am, in haste, D. Sir, yours most sincerely,

"JO. RUTHERFOORD.

"Saturday, past 8 P.M."

387. Letter, Mrs. Alison Cockburne [15th Nov. 1777], addressed to the Rev. Dr. Douglas, Minister of Galashiels. It contains the following description of Sir Walter Scott when a youth of about six years of age, first printed by Mr. Lockhart in his *Life of Scott*:—

"I last night supped in Mr. Walter Scott's. He has the most extraordinary genius of a boy I ever saw. He was reading a poem to his mother when I went in. I made him read on: it was the description of a shipwreck. His passion rose with the storm. He lifted his eyes and hands. 'There's the mast gone!' says he; 'crash it goes!—they will all perish!' After his agitation, he turns to me, 'That is too melancholy,' says he; 'I had better read you something more amusing.'

"Amusing! I preferred a little chat, and asked his opinion of Milton and other books he was reading, which he gave me wonderfully. One of his observations was, 'How strange it is that Adam, just new come into the world, should know everything—that must be the poet's fancy,' says he. But when he was told he was created perfect by God, he instantly yielded. When taken to bed last night, he told his aunt he liked that lady. 'What lady?' says she. 'Why, Mrs. Cockburn; for I think she is a virtuoso like myself.' 'Dear Walter,' says Aunt Jenny, 'what is a virtuoso?' 'Don't you know? Why, it's one who wishes and will know everything.'—Now, sir, you will think this a very silly story. Pray, what age do you suppose this boy to be? Name it now, before I tell you. 'Why, twelve or fourteen.' No such thing; he is not quite six years old. He has a lame leg, for which he was a year at Bath, and has acquired the perfect English accent, which he has not lost since he came, and he reads like a Garrick. You will allow this an uncommon exotic.

"Edinburgh, Saturday night, 15th of 'the gloomy month'
when the people of England hang and drown themselves."

⁂ Mrs. Cockburne wrote the beautiful verses to the tune of "the Flowers of the Forest," *I've seen the smiling of fortune beguiling.* See the notices of her life, in *Illustrations to Johnson's Scots Musical Museum.*

Lent by
Miss Douglas.

388. Facsimile of a School Exercise, "On the Setting Sun," addressed by Walter Scott to Dr. Adam, in July 1783, in the *History of the High School of Edinburgh*, by William Steven, D.D. Edin. 1849. 12mo.

The lines are also given by Mr. Lockhart.

389. The Petition of Walter Scott, son of Mr. Walter Scott, Writer to the Signet, unto the Right Honourable the Lords of Council and Session, to be taken upon Trials for passing as Advocate, 13th May, 1791. With the attestation of his several Examinators, from June 1791 to July 1792. *See Facsimile Signatures*, p. 162.
Mr. Hope Scott.

390. A DEED, written on Parchment, by the Tutors of Mary, Countess of Buccleuch, with the Signatures of Sir John Scott of Scotstarvet, dated at Edinburgh, 15th August 1656, and the other Tutors of the chief Families of Scott. The Countess died in 1661, aged 13.

Lent by

Mr. LAING. Also Nos. 391, 392, 397. and 399.

391. BOND signed by John Scott of Sintoun, William Scott of Raeburne, and John Scott of Ronaldburn, at Edinburgh, 4th and 7th December 1686.

392. A SET OF PLAYING CARDS, with the Arms of the Scottish Nobility. Engraved at Edinburgh by Walter Scott, Goldsmith.

Under "The Town of Edinburgh Armes" is this engraved title, "Phylarcharum Scotorum Gentilicia Insignia Illustria a Gualtero Scot, Aurifice, Chartis lusorijs Expressa. Sculpsit Edinburgi, Anno Dom. CIↃ.IↃC.XCI." (1691.) (A few defects in this copy were supplied in facsimile from the one in the Library at Abbotsford.)

*** *Note by Sir Walter Scott in the copy of Phylarcharum Insignia—in the Abbotsford Library.*

"Walter Scott, Goldsmith in Edinburgh, was admitted a Member of the Incorporation 25th July 1656, having been previously married to the daughter of Alex. Reid, Elder, late Deacon of the Craft. Another Walter Scott is stated as having been admitted, 6th June 1701. It is not mentioned if he was a relation of the first, but there is a striking resemblance between their signatures. One of these Walters, probably the engraver of the Insignia, must have been dead 28th August 1706, on which day a daughter of umquhile Walter Scott was appointed to the Trades' Maiden Hospital. Walter Scott was elected Deacon of the Incorporation for the two years 1706-7 and 1707-8."

393. A TRUE HISTORY OF SEVERAL HONOURABLE FAMILIES OF THE RIGHT HONOURABLE NAME OF SCOTT, in the Shires of Roxburgh and Selkirk, and others adjacent. Gathered out of Ancient Chronicles, Histories, and Traditions of our Fathers. By

Capt. WALTER SCOT,
An old Souldier, and no Scholler,
And one that can Write nane,
But just the Letters of his Name.

Edinburgh: Printed by the heir of Andrew Anderson, Printer to his most Sacred Majesty, City and Colledge. 1688. 4to.

Presented "To Walter Scott, Esqre., from his obliged and faithful servant, Archd. Constable. It is the only copy of the first Edition I have ever seen.—A. C.

"PARK PLACE, *26th March* 1818."

*** This Work is by no means common, but not so rare as this note would imply. It was reprinted at Edinburgh, 1776, 4to, and at Hawick, 1786, 8vo; but the interest of the present Copy consists in having on the leaf opposite the title the following lines, written by Sir Walter Scott, in imitation of his namesake's style of composition (*see Facsimile Signatures*, page 163):—

"I, WALTER SCOTT of Abbotsford, a poor scholar, no soldier, but a soldier's lover.
In the stile of my namesake and kinsman, do hereby discover
That I have written the twenty-four letters twenty-four million times over;
And to every true-born SCOTT I do wish as many golden pieces
As ever were hairs in Jason's and Mædea's golden fleeces."

Lent from
THE ABBOTSFORD LIBRARY.

394. PEDIGREE OF THE SCOTT FAMILY. Drawn up and written by Sir Walter Scott, in his own hand, on a large sheet of vellum.

Lent by
LORD POLWARTH.

395. THE SPECULATIVE SOCIETY. Volume of Scroll Minutes of the Speculative Society from 14th November 1786 to 1st April 1795. The portion of the Minutes from 26th November 1791 are holograph of Sir Walter Scott. Folio.

Lent by
THE SPECULATIVE SOCIETY. Also No. 396.

396. CASH-BOOK OF THE SPECULATIVE SOCIETY, commencing 28th November 1786, ending 26th November 1839. 4to.

*** WALTER SCOTT, Advocate, was admitted a Member of the Speculative Society, Edinburgh, December 21, 1790. He acted as Secretary and Treasurer from 1791 to 1795, becoming one of the Honorary Members, January 28, 1794. Richard Fowler, who signs the Diploma, as one of the Vice-Presidents, graduated as Doctor of Medicine at Edinburgh in 1793. He afterwards practised as a Physician in Salisbury.

397. DIPLOMA. A Latin Diploma of the Speculative Society, conferring the degree of an Honorary Member on John Wilde, Advocate, Professor of Civil Law in the University of Edinburgh. Written and signed "GUALTERUS SCOTT, *a Secretis. Apud Edinburgum*, Feb. 1793."

*** JOHN WILDE was called to the Scottish Bar in 1785; joined the Speculative Society in the following year; was appointed Professor of Civil Law in November 1792, and an Honorary Member of the Speculative, according to this Diploma, February 5, 1793. A few years later he became deranged, but survived till 1840.

398. COMMISSION, WALTER SCOTT, Gent., to be Quartermaster in the Royal Edinburgh Volunteers. (Signed) CH. MAITLAND, Captain Commandant. 12th April 1797.

Lent by
MR. HOPE SCOTT.

399. LETTER TO THE LORD ADVOCATE IN FAVOUR OF MAJOR MAITLAND.

(1.) This Letter, in favour of Charles Maitland of Rankeillor, Major Commandant, written "in our official capacity as Officers and Committee of the Royal Edinburgh Light Dragoons," 9th June 1798, is signed

WM. RAE, Captain R.E.V.L.D.
J. GORDON, Lieut.
GEO. ROBINSON, Lieut.
WILLIAM FORBES, Cornet.
COLIN MACKENZIE, Member of Committee.
GEO. STEUART, Member of Committee.
WALTER SCOTT, Secy.

(2.) Copy of the above Letter, also in Sir Walter Scott's handwriting, without the signatures.

(3.) Letter, General SIR RALPH ABERCROMBY to the Lord Advocate, in reply, as follows:—

"*Edinburgh, June 26, 1798.*—MY LORD,—I have the honor to return herewith a letter addressed to your Lordship by the Officers of the Edinburgh Light Dragoons, recommending to your notice their Commandant, Major Maitland, to whose merit your Lordship has, as well as his brother officers, borne ample testimony. It would, on these reasons, give me much satisfaction, if I could point out in what manner Major Maitland could be employed on the North British Staff, but in his present situation it is incompatible with the rules of the service to give him any appointment in that line. I am sorry I cannot give your Lordship a more favourable answer, and have the honor to be, my Lord, your Lordship's most humble and most obedient servant, (Signed) RA. ABERCROMBY."

400. MISCELLANEOUS DOCUMENTS in the Ashestiel Manuscript (No. 284).

Lent by
MR. HOPE SCOTT.

(1.) Certificate of the Marriage of Walter Scott, Esq., in the Parish Church of St. Mary, Carlisle, 23 December 1797.

(2.) Commission signed by George the Third, appointing Mr. Walter Scott, Advocate, to be Sheriff-Depute of the Shire or Sheriffdom of Selkirk, 16 December 1799.

(3.) Commission by Walter Scott, Esq., to Mr. Charles Erskine, as Sheriff-substitute of Selkirkshire, 14 March 1800.

(4.) Commission by the Right Hon. Lord Napier, Lord Lieutenant of the County of Selkirk, to Walter Scott, Esq., appointing him Deputy-Lieutenant of said County, 27th March 1800.

(5.) Burgess Ticket of the Burgh of Selkirk in favour of Walter Scott, Esq., Advocate, Sheriff of Selkirkshire, 26 February 1800.

(6.) Burgess Ticket of the Burgh of Kirkwall to Walter Scott, Esq., Principal Clerk of Session, August 13, 1814.

401. Original Article on the First Series of "Tales of My Landlord," contributed in 1817 to the *Quarterly Review*, in the handwriting of Sir Walter Scott, apparently criticising and praising his own anonymous work. 4to. pp. 69.

Lent by

John Murray, Esq., London.

*** In the Introduction to the Chronicles of the Canongate, First Series, October 1, 1827, after describing an incident, he says:—"This incident, with several other circumstances illustrating the Tales in question, was communicated by me to my late lamented friend, William Erskine (a Scottish Judge by the title of Lord Kinnedder), who afterwards reviewed with far too much partiality the 'Tales of My Landlord,' for the *Quarterly Review* of January 1817. In the same article are contained other illustrations of the Novels, with which I supplied my accomplished friend, who took the trouble to write the review."

See Mr. Lockhart's statement regarding the Authorship of this Article (Life of Sir W. Scott, vol. v. pp. 174, 175). Some passages were no doubt written by Mr. Erskine, but the greater part apparently by Scott himself.

402. The First Volume of Minutes of the Bannatyne Club, founded by Sir Walter Scott in February 1823. The early Minutes are all signed by him as President.

On a separate leaf is the scroll of the original Scheme, with Sir Walter's corrections. Also the Scroll of a Minute written by Sir Walter (in the Secretary's absence) in 1824, regarding the proposed extension of the Club, at first restricted to thirty-one Members.

The Secretary of The Club.

*** *In looking over various letters of* Sir Walter Scott *to select a few autograph signatures for pages* 165, 166, *the Secretary of the Bannatyne Club may be excused in giving the following extract, which has reference to the institution of the Bannatyne Club in February following:—*

"I wish our Scottish Roxburghe Club could be set agoing, though it has lost a steady supporter in Sir Alexander Boswell. It strikes me that we might make it a very entertaining party, and preserve some curious antiquarian information.—I am, in great haste, dear David, very much yours, Walter Scott.

"Abbotsford, 3 *October*."

(II.)—ORIGINAL LETTERS.

Letters of Sir Walter Scott are innumerable. No attempt was made nor any wish expressed by the Committee to obtain such for Exhibition, with the exception of a few having either some personal interest, or (in those already quoted) referring to his various publications, and at the same time to serve as specimens of his autograph signatures at different periods of his life.] *See* Facsimile Signatures, pp. 163-166.

403. LETTER, dated 22d Nov. 1799, from Sir Walter Scott to William Riddell, Esq. of Comieston, soliciting his interest when applying for the Sheriffship of Selkirk.

Lent by
W. RIDDELL CARRE, ESQ.

404. LETTER OF SIR WALTER SCOTT, addressed "DR. LEYDEN, CALCUTTA."

MRS. WILLIAM PRINGLE.

"MY DEAR LEYDEN,—Your letter of the 10th January 1810, reached me about ten days since, and was most truly wellcome, as containing an assurance of that which, however, I never doubted—the continuation of your unabated friendship, and affectionate remembrance. I assure you, Charlotte and I think and speak of you very often, with all the warmth due to the recollection of our early days, when life and hope were young with all of us. You have, I hope, long ere now, received my third poem, 'The Lady of the Lake,' which I think you will like for *auld lang syne*, if not for its intrinsic merit. It have [has] been much more successful than its predecessors, for no less than 25,000 copies have disappeared in eight months, and the demand is so far from being abated, that another edition of 3000 is now at press. I send [sent] you a copy of the 4to by a son of Mr. Pringle of Whitebank; and his third son, William Pringle, being now on the same voyage to your shores, I beg to introduce him. He is one of the younkers mentioned in the Introduction to *Marmion* as a companion of my field Sports. I take the opportunity to send you a little print which I think you will set some value upon. It has just come out in London, and is reckoned very cleverly engraved. Poor old Camp, whom you will readily recognise, died about two years ago of old age, rather prematurely accelerated by good living. His place is supplied in some sort by a very sensible Scotch terrier: but to have a dog whom I can love as much as Camp I must bring back all that were with me, and you, my dear Leyden, among the foremost, in our woodland walks by Eskes romantic shore. . . .

"I have not yet received the Chinese affair, though Helen has forwarded the letter which accompanied it. I have no other connexion with the *Quarterly Review* than as I am, with Ellis, Heber, and most of your old acquaintance, more partial to its politics than to those of your old friend Brougham in the *Edinburgh Review*. But I will recommend the work to the conductor, and if Southey will take it in hand (to whom the Missionaries have been obliged for the countenance they have hitherto received in the *Quarterly*), I have no doubt your friends will be satisfied with the manner in which they are treated. . . .

"You will expect news of European friends; Heber is in excellent health, and amassing books, and discussing magnums as usual. Ellis has quite recovered, that is, he is in the state of health in which you knew him, never a very robust one. James Ballantyne is increasing in fortune and bulk; his brother is now a bookseller here *meo auspice*. You must know that repeated favours on my part had the same effect upon . . . . that those from a higher quarter produced on Jeshurun—he wax'd fat and kicked. But he is aware by this time he had done better to have kept his [temper] to himself, for he may place £5000 minus in his books to the breach of our connexion occasioned by his own folly and his partner's insolence.

"I expect this boy to call every moment, so I must close my letter. Mrs. Scott joins in sending you all the wishes of affectionate friendship. Pray take care of your health, and come home to us soon. We will find an ingleside and a corner of our hearts as warm for you as ever. My children are all well; and now I hear the door-bell, *vale et nos ama*. WALTER SCOTT.

"EDINBURGH, 20*th February* 1811."

*** *This letter could not have reached its destination, Dr. Leyden having sailed from Calcutta with the expedition against Java in March* 1811, *where he died of fever in August following.*

405. VOLUME OF SIXTY-FIVE ORIGINAL LETTERS, chiefly Private, on Matters of Business, etc., addressed to Mr. James Ballantyne, between the years 1808 and 1831.

Lent by

CHRISTOPHER DOUGLAS, ESQ.

*** This Volume of letters was given by Mr. John A. Ballantyne to Alexander Douglas, Esq., Writer to the Signet, one of his father's trustees.

406. VOLUME OF MISCELLANEOUS NOTES AND LETTERS, from Sir Walter Scott, etc., to Mr. John Stevenson, Bookseller, Edinburgh, with Printed Papers and Extracts relating to Scott, in one vol. 4to.

MR. T. G. STEVENSON.

407. AUTOGRAPH NOTES, etc., addressed by Sir Walter Scott to Charles Kirkpatrick Sharpe, Esq., in reference to "A Ballad Book," inscribed by Mr. Sharpe to Sir Walter in 1823. (Of this little volume only Thirty copies were printed.)

REV. W. K. R. BEDFORD.

*** These MS. Notes, etc., have since been given by Mr. Sharpe's nephew, the Rev. Mr. Bedford, to Mr. D. Laing, with a request to have a limited impression of the little volume in an amended form.

408. Letter from Sir Walter Scott to the late William Stewart Watson, approving the Likenesses painted by him in 1825.

Lent by
Mrs. Stewart Watson.

409. Letter or Notes by Sir Walter Scott in connexion with the *Traditions of Edinburgh* by the late Robert Chambers.

James Hay, Esq., Leith.

410. Letter from Sir Walter Scott to Mr. Charles Mackay, describing his Visit to the Theatre-Royal, Edinburgh, to witness the play of "Rob Roy," and his representation of the character of Bailie Nicol Jarvie.

Mr. C. G. Mackay.

411. Letter from Sir Walter Scott to his cousin, Mrs. Meik, on her eldest Son leaving for India.

Also Leaf from an old Family Bible, written by Sir Walter Scott at the request of his cousin, Mrs. Meik, formerly Barbara Scott.

Mr. Thomas Meik, C.E.

412. Letter of Thanks from Sir Walter Scott to the late Peter Maclaurin, Esq.

Mrs. Maclaurin.

413. Letter with the Sketch of a Tankard, from Sir Walter Scott to Charles Kirkpatrick Sharpe, Esq.

Rev. W. K. R. Bedford.

414. Letter from Sir Walter Scott to John Scott, Esq. of Scalloway.

R. T. C. Scott, Esq., J.P.

415. Letter, Sir Walter Scott to George H. Baird, D.D., Principal of the University of Edinburgh, and Convener of the General Assembly's Committee on Psalmody, in 1828.

Isaac Bayley, Esq.

*** The subject of enlarging the Psalmody used in the Church of Scotland had for several years been under the consideration of the General Assembly. Principal Baird, when appointed Convener of the Committee, invited the assistance of several authors of distinction, and amongst others, he applied to Sir Walter Scott, who seems to have mistaken the object in view, as if it had been meant to supersede the present Metrical version of the Psalms. In submitting to the Assembly, June 2, 1828, a Report on this subject, Principal Baird disclaimed any idea of altering this Version; and read the following letter from Sir Walter Scott, which is here printed in full, as it will be read with special interest, at least by Scottish Presbyterians.

Dr. Chalmers, in seconding the approval of the Report, pointed out the great difficulty there was in writing poetry for such a purpose, and thought the Committee should cull from unbidden effusions, instead of calling on poets to write. He entirely coincided in the opinion so well expressed in the letter of SIR WALTER SCOTT, which at once combined high poetical feeling with humble piety. He considered our Metrical version to have a charm peculiar to itself; besides, these Psalms were deeply identified and incorporated with the feelings of the people, who, to use the strong expression of Dr. Baird, though not too strong for the subject, would "consider it sacrilege to make any alteration on them."

"DEAR SIR,—I am honoured with your letter, and I assure you I should feel happy if it were in my power to be of service to the undertaking which you recommend with so much propriety. Not to mention other requisites in which I feel my deficiency, I think my total unacquaintance with the original language of the Scriptures is of itself a complete incapacity. As I derive my acquaintance with the inspired writings solely from the prose translation, I must inevitably be liable to transfer into any poetical version of the Psalms every imperfection and amplification which may exist, and the translation into the poetical version which would thus be the shadow of a shade. Besides, after all, I am not sure whether the old-fashioned version of the Psalms does not suit the purposes of public worship better than smoother versification and greater terseness of expression. The ornaments of poetry are not perhaps required in devotional exercises, nay, I do not know whether, unless used very sparingly and with great taste, they are altogether consistent with them. The expression of the old metrical translation, though homely, is plain, forcible, and intelligible, and very often possesses a rude sort of majesty, which perhaps would be ill exchanged for mere elegance. Their antiquity is also a circumstance striking to the imagination, and possessing a corresponding influence upon the feelings. They are the very words and accents of our early Reformers—sung by them in woe and gratitude, in the fields, in the churches, and on the scaffold. The parting with this very association of ideas is a serious loss to the cause of devotion, and scarce to be incurred without the certainty of corresponding advantages. But if these recollections are valuable to persons of education, they are almost indispensable to the edification of the lower ranks, whose prejudices do not permit them to consider, as the words of the inspired poetry, the versions of living or modern poets, but persist, however absurdly, in identifying the original with the ancient translation.

"I would not have you suppose, my dear Sir, that I by any means disapprove of the late very well chosen Paraphrases. But I have an old-fashioned taste in sacred as well as prophane poetry: I cannot help preferring even Sternhold and Hopkins to Tate and Brady, and our own Metrical version of the Psalms to both. I hope, therefore, they will be touched with a lenient hand; and I have written a long letter that I might satisfy you in what a serious point of view I regard anything connected with our National Worship, as well as of the consideration due to any request of yours. —I am, my dear Sir, your most faithful servant,

WALTER SCOTT.

"The Rev. PRINCIPAL BAIRD, etc."

---

416. THE ORIGINAL SCROLL, containing Instructions, wholly in the hand of SIR WALTER SCOTT, for executing his Trust-Disposition and Settlement, dated Abbotsford, 7th January 1831.

*** This scroll was found, after Sir Walter Scott's decease, in his writing-desk, in the Study at Abbotsford. Six pages entirely holograph with this title:—"INSTRUCTIONS for Mr. Wood to draw Sir Walter Scott's Disposition of his worldly goods and effects." Walter Scott of Lochore, in the county of Fife, Major of the 15th Regiment of the King's Hussars, John Gibson Lockhart, Esq., of Sussex, etc., to be Executors.

On the first page, in Sir Walter's Instructions concerning his funeral, the following words printed in italics are deleted:—"The present assignation, having for object:—1. The payment of my debts and funeral expenses, *commending my body to be laid in my Aisle before the high altar of Dryburgh Abbey. The funeral to be conducted in the plainest, without consistent with*"——

Mr. Bayley says, "Before finishing the sentence, Sir Walter may have recollected that in Scotland Testamentary deeds are never opened until after the funerals."

On the sixth page, signed in reference to his children, he adds, "which have gone so far to make me a happy father, W. S.

"ABBOTSFORD, *7th January* 1831."

Inside of the envelope, dated Abbotsford, 12th Feb. 1831, explanatory of these Notes, and on the outside, "To my Children—Rough Notes of Testamentary Dispositions."—"The formal testament, extended and executed, is deposited in the iron chest of Robert Cadell, Esq., Bookseller, in January 1831."—Mr. John G. Wood, Writer to the Signet, above mentioned, who executed the deed, was related to Mr. Cadell.

417. A FUNERAL LETTER, signed by Major Sir Walter Scott, to attend the Funeral of Sir Walter Scott, his father, from Abbotsford to Dryburgh Abbey, on September 26, 1832, as follows:—

SIR,

The Honor of your Company on Wednesday, the 26 Inst., at One o'clock afternoon, to attend the funeral of Sir Walter Scott my father, from this house to the Burial Ground in Dryburgh Abbey, will oblige,

Your mo. ob. Servt.,

WALTER SCOTT.

ABBOTSFORD, 22 *Sept.* 1832.

Lent by

MISS DUNLOP.—The Letter Exhibited addressed to Mr. Mercer of Coatgreen.

418. SIR J. E. ALEXANDER'S SKETCH OF THE FUNERAL PROCESSION AT DRYBURGH, September 26, 1832.

Lent by

COL. SIR JAMES E. ALEXANDER.

In Tait's *Edinburgh Magazine*, November 1832, p. 196, there is an article, "FUNERAL OF SIR WALTER SCOTT. By an Eye-witness." It is anonymous, but the writer was SIR THOMAS DICK LAUDER, Bart., as appears from a letter addressed by him to Abraham Cooper, Esq., R.A., dated Nov. 30, 1835, in a volume of letters and engravings, chiefly in reference to Illustrations from Sir Walter Scott's Works, among the Egerton MSS. in the British Museum. The internal evidence fully confirms this. As the account is very minute and picturesque, some passages may be extracted as a suitable illustration of Sir James E. Alexander's interesting sketch of the Procession, of which a reduced facsimile is given on the opposite page.

The writer, after describing his journey from Edinburgh and his meditations suggested by the sad occasion, says:—

"But our dreams were at length abruptly broken, by the appearance of some of our acquaintances who issued from the house; and the sight of their weeds of woe immediately recalled our thoughts to the garb of grief which we also wore, and to the sad object of our present visit.

"Passing through the Gothic hall, we met with no one till we entered the library, where we found a considerable circle of gentlemen already assembled. These were chiefly from the neighbouring districts; but there were a few whom we recognised as having come from Edinburgh and other places equally distant. . . . But footsteps came slowly and heavily treading through the small armoury. They were those of the servants of the deceased, who, with full eyes, and yet fuller hearts, came reverently bearing the body of him whose courteous welcome had made that very porch so cheerful to us. We were the only witnesses of this usually unheeded part of the funeral duties. Accident had given to us a privilege which was lost to the crowd within. We instinctively uncovered our heads, and stood subdued by an indescribable feeling of awe as the corpse was carried outwards; and we felt grateful, that it had thus fallen to our lot to behold the departure of these the honoured and precious remains of Sir Walter Scott, from the house of Abbotsford, where all

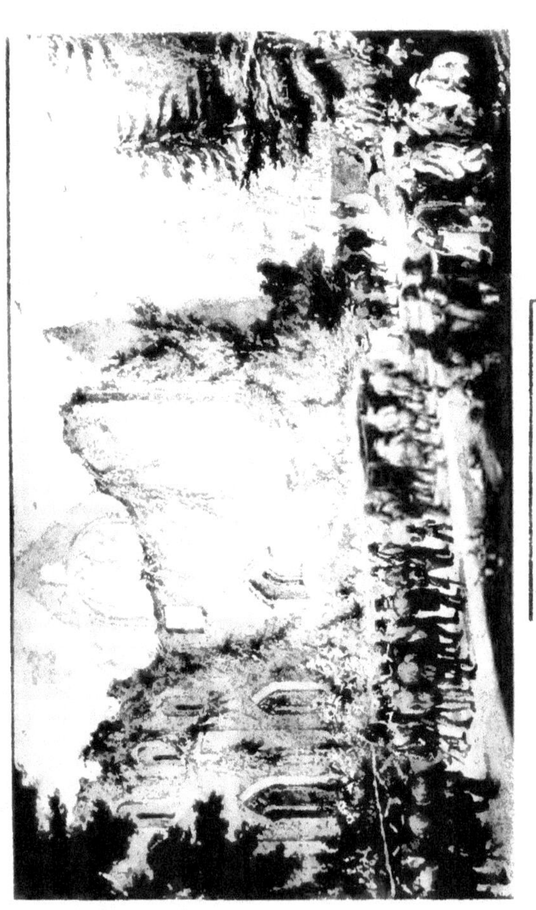

his earthly affections had been centred; and which had so long been to him the source of so much innocent and laudable enjoyment, that it may be matter of speculation, whether the simple pleasures which he reaped in the construction of this house and place, were not greater than any he derived from the almost unparalleled celebrity of his name as an author. The coffin was plain and unpretending, covered with black cloth, and having an ordinary plate on it, with this inscription,

SIR WALTER SCOTT OF ABBOTSFORD, BART., AGED 62.

. . . .

"Having followed the coffin until we saw it deposited in the hearse, which stood on the outside of the great gate of the court-yard, we felt ourselves unequal to returning into the apartment where the company were assembled; and we continued to loiter about, seeking for points of recollection which might strengthen the chain of association we wished to indulge in. Our attention was attracted, by observing the window of the study open, and we were led to look within, impelled by no idle or blameable curiosity, but rather like a pilgrim approaching the shrine where his warmest adoration has ever been paid. Our eyes penetrated the apartment with a chastened look, such as we should have used if the great magician himself had been seated in the chair of this his sacred penetralium. The different articles in the room seemed to remain much in the same places they occupied when we had last seen them. All the little circumstances attendant on our last visit to this sanctuary of the poet came crowding upon us. Thither Sir Walter had conducted us himself; there he had acted the part of our cicerone with all his native wit and playfulness. His figure was in our eyes; and his voice, nay, his very words were in our ears. But, alas! the deep tones of the venerable old Principal Baird, whose voice was heard in earnest and impressive prayer, came upon us through an opposite door, from the library beyond; and the affecting allusions which he uttered, again brought us back to the afflicting truth, that Sir Walter Scott was gone from us for ever!

. . . .

"The effect of the procession when crossing the Fly Bridge over the Tweed, and still more when winding around that high and long sweep of the road which is immediately opposite to the promontory of Old Melrose, was extremely striking and picturesque: and the view looking back from the high ground towards the Eildon hills and Melrose, over the varied vale of Tweed, till the eye was arrested by the distant mountains, then seen under a rich Claude effect; and the devious course of the river, betrayed by fragments of water that sparkled here and there amid the yellow stubbles and green pastures, was exquisitely beautiful. But nothing gave so much interest to this glorious scene as the far-off woods of Abbotsford, then dimmed by the warm haze, and melting, as it were, from their reality, and so reminding us even yet more forcibly of the fleeting nature of all the things of this perishable world."

After mentioning the names of the Pall-bearers and the approach to the old picturesque ruins of Dryburgh Abbey, until reaching the place of interment, the narrative proceeds:—

"In such a scene as this, then, it was, that the coffin of SIR WALTER SCOTT was set down on trestles placed outside the iron railing; and here that solemn service, beginning with those words so cheering to the souls of Christians, '*I am the resurrection and the life*,' was solemnly read by Mr. Williams. The manly soldierlike features of the chief mourner (Major Sir W. Scott), on whom the eyes of sympathy were most naturally turned, betrayed at intervals the powerful efforts which he made to master his emotions, as well as the inefficiency of his exertions to do so. The other relatives who surrounded the bier were deeply moved; and, amid the crowd of weeping friends, no eye, and no heart, could be discovered that was not altogether occupied in that sad and impressive ceremonial which was so soon to shut from them for ever, him who had been so long the common idol of their admiration, and of their best affections. . . . It was not until the harsh sound of the hammers of the workmen who were employed to rivet those iron bars covering the grave to secure it from violation, had begun to echo from the vaulted roof, that some of us were called to the full conviction of the fact, that the earth had for ever closed over that form which we were wont to love and reverence; that eye which we had so often seen beaming with benevolence, sparkling with wit, or lighted up with a poet's frenzy; those lips which we had so often seen monopolizing the attention of all listeners, or heard rolling out, with nervous accentuation, those powerful verses with which his head was continually teeming; and that brow, the perpetual throne of generous expression and liberal intelligence. Overwhelmed by the conviction of this afflicting truth, men moved away without parting salutation, singly, slowly, and silently. The day began to stoop down into twilight; and we, too, after giving a last parting survey to the spot where now repose the remains of our Scottish Shakespeare, a spot lovely enough to induce his sainted spirit to haunt and sanctify its shades, hastily tore ourselves away."

1785 _ No 388

Walter Scott

1791 _ No 389

remit to the Dean & Faculty of Advocates to take Trial of your Petitioner's Skill in Law, in the ordinary way, and to report

Walter Scott

Edinburgh 13th May 1791

The Lords having heard this Petition they remit to the Dean and Faculty of Advocates to take Trial of the Petitioners Skill in Law in the ordinary way, and to Report

Hay Campbell
J. P. D.

Edinburgh 14 June 1791

The Dean of Faculty remits the Petitioner to the private Examinators on the Civil Law to assign him a day for his Trial thereon he having promised on his honor to give no treat or entertainment on account thereof and producing to the Examinators proper Certificates of his being twenty years of age

Henry Erskine D. F.

Gualterus Scott advocatus

[illegible]
[illegible]
A.D. 1793

My dear Sir

Will you pardon the vanity of an author in hoping a copy of a new edition of his work may not be unacceptable to you as a man of letters & an ancient borderer. It contains some lines on p. 138 relative to the Homes of Wedderburn & the Cranstons (my own Maternal ancestors) & with a few others I have written added since the Quarto edition. I am ever with great regard

Dear Sir
yours obliged & faithful
servant

W Scott

Castle Street
Tuesday —

Mrs Scott
from her affectionate son
The Author

Edinburgh 20th July 1809

Received the contents of the annexed precept for five hundred pounds

Walter Scott

15 Decem

15 Dec 1814

£600 . 0 . 0 Stg   Edinburgh 12 Sept. 1814

Three months after date pay to my order Six hundred pounds Sterling value received

Walter Scott

Messrs John Ballantyne & Co Booksellers Edinr

Accepted John Ballantyne & Co

(In dorso)

Walter Scott

James Ballantyne & Co.

Duncan & Cleghorn

I Walter Scott of Abbotsford, a poor scholar, no soldier but a soldier's lover

In the style of my namesake and kinsman do hereby discern

That I have written the twenty-four letters twenty-four million times over

And to every true-born Scot I do wish as many golden pennies

As ever were heard in James and Mathew's golden pieces

[illegible]

[illegible] our Scottish Roxburghe club [illegible] though it has lost a strong supporter in Sir Alexander Boswell [illegible]

Dear David

Very much yours

Walter Scott

Abbotsford

13 October

[illegible]

No more at present but [illegible]

[illegible] Yours truly

2 Sept. Walter Scott Abbotsford

[illegible]

Dear Sir

I found among my papers the enclosed ballad prepared for your Chronicle of sundry unconsidered trifles. It was never used & I have since taken notice of it though it occurs in Hall's copies and was popular when I was a boy. It is I think well written & on an interesting subject. You will judge for yourself as to using it. Farewell for a long while and best wishes

Yours very truly

Walter Scott

Abbotsford

16 Sept. 1831

(ILLUSTRATIONS.—No. XXXII.)

MASK OF SIR WALTER SCOTT, TAKEN AFTER DEATH, SEPTEMBER 1832.

IN the Life of Sir Walter Scott is this paragraph :—" It was considered due to Sir Walter's physicians, and to the public, that the nature of his malady should be distinctly ascertained. The result was, that there appeared the traces of a very slight mollification in one part of the substance of the brain."[1] In this examination the upper part of the cranium was removed, which shows that the Mask had been taken subsequently, —no doubt under the directions and inspection of the medical gentlemen referred to.

Although rather painful, or at least by no means an agreeable object for observation, there was perhaps nothing in the whole Exhibition of greater interest than the original Mask, which Mr. HOPE SCOTT permitted, for that purpose, to be brought to Edinburgh. It is reduced in size, and is here represented in two positions. Some years later, from this Mask, a Cast in bronze, by Mr. John Steell, R.S.A., was executed for Mr. Hope Scott, and is exhibited to visitors at Abbotsford.

At Abbotsford there is another Mask of Sir Walter Scott, taken during life. Mr. Hope Scott kindly offered the choice of the two for Exhibition. As the one had no history or description attached to it,[2] there

[1] Lockhart's *Life of Scott*, 1838, vol. vii. p. 394 ; 1839, vol. x. p. 219. In a footnote a copy of the Report is given, signed by Dr. Clarkson, September 23, 1832. This Report, as mentioned in a previous page of the Illustrations (No. IV.), p. 51, led Mr. George Combe, in his great zeal for the cause of Phrenology, to address a letter to the Editor of the *Phrenological Journal*, August 16, 1838 (vol. xii. pp. 44-49), in which he complains of the paucity and vagueness of the Report regarding the *post-mortem* examination of the brain. But this discussion " On the Phrenological Development of Sir Walter's Head," principally founded upon Macdonald's bust, is quite unsuited for this place.

[2] Mr. Combe, in his letter quoted under No. IV. of the Illustrations, p. 51, evidently refers to the second Mask when he says,—" I have seen a cast purporting to be one of Sir Walter Scott's head, and which is said to have been taken in Paris ; but it is widely at variance with Mr. Macdonald's bust, and also with my recollection of Sir Walter's head, which I have seen at least a thousand times, and closely observed."—*Phrenological Journal*, vol. xii. p. 48.

could be no hesitation in selecting the Mask taken after death, from its very remarkable character and undoubted authenticity. It is therefore to be kept in mind that this Mask exhibits the proportions and actual appearance of the head, subsequent to the state of mental depression and suffering, in his declining days.

In connexion with this Mask, the following extract may not be considered as out of place. Sir Henry Holland, Bart., M.D., in his *Recollections of Past Life*, Lond. 1872, describes his intercourse with Sir Walter Scott at various periods. Of his latter days he says—

"I saw him frequently on his way to Italy at the house of his son-in-law, Lockhart—already an altered man in effect of the first slight paralytic seizure, and painfully showing this alteration in the effort to recover the stories and events partially lost to his memory.

"Such struggle of the mind with its own decay is a sad spectacle in every case—in Walter Scott it was especially so. It was not possible either to aid him or to arrest the effort. I saw him again in London on the day of his return from the Continent, and each day of his stay here—in a state of hopeless paralysis and very imperfect consciousness. His wishes, as far as they could be understood, all pointed to Abbotsford."—(*Recollections of Past Life*, by Sir Henry Holland, p. 84. Lond. 1872. Post 8vo.)

The Eildon Hills.

Fourth Division.

HISTORICAL AND PICTORIAL ILLUSTRATIONS OF SCOTT'S WORKS.

I.—PORTRAITS OF HISTORICAL PERSONAGES.

II.—PAINTINGS AND WATER-COLOUR DRAWINGS CHIEFLY BY SCOTTISH ARTISTS, ILLUSTRATING HISTORICAL EVENTS, OR THE WAVERLEY NOVELS.

III.—LANDSCAPE ILLUSTRATIONS TO SCOTT'S POEMS AND NOVELS.

IV.—DRAWINGS AND ENGRAVINGS ILLUSTRATIVE OF SCOTT'S WORKS.

V.—ODDS AND ENDS; INCLUDING SOME PERSONAL RELICS.

I. PORTRAITS OF HISTORICAL PERSONAGES.

419. KING JAMES THE FOURTH, KING OF SCOTLAND. On Canvas.
3 ft. 1¼ x 2 ft.

Lent by — *Artist.*

SIR WILLIAM STIRLING MAXWELL, BART. — DANIEL MYTENS.

Born 1472. Slain at Flodden in September 1513.

This Portrait, representing the King with a hawk on his hand, is engraved in Pinkerton's *Iconographia Scotica*, 1797. It appears to have belonged to King Charles I., from the description given in the Catalogue of the King's pictures, as "done after an ancient water-coloured piece, by DANIEL MYTENS," who flourished in the reign of James I. of England. It afterwards (about 1799) was purchased by the Earl of Buchan, and when his Lordship's collection was sold by auction at Edinburgh, a few years ago, it was secured by the present proprietor.

420. ELIZABETH QUEEN OF ENGLAND. Crowned. In a rich ornamental dress. On Panel. 11¾ in. x 9½ in.

DAVID LAING, ESQ. — MARK GERARD (?)

Born 1533. Died 1603.

Of this Portrait, or a repetition, there is an old engraving in a French "History of the Netherlands," probably one of the editions of Meteren, about 1606, marked "Crispiaen vandenqueboeren Sculp. H. I. cobsen exc."

421. MARY QUEEN OF SCOTS. On Panel. 12½ in. x 10¼ in.

JAMES T. GIBSON CRAIG, ESQ. — UNKNOWN.

Born 1542. Beheaded 1587.

422. KING JAMES THE SIXTH. On Panel. 1 ft. 4¼ in. x 1 ft. 1⅛ in.

JAMES T. GIBSON CRAIG, ESQ. — UNKNOWN.

Born 1566. Crowned King of Scotland 1567. Succeeded to the Crown of England 1603. Died 1625.

423. ANNE OF DENMARK, Wife of James VI. On Panel. The companion Portrait. 1 ft. 4½ in. x 1 ft. 1⅛ in.

JAMES T. GIBSON CRAIG, ESQ. — UNKNOWN.

Born 1574. Married 1589. Died 1618-9.

424. CHARLES PRINCE OF WALES, afterwards King Charles the First.
9 in. x 7⅛ in.

JAMES T. GIBSON CRAIG, ESQ. — HONTHORST.

Born 1600. Crowned 1625. Beheaded 1649.

425. JAMES FREDERICK EDWARD STUART, Chevalier de St. George.
Lent by 2 ft. 11¼ in. x 2 ft. 3¾ in.
SIR WILLIAM STIRLING MAXWELL, BART. *Artist.*
Born 1688. Died 1766. UNKNOWN.

426. JAMES FREDERICK EDWARD STUART, Chevalier de St. George.
2 ft. 1 in. x 1 ft. 7 in.
THE EARL OF BREADALBANE. UNKNOWN.

427. PRINCE CHARLES EDWARD STUART. 2 ft. 1 in. x 1 ft. 7 in.
THE EARL OF BREADALBANE. DOMINICO DUPRA.
Born 1720. Died 1778.

428. PRINCE CHARLES EDWARD STUART. 2 ft. 4 in. x 1 ft. 11 in.
SIR WILLIAM STIRLING MAXWELL, BART. DOMINICO DUPRA.

429. PRINCE CHARLES EDWARD STUART. Miniature, to which is attached "The Highlander Ribbon." This pattern of Ribbon is said to have been made for the Prince at Lyons.
JAMES DRUMMOND, ESQ., R.S.A. UNKNOWN.

430. HENRY BENEDICT STUART, Cardinal York. 2 ft. 2½ in. x 1 ft. 9½ in.
SIR WILLIAM STIRLING MAXWELL, BART. DOMINICO DUPRA.
Born 1725. Died 1807.

431. HENRY BENEDICT STUART, Cardinal York. 2 ft. 2 in. x 1 ft. 8 in.
JAMES DRUMMOND, ESQ., R.S.A. UNKNOWN.

432. GEORGE HERIOT, Goldsmith.
THE GOVERNORS OF GEORGE HERIOT'S HOSPITAL.
Born 1563. Died 1624.
This Picture, attributed to Scougal, was engraved in 1743 by Jo. and Chas. Esplens. (See No. 444.)

433. JAMES GRAHAM, Marquis of Montrose. 3 ft. 5 in. x 2 ft. 5 in.
THE EARL OF DALHOUSIE. HONTHORST.
Born 1612. Died 1650.
Engraved by James Faed for the *Memoirs of the Marquis of Montrose*, by Mark Napier, Esq.

434. JAMES GRAHAM, Marquis of Montrose. 2 ft. 4 in. x 2 ft.
LADY COLQUHOUN. GEORGE JAMESONE.
Engraved by Robert C. Bell for Mr. Napier's work.

435. JOHN GRAHAM of Claverhouse, Viscount Dundee.
2 ft. 4¾ in. x 2 ft. 0½ in.
LADY ELIZABETH-JANE LESLIE-MELVILLE CARTWRIGHT. UNKNOWN.
Born 1643. Died 1689.
Engraved by T. G. Flowers for *The Life and Times of John Graham of Claverhouse*, by Mark Napier.

436. JOHN GRAHAM of Claverhouse. 4 ft. × 3 ft. 3 in.

Lent by — *Artist.*

EARL OF STRATHMORE. — SIR GODFREY KNELLER.

Engraved for Lodge's *Portraits of Illustrious Personages of Great Britain*; Napier's *Life of Claverhouse*, and for other works.

HISTORICAL AND OTHER ENGRAVED PORTRAITS.

437. ELIZABETA, D. G. Angliæ, Franciæ, Hiberniæ, et Verginiæ Regina. Fidei Unicum Propugnaculum.

In honorem Serenissimæ Suæ Majestatis hanc effigiem fieri curabat Joannes Woutnelius belgæ. Anno 1595.

SIR W. STIRLING MAXWELL, BART.

*** This beautiful print represents the Queen standing full-length, the globe in one hand, a sceptre in the other. A pillar at each side of the picture, and a table at her right hand, on which is an open book. There are also two verses of poetry.

438. MARY QUEEN OF SCOTS.

DAVID LAING, ESQ. Also Nos. 439 to 444, and 446.

*** The Portrait is in an oval, surrounded by emblematic figures, and a representation of the beheading of the Queen, with another scene in which the executioner is holding up her head. Above is a crowned shield, impaled with the arms of France and Scotland. This rare print, which has no engraver's name nor date, is attributed by Prince A. Labanoff to Jerome Wierix, who died in 1608. The date was probably 1588. Underneath are twenty lines of Latin verse, beginning "*En tibi magnanimæ spirantia Principis ora*," signed "G. C. Scotus." These lines are given in Labanoff's Catalogue, p. 192, but he omits to state that the author was George Crichton, a native of Edinburgh, who became Regius Professor of Greek in the University of Paris. He was author of numerous Latin tracts, from 1583 to 1610; and died at Paris 1611, aged 56.

439. SERENISSIMA MARIA REGINA IACOB. MAG. BRIT. REG. MATER.—The most excellent Princesse MARY QUEENE OF SCOTLAND AND DOWAGER OF FRANCE, Mother to oure Soueraigne lord James of greate Britaine, France, and Ireland King.

R. ELSTRACK, *sculpsit.* Are to be sold by Compton Holland ouer against the Exchange.

440. JACOBUS VI. Scotiæ Rex, et Primus eo Nomine Angliæ, Franciæ, et Hiberniæ maximo applausu electus Rex, etc.

Ampliss. etc. D. Philippo d'Ayala, etc. P. de Judeis, Antwerp. D.D.

The picture is a head size; on the right side is a crowned shield of the Arms of Great Britain and France: and opposite "A°. 1603. Aetatis suæ 37."

441. ANNA FRIDERICI III. Danorum Regis F. Jacobi VI. Scotorum Anglorumq. Primi Electi Regis Uxor, Lectissima Heroina.

No Engraver's name. A companion print to the former, by a different engraver.

442. JAMES, KING OF GREAT BRITAIN, etc.

A full-length Portrait with Crown, Sceptre, etc., seated, prefixed to "A Collection of His Maiesties Workes." London, 1616, folio.

SIMON PASSEUS, *sculp.* Lond. JOH. BILL, *excudit.*

"Crounes haue their compasse, length of dayes their date,
Triumphes their tombes, felicitie her fate:
Of more then earth, can earth make none partaker,
But knowledge makes the KING most like his Maker."

443. JACOBUS D. G. Angliæ, Scotiæ, Franciæ et Hiberniæ. Rex Fidei. Defensor, Primus Magnæ Britanniæ Monarcha.

C. JOHNSON, *pinx.* R. WHITE, *Sculp.*, 1696.

On a scroll at top of print—*Beati Pacifici.*

444. GEORGE HERIOT, Jeweller to King James VI., who, besides founding and endowing his stately Hospital at Edinburgh, bequeathed to his relations above £60,000 sterling. Obiit 1623, Aetatis anno LXIII. *Under this title (which contains a statement that would require some confirmation), is the inscription:—*

To the Right Honourable John Couts, Esq., Lord Provost of Edinburgh, the Town Council, etc., Governors and Treasurer of Heriot's Hospital, this plate is humbly dedicated by your Honours most humble Servants,

SCOUGAL, *pinx.* JO. AND CHA^{S}. ESPLENS, 1743.

445. JAMES EDWARD STUART, Chevalier de St. George.

Engraved by MM. Horthemels. In an oval frame. This is one of those beautiful Jacobite portraits, without a name, which were engraved on the Continent, and is curious as illustrating one of the many ways employed to elude the vigilance of the Custom-house officers, while smuggling them into this country. He wears the Collar and Insignia of the Order of the Garter, but over the George there was neatly gummed an oval shield of the same size, on which is engraved the arms of Prince George of Denmark. This could easily be damped off when it fell into Jacobite hands; fortunately it had never been removed in this impression, and is now so attached that it can be raised to show the Order below.

Lent by

JAMES DRUMMOND, ESQ., R.S.A.

446. PRINCE CHARLES EDWARD STUART.

An engraving cut as an oval, and inserted within a most elaborately designed border, cut in paper, gilt and coloured, having at the under part, "Thomas Hunter *fecit*, Edinburgh, 1720. Aged 79." which is also cut out with scissors.

II.—PAINTINGS AND WATER-COLOUR DRAWINGS, CHIEFLY BY SCOTTISH ARTISTS, ILLUSTRATING HISTORICAL EVENTS, OR THE WAVERLEY NOVELS.

447. RETURN OF JEANIE DEANS. — 12½ in. × 9 in.
Lent by — *Artist.*
PROFESSOR MACLAGAN. — SIR WILLIAM ALLAN, *P.R.S.A.*, R.A.

448. THE BLACK DWARF. — 1 ft. 5⅜ in. × 1 ft. 1 in.
THE TRUSTEES OF THE NATIONAL GALLERY OF SCOTLAND. — SIR WILLIAM ALLAN, *P.R.S.A.*, R.A.

449. HEROISM AND HUMANITY. — 6 ft. 6 in. × 4 ft. 2½ in.
J. A. BUTTI, ESQ. — SIR WILLIAM ALLAN, *P.R.S.A.*, R.A.

Engraved by John Burnet for the Royal Association for Promotion of the Fine Arts in Scotland. 1842.

SIR WILLIAM ALLAN, *P.R.S.A.*, R.A., was born at Edinburgh in 1782. He died in 1850. See Illustrations, No. XXIX., page 101.

450. BRUCE AND THE SPIDER. — 6 ft. 1 in. × 4 ft. 1 in.
R. B. WARDLAW RAMSAY, ESQ. — WILLIAM BONNAR, R.S.A.

451. ROSE BRADWARDINE VISITING HER FATHER IN THE CAVE WITH FOOD. — 2 ft. 9 in. × 2 ft. 1 in.
JOHN INGLIS, ESQ. — WILLIAM BONNAR, R.S.A.

452. JEANIE DEANS IN THE ROBBERS' BARN. — 2 ft. 10 in. × 2 ft. 4 in.
JAMES BALLANTINE, ESQ. — WILLIAM BONNAR, R.S.A.

453. HARRIET, DUCHESS OF BUCCLEUCH, etc.
THOMAS BONNAR, ESQ. — WILLIAM BONNAR, R.S.A.

*** By some oversight this Painting was inserted among Portraits as No. 96. It was in the Exhibition of the Royal Scottish Academy, 1839, No. 157. The painting is thus more correctly described in the Catalogue :—

"ELIZABETH, late Duchess of Buccleuch, and Harriet, late Countess of Dalkeith, the unwearied benefactresses of the afflicted and the poor, visiting the cottage of a widow. The ladies are designed and painted from original portraits in the possession of his Grace the Duke of Buccleuch, by his Grace's special permission."

An engraving from the picture was published by Mr. Alexander Hill, 50 Princes Street, to whom it then belonged.

The Duchess Elizabeth, daughter of George Duke of Montagu, survived till November 1827. Her daughter-in-law, Harriet-Katherine, died August 24, 1814.

454. THE FIERY CROSS. — 6 ft. 5½ in. × 3 ft. 7 in.
THE MAYOR OF MANCHESTER. — J. LAMONT BRODIE.

455. THE LADY OF THE LAKE. 5 ft. 11 in. × 3 ft. 9 in.

Lent by *Artist.*

W. F. SALE, ESQ. J. LAMONT BRODIE.

456. BALFOUR OF BURLEY IN THE CAVE. 6½ in. × 5 in.

MRS. MARGARET SANSON. WILLIAM CARSE.

WILLIAM CARSE, a son of Alexander Carse, the painter, died in early life about 1846.

457. THE LADY OF AVENEL LEAVING GLENDEARG. 7½ in. × 6¼ in.

J. D. GILLESPIE, M.D. ALEXANDER CHISHOLM.

Engraved by T. S. Engleheart, as vignette title-page for first volume of *The Monastery*. 1830.

ALEXANDER CHISHOLM, born at Elgin in 1792. In 1818, went to London. Died at Rothesay in 1847.

458. AN ANTIQUARY. 1 ft. 3½ in. × 7½ in.

JAMES T. GIBSON CRAIG, ESQ. WILLIAM F. DOUGLAS, R.S.A.

459. THE ANTIQUARY. 2 ft. 10 in. × 2 ft. 2 in.

THOMAS BONNAR, ESQ. WILLIAM F. DOUGLAS, R.S.A.

460. MORTON AWAITING HIS DEATH AT THE HANDS OF THE CAMERONIANS IN THE FARMHOUSE OF DRUMSHINNEL. 3 ft. 5⅞ in. × 2 ft. 8 in.

GEORGE ARMSTRONG, ESQ. WILLIAM F. DOUGLAS, R.S.A.

Engraved by R. C. Bell as one of the Illustrations of *Old Mortality*, for the Royal Association for Promotion of the Fine Arts in Scotland.

461. THE DAY AFTER PRESTONPANS. 1 ft. 8 in. × 1 ft. 4 in.

JAMES CLARK, ESQ. JAMES DRUMMOND, R.S.A.

462. MAURICE DRUMMOND, ABBOT OF INCHAFFRAY, BLESSING THE SCOTTISH ARMY BEFORE THE BATTLE OF BANNOCKBURN.

4 ft. 1½ in. × 2 ft. 9 in.

JAMES BALLANTINE, ESQ. JAMES DRUMMOND, R.S.A.

463. MONTROSE LED PRISONER THROUGH EDINBURGH, 1650.

6 ft. 1 in. × 3 ft. 8½ in.

THE ARTIST. JAMES DRUMMOND, R.S.A.

464. THE PORTEOUS MOB, 1737. 5 ft. × 3 ft. 7 in.

JAMES DRUMMOND, R.S.A.

THE TRUSTEES OF THE NATIONAL GALLERY OF SCOTLAND AND ROYAL ASSOCIATION FOR PROMOTION OF THE FINE ARTS IN SCOTLAND.

Engraved in Mezzotinto by Edward Burton for the Royal Association for Promotion of the Fine Arts in Scotland. 1862. 25 in. × 20¼ in.

465. JEANIE DEANS AND THE ROBBERS. 2 ft. 3 in. × 1 ft. 8 in.

Lent by *Artist.*

THE TRUSTEES OF THE NATIONAL GALLERY OF SCOTLAND. THOMAS DUNCAN, R.S.A., A.R.A.

466. FATHER CLEMENT AND CATHARINE GLOVER, the "Fair Maid of Perth." 2 ft. 4½ in. × 1 ft. 9½ in.

A. DENNISTOUN, ESQ. THOMAS DUNCAN, R.S.A., A.R.A.

Engraved by J. Horsburgh for Volume second of *The Fair Maid of Perth.* 1832.

467. CUDDIE HEADRIGG. 2 ft. 4¼ in. × 1 ft. 11 in.

JOHN WHITE, ESQ. THOMAS DUNCAN, R.S.A., A.R.A.

468. PRINCE CHARLES COMING DOWN THE CANONGATE. 6 ft. 7 in. × 4 ft.

THE TRUSTEES OF THE LATE ALEX. HILL, ESQ. THOMAS DUNCAN, R.S.A., A.R.A.

Engraved in Line by Frederick Bacon, and published by Alexander Hill. 1845. 30¼ in. × 19 in.

469. PRINCE CHARLES AND FLORA MACDONALD IN THE CAVE. 6 ft. 6 in. × 4 ft. 7½ in.

THE TRUSTEES OF THE LATE ALEX. HILL, ESQ. THOMAS DUNCAN, R.S.A., A.R.A.

Engraved by H. T. Ryall in Mezzotinto, and published by Alexander Hill. 1846. 30¼ in. × 20½ in. Mr. Duncan also did an etching from this picture.

Nos. 468 and 469 are now the property of Robert Jardine of Castlemilk, Esq., M.P.

470. QUEEN MARY AT LOCHLEVEN. 6 ft. 4½ in. × 4 ft. 2 in.

DR. J. D. GILLESPIE. THOMAS DUNCAN, R.S.A., A.R.A.

THOMAS DUNCAN, R.S.A., A.R.A., was born at Kinclaven, Perthshire, in 1807. Studied his art in Edinburgh, where he settled; and succeeded Sir William Allan as Head Master of the School of Design. Was elected Associate of the Royal Academy in 1843, and died in 1845. He painted portraits, historical and fancy subjects.

471. TRUDCHEN (*Quentin Durward*). 3 ft. × 2 ft. 3½ in.

MRS. CUMINE PEAT. WILLIAM DYCE, R.A., *H.*R.S.A.

WILLIAM DYCE, *H.*R.S.A., R.A., was born in 1806 at Aberdeen, studied in Rome, and settled in Edinburgh in 1829, where in 1837 he was appointed Master of the School of Design. Removed to London in 1839, on being appointed Superintendent of the Government School of Design. Painted frescoes for the House of Lords. Was elected R.A. in 1848, and died in 1864. Mr. Dyce was also an admirable etcher and an accomplished musician.

472. ROLAND GRAEME'S INTRODUCTION TO THE KNIGHT OF AVENEL. 3 ft. 1½ in. × 3 ft. 3½ in.

MRS. P. A. FRASER. PATRICK ALLAN FRASER, *H.*R.S.A.

473. Scene from "The Talisman." 1 ft. 8½ in. × 1 ft. 3½ in.

Lent by — *Artist.*

H. G. Watson, Esq. — Sir John Watson Gordon, *P.*R.S.A., R.A.

Engraved by S. Sangster, as vignette title-page for *The Talisman*, 1832.

474. Scene from "The Talisman." 4 ft. 2 in. × 3 ft. 3½ in.

H. G. Watson, Esq. — Sir John Watson Gordon, *P.*R.S.A., R.A.

Engraved by Charles Rollo for *The Talisman*, 1832.

475. The Curlers. 5 ft. 9 in. × 1 ft. 11 in.

"There was the finest fun amang the curlers ever was seen."
Guy Mannering, chap. xxxii.

Gilbert Stirling, Esq. — Sir George Harvey, *P.*R.S.A.

Engraved by William Howison, in Line, and published for George Harvey by Alexander Hill, Edinburgh. 29 in. × 11 in.

476. Covenanters Preaching. 3 ft. 6¼ in. × 2 ft. 8½ in.

The Glasgow Corporation. — Sir George Harvey, *P.*R.S.A.

Engraved in Mezzotinto by John Bromley. Published in 1834 for George Harvey by Hodgson, Boys, and Graves. 2 ft. × 1 ft. 6 in.

477. The Battle of Drumclog. 5 ft. 2 in. × 3 ft. 3⅝ in.

James Muspratt, Esq. — Sir George Harvey, *P.*R.S.A.

Engraved in Mezzotinto by C. E. Wagstaff. Published by Hodgson and Graves, London. 2 ft. 5 in. × 1 ft. 6½ in.

478. Richie Moniplies. 4 ft. 1½ × 2 ft. 5½ in.

John Williamson, Esq. — George Hay, A.R.S.A.

479. Rose Bradwardine. 1 ft. 1½ × 10¼ in.

A. B. Shand, Esq. — Robert Herdman, R.S.A.

480. Queen Mary. "The last scene of all." 3 ft. 1½ × 2 ft. 7 in.

James Blaikey, Esq. — Robert Herdman, R.S.A.

481. Louis XI. and Oliver Dain (*Quentin Durward*). 2 ft. 3 in. × 1 ft. 10 in.

Patrick Allan Fraser, Esq. — W. B. Johnstone, R.S.A.

William B. Johnstone, R.S.A., born at Edinburgh in 1804. Was elected A.R.S.A. in 1840; in 1848, R.S.A.; and in 1850, Treasurer to the Academy. In 1858 he was appointed principal Curator and Keeper of the National Gallery of Scotland. He died in 1868.

482. DAVIE GELLATLY'S MODE OF DELIVERING A LETTER.
2 ft. 5 in. x 1 ft. 9 in.

Lent by — *Artist.*

G. B. SIMPSON, ESQ. — WM. B. KIDD, *H.*R.S.A.

483. PETER PEEBLES IN THE PARLIAMENT SQUARE. 9½ in. x 7½ in.
J. D. GILLESPIE, ESQ., M.D. — WM. B. KIDD, *H.*R.S.A.

Engraved by J. Horsburgh for title-page of *Redgauntlet.* Vol. II. 1832.

484. THE DOOR OF THE OLD EDINBURGH GUARD-HOUSE.
1 ft. 11¼ in. x 1 ft. 7 in.
DAVID BRYCE, ESQ., R.S.A. — WM. B. KIDD, *H.*R.S.A.

485. THE STUDY AT ABBOTSFORD. 2 ft. x 1 ft. 6 in.
W. P. ADAM, ESQ., M.P. — SIR EDWIN LANDSEER, R.A., *H.*R.S.A.

Engraved by C. Westwood.

486. BAILIE MACWHEEBLE AT BREAKFAST (*Waverley*). 2 ft. 2½ in. x 1 ft. 7½ in.
JAMES T. GIBSON CRAIG, ESQ. — JAMES E. LAUDER, R.S.A.

Engraved by R. C. Bell, for the Association for the Promotion of the Fine Arts in Scotland.

JAMES ECKFORD LAUDER, R.S.A., was born at Edinburgh in 1812. Studied at the Trustees' Academy. Was elected A.R.S.A. in 1839, and R.S.A. in 1846. He died in 1869.

487. THE GLEE MAIDEN. 3 ft. x 2 ft. 4 in.
PATRICK ALLAN FRASER, ESQ. — R. SCOTT LAUDER, R.S.A.

488. RAVENSWOOD AND LUCY ASHTON. 2 ft. 1 in. x 1 ft. 8 in.
FRANCIS FARQUHARSON, ESQ. — R. SCOTT LAUDER, R.S.A.

489. THE BRIDE OF LAMMERMOOR. 4 ft. 1½ x 3 ft. 2½ in.
MRS. MELVILLE. — R. SCOTT LAUDER, R.S.A.

ROBERT SCOTT LAUDER, R.S.A., born at Silver Mills, Edinburgh, in 1803. Was a pupil at the Trustees' Academy. In 1833 he went to Italy, where he studied for five years. Retiring in 1838, he settled in London. He returned to Edinburgh in 1850 on his appointment as principal teacher in the Trustees' Academy. He died in 1869.

490. SCENE.—THE MEETING OF MARK AND THE REFORMER WITH CHRISTIE OF THE CLINTHILL AND EDWARD GLENDINNING (*The Monastery*). 2 ft. 4 in. x 1 ft. 11 in.
MRS. FINLAYSON. — MACARTNEY.

491. JEANIE DEANS BEGGING THE LIFE OF HER SISTER FROM QUEEN CAROLINE. 3 ft. 11½ in. × 3 ft. 5⅞ in.

Lent by — *Artist.*

ALEXANDER DENNISTOUN, ESQ. — J. G. MIDDLETON.

492. JEANIE DEANS ON HER WAY TO LONDON. 2 ft. 3½ in. × 1 ft. 6 in.

ROBERT MERCER, ESQ. — W. Q. ORCHARDSON, A.R.A., *H.*R.S.A.

493. GLENDINNING AND THE MONK. 2 ft. 4½ in. × 1 ft. 10¾ in.

ROBERT MERCER, ESQ. — JOHN PETTIE, A.R.A., *H.*R.S.A.

494. BAILIE NICOL JARVIE IN THE CLACHAN OF ABERFOYLE. 2 ft. 8½ in. × 2 ft. 2½ in.

ROBERT ROBERTSON, ESQ. — ALEXANDER RITCHIE.

ALEXANDER ABERNETHY RITCHIE was born at Edinburgh in 1816, and died there in 1850. He also etched with much cleverness.

495. WALLACE, THE DEFENDER OF SCOTLAND. An Allegory.

ROBERT CARFRAE, ESQ. — DAVID SCOTT, R.S.A.

In three compartments. The centre represents Wallace in single combat with Edward I. as representing England (3 ft. × 2 ft. 6 in.), on one side the Scottish mode of battle, on the other the English (each 2 ft. 2 in. × 1 ft. 8 in.)

DAVID SCOTT, R.S.A., was a native of Edinburgh, where he was born in 1806. His father wished him to be an engraver, but he soon left it for painting. He became a member of the Royal Scottish Academy in 1830. His greatest work was a picture on a very large scale, of Vasco de Gama passing the Cape, a work of rare power and grandeur. But what he is best known by are his designs from Coleridge's *Ancient Mariner*, full of imagination and individuality of character. They were etched by himself in outline. He died in 1849.

496. PRINCE CHARLES AT HOLYROOD. Original Sketch. 9 in. × 7 in.

ROBERT MERCER, ESQ. — WILLIAM SIMSON, R.S.A.

497. PRINCE CHARLES READING GENERAL COPE'S LETTER, WHILE AT HOLYROOD. 1 ft. 8 in. × 1 ft. 3½ in.

F. A. HILL, ESQ. — WILLIAM SIMSON, R.S.A.

Engraved in line by J. Horsburgh.

WILLIAM SIMSON, R.S.A., was a native of Dundee, where he was born in 1800. He received his Art education at the Trustees' School, Edinburgh. At first he painted landscape and sea pieces. On his return from Italy in 1838, he settled in London, devoting himself mostly to figure pictures. He died in London in 1847.

498. WHITTAKER READING THE LIST OF GUESTS FOR THE RESTORATION FEAST, (*Peveril of the Peak*). 2 ft. 2½ in. × 1 ft. 10.

A. B. SPENCE, ESQ. — J. OSWALD STEWART.

III.—LANDSCAPE ILLUSTRATIONS TO SCOTT'S POEMS AND NOVELS.

499. RUINS OF THE ANCIENT CASTLE OF THE PEVERILS, NEAR WHITTINGTON.
2 ft. 5½ in. × 2 ft.

Lent by — *Artist.*

DANIEL BRUCE, ESQ. — GEORGE BARRET.

500. HOY HEAD, ORKNEY. 4 ft. 1½ in. × 2 ft. 7½ in.
G. B. SIMPSON, ESQ. — JOHN CAIRNS.

501. STROMNESS BAY, ORKNEY. 3 ft. 8 in. × 2 ft. 3½ in.
G. B. SIMPSON, ESQ. — JOHN CAIRNS.

502. EDINBURGH: View of the City, about the year 1765.
7 ft. 5 in. × 3 ft. 5 in.
R. B. WARDLAW RAMSAY, ESQ. — W. DE LA COUR.

503. SHIPWRECK NEAR THE FITFUL HEAD. 1 ft. 3½ in. × 10½ in.
JAMES T. GIBSON CRAIG, ESQ. — THOMAS FENWICK.

504. BEN VENUE FROM THE SILVER STRAND. 3 ft. 4½ in. × 2 ft. 4 in.
G. B. SIMPSON, ESQ. — ALEXANDER FRASER, R.S.A.

505. BOTHWELL CASTLE, ON THE CLYDE. 3 ft. 7 in. × 2 ft. 10 in.
G. B. SIMPSON, ESQ. — ALEXANDER FRASER, R.S.A.

506. INTERIOR OF ROSLIN CHAPEL. 1 ft. 5¾ in. × 1 ft. 0¾ in.
DAVID LAING, ESQ. — PATRICK GIBSON, R.S.A.

PATRICK GIBSON, R.S.A., Landscape Painter, a native of Edinburgh, was an Exhibitor in 1808, and an active friend of the Scottish Academy. As a landscape painter, he was too fond of composition subjects. During the latter period of his life, he resided at Dollar, Clackmannanshire, holding the office of Teacher of Drawing in the Dollar Institution. Mr. GIBSON died at Dollar, in 1829, in the forty-sixth year of his age.

507. INTERIOR OF ROSLIN CHAPEL. 2 ft. × 1 ft. 8 in.
JAMES BALLANTINE, ESQ. — H. HANSEN.

508. LOCH KATRINE. 6 ft. × 3 ft. 8 in.
SIR ANDREW ORR. — HORATIO MACCULLOCH, R.S.A.

HORATIO MACCULLOCH, R.S.A., was born at Glasgow in 1805. He was for a short time in Edinburgh in 1825, but finally settled there, where he died in 1867. He was elected A.R.S.A. in 1834, and R.S.A. in 1838.

509. LINLITHGOW PALACE. 2 ft. 10½ in. × 2 ft. 2½ in.

Lent by *Artist.*

THOMAS S. AITCHISON, ESQ. ALEXANDER NASMYTH.

ALEXANDER NASMYTH was born at Edinburgh in 1758. The earliest part of his professional education was received in his native city, he then studied in London under Allan Ramsay. He also travelled for some years in Italy, and returning practised as a landscape and occasionally as a portrait painter, his best known picture of the latter class being that of Robert Burns, well known from the engraving by W. Walker. This Picture is now in the Scottish National Gallery, having been bequeathed to it by the Poet's son, Colonel Robert Burns, H.E.I.C.S. He died in 1840.

510. THE HEART OF MIDLOTHIAN. 1 ft. 3 in. × 10⅝ in.

WILLIAM D. CLARK, ESQ. PATRICK NASMYTH.

PATRICK NASMYTH, son of the preceding, was born at Edinburgh 1786 or 1787. Went to London when about twenty years of age, and there gained great eminence as a landscape painter. He died at Lambeth in 1831.

511. HEAD OF LOCHLOMOND. 1 ft. 11½ in. × 1 ft. 3½ in.

MRS. MARGARET SANSON. MISS JANE NASMYTH.

512. VIEW OF EDINBURGH FROM THE NORTH, about the year 1760.

4 ft. 1½ in. × 1 ft. 11 in.

DAVID LAING, ESQ. ROBERT NORIE.

ROBERT NORIE was one of a family of house painters of reputation in Edinburgh, who ornamented the walls and ceilings of houses in Edinburgh and elsewhere with landscapes and fancy subjects. Alexander Runciman, the historical painter, was his apprentice. Norie died in 1766.

513. BOTHWELL CASTLE. 3 ft. 7¼ in. × 2 ft. 2 in.

JAMES T. GIBSON CRAIG, ESQ. ALEXANDER RUNCIMAN.

ALEXANDER RUNCIMAN was born at Edinburgh in 1736, and died in 1785. Studied in Italy, and thereafter settled in Edinburgh, where he was appointed master of the Trustees' Drawing School. He painted Penicuik House with subjects from Ossian, and the Cowgate Chapel with Scripture pieces. He also executed a series of etchings from his own designs.

514. CULLODEN MOOR. 4 ft. 1½ in. × 3 ft. 3½ in.

JOHN WHITE, ESQ. WM. SIMSON, R.S.A.

515. FAST CASTLE. 3 ft. 5 in. × 2 ft. 5½ in.

M. N. MACDONALD HUME, ESQ. REV. JOHN THOMSON.

516. FAST CASTLE. Another picture of the same dimensions, but treated differently. 3 ft. 5 in. × 2 ft. 5½ in.

Lent by — *Artist.*

M. N. MACDONALD HUME, ESQ. — REV. JOHN THOMSON.

The REV. JOHN THOMSON, *H.*R.S.A., was born in the Manse of Dailly, Ayrshire, in 1778. In addition to being a landscape painter of a very high order, he was a most accomplished scholar and an excellent musician. He became parish minister of Duddingstone in 1805; where he died October 28, 1840.

517. LOCAL SCENERY OF, AND SCENE IN, "THE ANTIQUARY." 2 ft. 10½ in. × 1 ft. 8½ in.

DAVID CORSAR, ESQ. — W. F. VALLANCE.

518. STUDY AT ABBOTSFORD. Sketch in Water-Colour.

DAVID SIMPSON, ESQ. — SIR WILLIAM ALLAN, *P.*R.S.A.

519. HEAD OF COLLEGE WYND—Situation of the House where Sir Walter Scott was Born. Also,

SIR WALTER SCOTT'S FIRST SCHOOL, POTTERROW.

THE ARTIST. — MRS. STEWART SMITH.

520. SOUTH GRAY'S CLOSE, EDINBURGH, in which stands Dr. Rutherford's House. Sketch by JAMES DRUMMOND, R.S.A. Also

HIGH SCHOOL WYND, EDINBURGH. And

DUNBAR'S CLOSE. Cromwell's Headquarters while in Edinburgh—Looking towards the New Town, with the Scott Monument.

THE ARTIST.

ADDITIONAL PORTRAITS.

521. ROB ROY. Copy of Original Picture.

KENNETH MACLEAY, ESQ. — ANDREW HENDERSON.

522. JOHN GRAHAM of Claverhouse. Copy by James Ramage, in sepia, from Kneller's Portrait.

WILLIAM MACDONALD, ESQ. Also No. 523.

523. JOHN DUKE OF ARGYLE. Copy by James Ramage, in sepia, from Kneller's Portrait.

Born 1678. Died 1743.

524. MINIATURE OF MRS. COCKBURNE (ALISON RUTHERFORD), Authoress of *The Flowers of the Forest*. Born 1710-12, died 1794.

Lent by — *Artist.*

A. D. COCKBURN, ESQ. — MISS ANNE FORBES.

525. MINIATURE OF ANNE DUFF, COUNTESS OF DUMFRIES.

JAMES T. GIBSON CRAIG, ESQ. — MISS ANNE FORBES.

526. LADY FORBES OF PITSLIGO.

*** As this Lady is called MISS STUART by Mr. Lockhart and others, it has been supposed the note at page 20, No. 101, is erroneous. We may therefore briefly state that her marriage is thus recorded :—

"1797, *January* 17.—At Edinburgh, William Forbes, Esq., eldest son of Sir William Forbes, Bart., of Pitsligo, to Miss Belsches, daughter of Sir John Wishart Belsches, Bart., of Fettercairn." John Belsches, Advocate (of the family of Invermay), married the Lady Jane Leslie, eldest daughter of David Earl of Leven and Melville. Soon after this he succeeded to a baronetcy, and was styled Sir John Wishart Belsches of Fettercairn; but subsequent to the marriage of his daughter he had dropped the surnames of Wishart and Belsches, and assumed the name of Stuart only, in terms of the deed of settlement of his great-grandfather in 1708. Her father, Sir John Stuart, who (as John Belsches) passed Advocate in 1774, was appointed one of the Barons of Exchequer in Scotland in 1807. His only child, Williamina, Lady Forbes, died in Devonshire, December 5, 1810, leaving four sons and two daughters; her husband had succeeded to the baronetcy on the death of his father, Sir William Forbes, in 1806.—(See Playfair's *Baronetage of Scotland*, 1811, page cix.)

The Hon. Sir John Stuart of Fettercairn, Baronet, one of the Barons of Exchequer, died at Greenhill, Edinburgh, December 4, 1821.

527. JOCK GRAY, the Original of Davie Gellatly.

THE ARTIST. — W. SMELLIE WATSON, R.S.A.

528. DAVID RITCHIE, the Original of the Black Dwarf.

DAVID B. ANDERSON, ESQ.

529. SIX JACOBITE MINIATURES AND ONE BRONZE MEDAL.

ROBERT HAY, ESQ.

---

530. MR. CHARLES MACKAY as "Bailie Nicol Jarvie."

SIR WILLIAM ALLAN, *P.R.S.A.*, R.A., *pinxt.* — J. HORSBURGH, *Sculp.*

531. GEORGE M. KEMP, Architect of the Scott Monument.

Engraved by Francis Croll from the Bust by Alex. Handyside Ritchie, A.R.S.A.

IV.—DRAWINGS, ETC., ILLUSTRATIVE OF SCOTT'S WORKS.

532. OLD MORTALITY.

Engraved as a woodcut frontispiece to the Waverley and other editions. 12mo.

Lent by — *Artist.*

MR. D. LAING. — SIR WILLIAM ALLAN, *P.*R.S.A.

533. SCENE FROM "WAVERLEY."

JOHN FAED, R.S.A.

Engraved by Lumb Stocks.

MESSRS. A. & C. BLACK. Also Nos. 534 to 538 inclusive. These drawings were engraved for the Library edition of the Waverley Novels.

534. SCENE FROM "WAVERLEY."

JOHN FAED, R.S.A.

Engraved by Charles Rolls.

535. SCENE FROM "GUY MANNERING."

JOHN FAED, R.S.A.

Engraved by Lumb Stocks.

536. SCENE FROM "THE ABBOT."

THOMAS FAED, R.A., *H.*R.S.A.

Engraved by Francis Croll.

537. SCENE FROM "THE HEART OF MIDLOTHIAN."

THOMAS FAED, R.A., *H.*R.S.A.

Engraved by E. Goodall.

538. SCENE FROM "ROB ROY."

R. R. M'IAN, A.R.S.A.

Engraved by G. Stephenson.

539. FIVE DRAWINGS, ILLUSTRATIVE OF "WAVERLEY."

HEATH.

MR. W. M'DONALD, also Nos. 540 and 541.

540. EIGHT DRAWINGS, ILLUSTRATIONS FOR "TALES OF A GRANDFATHER."

LIZARS and CORBOULD.

541. Jenny Geddes.

Artist.

W. H. Lizars.

542. Queen Mary at the Place of Execution.

Lent by

Mr. T. Bonnar. Also No. 543. — David Scott, R.S.A.

543. James the First appointing Sheriffs.

David Scott, R.S.A.

544. Dryburgh Abbey.

Mr. W. M'Donald. — William Banks.

545. The Bass.

Mr. W. Paterson. — Sam. Bough, A.R.S.A.

546. John Knox's House.

Mr. D. Laing. — James Drummond, R.S.A.

547. The Shaft of the Old Cross of Edinburgh, as it stood in the Grounds of Drum.

The Artist. Also Nos. 548, 549, and 550. — James Drummond, R.S.A.

548. Cardinal Beaton's Palace, Edinburgh. Demolished in 1870.

James Drummond, R.S.A.

549. Queen Mary's Room, Craigmillar Castle.

James Drummond, R.S.A.

550. Smailholm Tower. Sketch.

James Drummond, R.S.A.

551. Steinie, the Son of Mucklebackit.

Mr. W. M'Donald. Also Nos. 553 to 562. — John Ewbank, S.A.

552. Sepia Drawing of Tantallon Castle.

John Ewbank, S.A.

553. Five Views of Edinburgh.

554. Thirteen Drawings of Edinburgh.

John Ewbank, S.A.

555. Nine Drawings of Melrose, Abbotsford, etc.

John Ewbank, S.A.

556. Views of Edinburgh.

John Ewbank, S.A.

557. Pencil Drawing of Castle Campbell. *Artist.*
Robert Gibb, R.S.A.

558. Dunkeld.
Robert Gibb, R.S.A.

559. Nine Drawings in Bistre.
Robert Gibb, R.S.A.

Robert Gibb, R.S.A., born in Dundee. Landscape Painter. Died in 1837.

560. West Bow. Walter Geikie, R.S.A.

Walter Geikie, R.S.A., born at Edinburgh in 1795. Elected A.R.S.A. in 1831, and R.S.A. in 1834. He was deaf and dumb. His very clever and spirited "*Etchings Illustrative of Scottish Character and Scenery*, executed after his own Designs; with Biographical Introduction by Sir Thomas Dick Lauder, Bart.," were published in a 4to volume at Edinburgh, 1841. He died in 1837.

561. Frame—Four Drawings of Melrose, Two Drawings of Kelso.
W. H. Lizars.

562. Five Drawings of Border Abbeys.
W. H. Lizars.

William Home Lizars, born at Edinburgh in 1778; he died in 1859. He intended to follow Art as a profession, and showed great talents; but, from family circumstances, he was obliged to undertake the management of the Engraving business of his late Father.

563. Cuchullin Mountains, Isle of Skye.
The Artist. Also No. 564. Kenneth MacLeay, R.S.A.

564. Goatfell and the Mountains of Arran, from Brodick Bay.
Kenneth MacLeay, R.S.A.

565. View of Roslin, in Water-colour.
Mrs. Sanson. H. W. Williams.

566. Melrose Abbey.
Mr. W. M'Donald. H. W. Williams.

Hugh William Williams was a native of Wales, and settled in Edinburgh towards the end of the last century. He spent some years in Greece and Italy, and published in 1820 his Travels in those countries. But he is best known by the series of Engravings from his beautiful drawings of "Views in Greece," 1827-1829, 2 vols. 4to. As works of art, his water-colour drawings take a very high place. He died at Edinburgh in 1829.

567. View of Abbotsford, in Water-colour.
Mrs. Sanson. J. F. Williams, R.S.A.

J. F. Williams, a native of Perthshire, was for many years employed as a scene painter. As a member of the Royal Scottish Academy he held the office of Treasurer for several years. He died in 1846.

(2.)—ENGRAVINGS OF VIEWS, ETC., ILLUSTRATIVE OF HISTORICAL EVENTS.

568. THE BATTLE OF CULLODEN.

This is a print of great rarity, and was published within less than a month after the battle. Above the Engraving is inscribed:—"A Representation of the Battle on Drumossie Moor, near Culloden, about 2 miles E^t of Inverness, on April 16, 1746, where 2509 of the Rebels was kill'd in Battle, 1500 in the pursuit, and 1800 taken Prisoners—in all, 5809."

Under the Print is, first, the "Order of March" of King George's Army, with a Plan, and the name of each detachment. In the centre, another Plan, "The Order of Battle;" to the left of this is the name of each General and his division, headed "The King's Army—The Duke." To the right the Prince's Army, giving the names of Generals of Divisions, and the name and number of each clan: this is called "The Rebel Army—The Young Pretender," etc.

Printed for John Bowles, at the Black Horse in Cornhill. Published, according to Act of Parliament, May 14, 1746. Size of Print, 19½ in. × 14 in.

Lent by

JAMES DRUMMOND, R.S.A. Also No. 569.

569. THE BATTLE OF CULLODEN. April 16, 1746.

There is a long inscription under the print, giving an account of the battle.

A. HECKEL, *Delin.* Published, according to Act of Parliament, May 1, 1747. L. S., *Sculp*—Printed for and Sold by Thomas Bowles, in St. Paul's Churchyard; and John Bowles, at the Black Horse in Cornhill.

570. EDINBURGH: Views drawn by JAMES GORDON, A.M., Minister of Rothiemay (1641-1686), and engraved in Holland, about 1647.

DAVID LAING, Esq. Also Nos. 571 to 575.

1. THE ROYAL PALACE OF HOLY ROOD HOUSE. J. G., *delin.* F. W. (as a monogram), *fecit.*

   ⁎ This and the next View are alike, representing the old Palace before its destruction by fire in 1650, somewhat larger in size.

2. PALATIUM REGIUM EDINENSE, QUOD ET CŒNOBIUM S. CRUCIS. The Royal Palace of Holy-rood-hous. By J. G.

3. CASTRUM EDINENSE QUOD ET OLIM AR PUELLARUM. The Castell of Edinborrowgh from the west Porte. By J. G.

4. CURIA SUPREMI CONVENTUS ORDINUM REGNI SCOTIAE, VULGO DOMUS PARLIAMENTJ. The Parliament House in Edinborrowgh. By J. G.

5. HERIOTI ORPHANOTROPHIUM. Heriot's Hospital. By J. G.

   ⁎ The last four Views are sometimes met with on a double sheet of paper, in a large work, published by Frederick de Wit, at Amsterdam, without date, but apparently between the years 1690 and 1700.

571. Six Views of Edinburgh, Leith from the East Road, Castles of Dumbarton, Edinburgh, and Stirling, etc.

Engraved or Etched from his own Drawings by Paul Sandby, 1751-1753.

572. The Ceremony of Laying the Foundation-Stone of the New College of Edinburgh, November 16, 1789. D. Allan, *del. et incid. Edinb.*

Also, another Impression of the same interesting Etching, in which the masons shed where the principal figures are standing is removed, and in its place a small view of the proposed building, suspended on a pole, is given. The Artist, David Allan (*b.* 1744, *d.* 1796), is too well known to require any notice.

573. Select Views in Edinburgh, accompanied with Historical and Explanatory Notices. Etched by Patrick Gibson, Edinburgh, 1818.

⁎ This work, containing six plates, royal 4to, was not continued. Mr. Gibson's etchings are in a bold masterly style, not unworthy of Canaletto or Piranesi. See Note to No. 506.

574. Heriot's Hospital, Edinburgh. Founded by George Heriot, King's Goldsmith, in 1623.

Inventory of Original Documents in the Archives of Heriot's Hospital.

Edinburgh: Printed for the Governors, 1857. 8vo. Portrait, engraved title, etc., 4 leaves and pp. 52.

⁎ This Inventory was prepared and printed, after the mass of Original Documents and Letters, which was preserved in this noble Institution, had been carefully arranged and handsomely bound.

Among the Original Letters are many interesting autographs of George Heriot, including signatures of King James the Sixth and First, his wife Queen Anne of Denmark, Dr. Balcanqual, Archbishop Laud, and others. Two Volumes of these Original Documents were exhibited.

575. Original Letters and Documents of the above Series described in the Inventory. Two of the above Volumes exhibited by permission of the Governors of Heriot's Hospital.

576. History of George Heriot's Hospital, with a Memoir of the Founder, etc., by William Steven, D.D. New edition, revised and enlarged by Fred. W. Bedford, D.C.L., Edinburgh, 1859. 12mo.

(3)—ENGRAVED ILLUSTRATIONS TO SCOTT'S WORKS ISSUED BY THE ROYAL ASSOCIATION FOR THE PROMOTION OF THE FINE ARTS IN SCOTLAND.

The Set Lent for Exhibition.

577. WAVERLEY. In a Series of Eight Designs. 1865.

	Designer.	*Engraver.*
1. TULLY-VEOLAN.	W. L. LEITCH.	W. MILLER.
2. WAVERLEY AND ROSE BRADWARDINE AT THEIR STUDIES.	R. HERDMAN, R.S.A.	F. HOLL.
3. THE HOLD OF A HIGHLAND ROBBER.	J. B. MACDONALD, A.R.S.A.	R. C. BELL.
4. SCENE AT CAIRNVRECKAN.	P. GRAHAM, A.R.S.A.	J. STEPHENSON.
5. FERGUS MACIVOR INTRODUCES WAVERLEY TO THE PRINCE.	J. B. MACDONALD, A.R.S.A.	LUMB STOCKS.
6. BAILIE MACWHEEBLE AT BREAKFAST.	J. E. LAUDER, R.S.A.	R. C. BELL.
7. BARON BRADWARDINE IN HIDING.	P. GRAHAM, A.R.S.A.	W. FORREST.
8. WAVERLEY'S LAST VISIT TO FLORA MACIVOR.	R. HERDMAN, R.S.A.	LUMB STOCKS.

578. GUY MANNERING. In a Series of Six Designs. 1866.

1. ELLANGOWAN CASTLE by Moonlight.	J. M'WHIRTER, A.R.S.A.	W. RICHARDSON.
2. THE DEPARTURE OF THE GIPSIES FROM ELLANGOWAN.	CLARK STANTON, A.R.S.A.	LUMB STOCKS.
3. DANDIE DINMONT AND HIS TERRIERS.	GOURLAY STEELL, R.S.A.	J. STEPHENSON.
4. HARRY BERTRAM IN THE KAIM OF DERNCLEUGH.	W. M'TAGGART, R.S.A.	J. LE CONTE.
5. THE PARTY AT COLONEL MANNERING'S ON THE EVE OF BERTRAM'S RETURN.	ROBERT HERDMAN, R.S.A.	F. HOLL.
6. THE CAPTURE OF DIRK HATTERAICK.	J. B. MACDONALD, A.R.S.A.	R. C. BELL.

579. The Antiquary. In a Series of Six Designs. 1867.

1. The Antiquary and Lovel entering the Sanctum.

	Designer.	*Engraver.*
	R. Herdman, R.S.A.	R. C. Bell.

2. Sir Arthur and Miss Wardour setting out along the Shore.—Sunset.

	J. M'Whirter, A.R.S.A.	W. Richardson.

3. The Storm.

	Sam. Bough, A.R.S.A.	W. Forrest.

4. The Interview between Miss Wardour and Edie Ochiltree at the Grated Window of the Flagged Parlour.

	W. M'Taggart, R.S.A.	J. Le Conte.

5. The Kaim of Kinprunes.

	J. B. Macdonald, A.R.S.A.	T. Brown.

6. Sir Arthur and Dousterswivel in the Ruins of St. Ruth.

	Waller H. Paton, R.S.A.	W. Richardson.

580. Rob Roy. In a Series of Six Designs. 1868.

1. Cattle-Lifting.

	Gourlay Steell, R.S.A.	J. Stephenson.

2. Diana Vernon and Frank Osbaldistone in the Library —The Glove Scene.

	R. Herdman, R.S.A.	R. C. Bell.

3. Rob Roy parting the Duellists, Rashleigh and Francis Osbaldistone.

	J. B. Macdonald, A.R.S.A.	J. Le Conte.

4. The Clachan of Aberfoyle and Loch Ard—Morning.

	J. M'Whirter, A.R.S.A.	W. Miller.

5. The Escape of Rob Roy at the Ford.

	Sam. Bough, A.R.S.A.	W. Forrest.

6. Loch Lomond.

	Sam. Bough, A.R.S.A.	T. Brown.

581. Old Mortality. In a Series of Six Designs. 1869.

1. The Graveyard—Old Mortality at the Tombs.

	J. M'Whirter, A.R.S.A.	W. Richardson.

2. Lady Margaret Bellenden in Mause Headrigg's Cottage.

	W. F. Douglas, R.S.A.	J. Le Conte.

3. LADY MARGARET AND MAJOR BELLENDEN FINDING EDITH ON THE BATTLEMENTS WATCHING FOR THE APPROACH OF THE TROOPS.

Designer.	*Engraver.*
R. HERDMAN, R.S.A.	T. BROWN.

4. MAJOR BELLENDEN INTERCEDING WITH CLAVERHOUSE FOR THE LIFE OF HENRY MORTON.

W. CRAWFORD, A.R.S.A. — F. HOLL.

5. THE BATTLE OF BOTHWELL BRIDGE.

SAM. BOUGH, A.R.S.A. — W. FORREST.

6. MORTON AWAITING HIS DEATH AT THE HANDS OF THE CAMERONIANS IN THE FARMHOUSE OF DRUMSHINNEL.

W. F. DOUGLAS, R.S.A. — R. C. BELL.

ROBERT CHARLES BELL was a native of Edinburgh, where he studied the art of engraving under John Bengo. He engraved a number of important plates, but his finest works were undoubtedly his small vignetted portraits. He died at Edinburgh, September 1872, in the 66th year of his age.

582. THE PIRATE. In a Series of Five Designs. Also a PORTRAIT OF SIR WALTER SCOTT. 1871.

1. PORTRAIT OF SIR WALTER SCOTT IN HIS STUDY, 39 Castle Street.

SIR J. WATSON GORDON, P.R.S.A., R.A. — R. C. BELL.

2. THE UDALLER'S HOME—MAGNUS TROIL AND HIS FAMILY.

R. HERDMAN, R.S.A. — THOMAS BROWN.

3. THE STORM, WITH MORDAUNT RESCUING CLEVELAND.

SAM. BOUGH, A.R.S.A. — W. RICHARDSON.

4. NORNA PERFORMING HER CURATIVE SPELL ON MINNA TROIL.

JOHN A. HOUSTON, R.S.A. — J. LE CONTE.

5. THE ALTERCATION BETWEEN THE PEDLAR AND CLEVELAND AT THE FAIR OF KIRKWALL.

KEELEY HALSWELLE, A.R.S.A. — THOMAS BROWN.

6. MINNA TAKING THE PISTOL FROM BUNCE TO DEFEND HERSELF AND HER SISTER.

W. E. LOCKHART, A.R.S.A. — J. LE CONTE.

583. THE LADY OF THE LAKE. In a Series of Six Designs.

1. THE DEATH OF THE GALLANT GREY.

GOURLAY STEELL, R.S.A. — LUMB STOCKS.

2. THE TROSSACHS.

HORATIO MACCULLOCH, R.S.A. — WILLIAM FORREST.

3. THE LADY OF THE LAKE.

R. HERDMAN, R.S.A. — THOMAS BROWN.

	Designer.	*Engraver.*
4. Loch Katrine.	Peter Graham, A.R.S.A.	W. Richardson
5. The Cross of Fire.	James Drummond, R.S.A.	R. C. Bell.
6. Fitz-James and Roderick Dhu.	J. B. Macdonald, A.R.S.A.	Lumb Stocks.

584. A Series of One Hundred and Twenty Engravings illustrating the Abbotsford Edition of the Novels of Sir Walter Scott. The original India proof impressions before Letters.

Edinburgh: The Royal Association for the Promotion of the Fine Arts in Scotland. 1851. Bound in Two Volumes, large folio.

Lent by
Robert Horn, Esq.

585. Illustrations of Walter Scott's "Lay of the Last Minstrel," consisting of Twelve Views on the Rivers Borthwick, Ettrick, Yarrow, Teviot, and Tweed.

Engraved by J. Heath, R.A., from designs taken on the spot by John C. Schetky, of Oxford. With Anecdotes and Descriptions. London: Printed for Longman, Hurst, Rees, and Orme. 181[illegible]. Royal 8vo.

The descriptions were revised by Walter Scott, Esq.

Mr. [illegible]. Also Nos. 586 and 587.

586. Graphic Illustrations to Sir Walter Scott's Works.

Scenes described in the Novels and Tales, from drawings by A. Nasmyth, engraved by Lizars. (Waverley to Rob Roy.) Edinburgh, 1821. 16 Plates. 8vo.

587. A Series of Sketches of the existing Localities alluded to in the Waverley Novels.

Etched from Original Drawings. By James Skene, Esq. Robert Cadell, Edinburgh. 1831. Royal 8vo.

588. Landscape Illustrations of the Waverley Novels, with Descriptions of the Views.

Vol. I. Waverley to Legend of Montrose. Vol. II. Ivanhoe to Woodstock.) London: Charles Tilt, Fleet Street. 1832. Two Vols. Royal 8vo.

589. The Book of Waverley Gems: in a Series of Engraved Illustrations of Incidents and Scenery in Sir Walter Scott's Novels.

Henry G. Bohn, Esq.

Engravings by Heath, Finden, Rolls, etc., after pictures by Leslie, Stothard, Cooper, Howard, etc., with illustrative letterpress. London, 1862. 8vo.

V.—ODDS AND ENDS,

Including some Personal Relics.

590. Drawing of the Lennox or Darnley Jewel, in Gold and Colours.

Lent by

Mr. Gibson Craig.

*** The old description of this interesting Relic is as follows:—"A Golden Heart set with Jewels and ornamented with emblematical figures enamelled, and Scottish mottoes." Mr. Fraser Tytler prepared, by Her Majesty's command, an elaborate description of the various emblems and mottoes, clearly showing that this curious and ancient Jewel contains internal evidence that it was made for Margaret Countess of Lennox in memory of her husband the Regent, as a present to her Royal Grandson James VI. of Scotland.

591. Drawings of the Bloody Banner and other Covenanters' Banners borne at Drumclog and Bothwell Brig. By James Drummond, R.S.A.

The Artist.

*** On the "Bluidy Banner," which is of blue silk, is inscribed in Hebrew characters, "Jehovah Nissi" (The Lord is my Banner); this in gilt letters. Next, in large white letters, "For Christ and His Truths;" and then, painted in red, the motto from which it derives its name, "No Quarters for ye Active Enimies of ye Covenant."

The other Banners belonged to the parishes or districts of East Monkland, Avendale, Garscube, Phinick, Shotts, and Irongray. Also of one, afterwards carried (not very creditably) by a body of Burgher Seceders, who volunteered to defend the University of Edinburgh against the Highlanders in 1745.—(See *Proceedings of the Society of Antiquaries of Scotland*, vol. iii. p. 253.)

592. Key of Lochleven Castle.

William Patrick Adam, Esq., M.P.

*** Presented by Sir Walter Scott to Lord Chief-Commissioner Adam. (See *Blair-Adam Tracts*, No. I., 1834.)

593. Antique Key of Brass, or some Yellow Metal.

Lady Elizabeth-Jane Leslie-Melville Cartwright.

Inscribed on bowl *Marie Rex*, and on wards 1565. Found in Loch Leven; and supposed to be a Chamberlain's Key or Badge of Office.

594. BRIDLE-BIT found in a Vault of the Hermitage Castle, along with some Remnants of Ancient Armour and several Human Bones.

Lent by

THE EARL OF DALHOUSIE.

_ The Vault was that in which Sir Alexander Ramsay of Dalhousie was starved to death by order of William Douglas, called the Knight of Liddesdale. "The Bit was presented to me by Mr. Elliot, Tenant in Millburnhall.—W. S. *October* 1795."—Given by Sir Walter Scott to George, ninth Earl of Dalhousie.

595. GEORGE HERIOT'S "LOVING CUP."

THE GOVERNORS OF GEORGE HERIOT'S HOSPITAL.

_ "In 1792, John Stewart, Esq., presented to the Governors a curious antique cup, formed of a Nautilus shell, exquisitely mounted with silver, and said to have been the workmanship and the drinking-cup of George Heriot . . . This cup, of which the House-Governor is the conservator, is used on all public occasions when the Governors drink to the memory of the Founder."—(Steven's *History of George Heriot's Hospital*, edit. by Bedford, p. 132.)

596. MEG DODS'S PUNCH-BOWL.

MR. WALKER, Peebles.

_ This Bowl, which belonged to Miss Ritchie of The Yett, Peebles, was cracked by Sir Walter Scott, who, rather than encounter her wrath, stole unseen from the house with it in his handkerchief, and ordering his groom to follow him with the carriage, walked out on the road till the groom came up; and driving with all haste to Edinburgh had it clasped by some muggers who were plying their craft there at the time, and returned to Peebles with it next morning, thinking his anxiety for the Bowl would be some palliation of his offence: but he was met by Miss Ritchie at the door with a perfect torrent of abuse for "leaving *her decent house in sic a clandestean manner, at sic a late hour, and a' about a bit crokerie-ware that wasna worth fashin' ane's thoomb about.*"

597. PLAY BILL with CAST OF ROB ROY, on the occasion of the Visit of His Majesty George IV. to the Theatre-Royal, Edinburgh.

598. BABY-CLOTHES BASKET used for SIR WALTER SCOTT in his Infancy.

THE MISSES AYTOUN.

_ Presented by the Mother of Sir Walter Scott to Mrs. Aytoun, Mother of William Edmondstoune Aytoun, Author of the *Lays of the Scottish Cavaliers.*

599. SILVER FRUIT-KNIFE AND IVORY SIX-INCH RULE.

MR. R. T. C. SCOTT.

_ Presented by Sir Walter Scott to R. T. C. Scott of Melby, Shetland, on the 7th August 1814. See Lockhart's *Life*, vol. iii. pp. 160, 161.

600. (1.) SILVER SNUFF-BOX, in constant use by SIR WALTER SCOTT;

(2.) GOLD WATCH which belonged to LADY SCOTT.

DR. CLARKSON.

_ Presented to Dr. Clarkson by Sir Walter's Son, in acknowledgment of his long services, and the friendship entertained for him by the family.

601. PENCIL-CASE AND PENCIL which belonged to SIR WALTER SCOTT, and presented by him to the late Sir John Watson Gordon; with Letter from H. G. Watson, Esq., to James Simson, Esq., M.D.

Lent by
JAMES SIMSON, M.D.

602. LOCKET, with PHOTOGRAPH and HAIR of SIR WALTER SCOTT.
MISS CAMPBELL SWINTON.

603. SIR WALTER SCOTT'S PIPE.
MR. JAMES DOUGLAS.

604. BOX WITH STEEL AND FLINT.
MR. ALEXANDER NICHOLSON.

605. LOCKET of SIR WALTER SCOTT'S HAIR.
Presented by Sir Adam Ferguson to a friend.

606. GOLD WATCH AND CHAIN, and SILVER NECK CHAIN, worn by SIR WALTER SCOTT.
MR. ALEXANDER NICHOLSON.

---

607. THE STUDY AT ABBOTSFORD. Painted by SIR WILLIAM ALLAN, P.R.S.A., R.A. 1 ft. 2 in. × 11 in.

Lent by
T. WILLIAMS, ESQ.

608. PAINTING OF SIR WALTER SCOTT'S FAVOURITE DOG "CAMP." 2 ft. 9½ in. × 2 ft. 3½ in.

MR. T. G. STEVENSON. JAMES HOWE.

Also the Original MS. Notice of which the following is an Extract.

"Camp was got by a black and tan English terrier call[ed] Doctor, the property of Mr. Storie, Farrier in Rose Street, about 1800, out of a thoroughbred English brindled bull-bitch, the property of Mr. John Adams, of the Riding School, Adjutant to the Royal Edinburgh Volunteer Cavalry. He was of great strength and very handsome, extremely sagacious, faithful and affectionate to the human species, and possessed of a great turn for gaiety and drollery. Although he was never taught any tricks, he learned some of his own accord, and understood whatever was said to him as well as any creature I ever saw. His great fault was an excessive ferocity towards his own sprees, which sometimes brought both his master and himself into dangerous scrapes. He used to accompany me always in coursing, of which he was a great amateur, and was one of the best dogs for finding hares I ever saw, though I have since had very fine terriers. At last he met with an accident which gave him a sprain in the back, from which he never recovered, after which he could not follow when I went out on horseback. . . . .

"He is painted in two portraits of his owner by Raeburn. One at Dalkeith Palace, and one in my own possession.

"He lived till about twelve years old, and might have lived longer but for the severe exercise which he had taken when young, and a considerable disposition to voracity, especially where animal food was to be come by.

"I could add a number of curious anecdotes of his sagacity, but they are connected with a family loss since sustained, and are painful to recollect or detail.

"There is enough to illustrate Mr. Stevenson's picture which was painted by Mr. Howe, then a painter of animals of some merit. W. S.

"SHANDWICK PLACE, [illegible] *March* 11, 1828."

609. CALL-BOOK AT THE PALACE OF HOLYROOD (with very numerous Original Signatures), during the Visit of His Majesty George the Fourth to Scotland, in August 1822. Folio

Lent by

MR. D. LAING. Also Nos. 611 and 612.

610. VISITORS' BOOK AT DRYBURGH, in the years 1821 to 1835.

MR. JOHN T. ROSE.

611. ADVERSARIA: Notices Illustrative of some of the Earlier Works printed for the Bannatyne Club. Edinburgh, 1867. 4to.

Presented by the Secretary to the Members of the Club.

This Volume contains three Engraved Portraits, and four Facsimile Lithographs, including the Testimonial to the Secretary. See Illustrations, No. VI. p. 55.

612. THE BANNATYNE CLUB.—Lists of Members and the Rules, with a Catalogue of the Books printed for the Bannatyne Club since its Institution in 1823. Edinburgh, 1867. 8vo.

SUPPLEMENTAL NOTICES AND CORRECTIONS.

(1.) Some of the references in the List of ORIGINAL PORTRAITS, require to be corrected.

No. 58, add, See Illustrations, No. XXV.—No. 71, see No. XXVII. (B.)—No. 72, see No. XIX.—No. 73, read, A duplicate of No. 67.—No. 76, see No. XXVIII.—No. 78, see No. XXX.—No. 80, see No. XXIX.—No. 88, see No. XX.

(2.) No. 66. The title of this Engraved Portrait by SIR WILLIAM ALLAN is "SIR WALTER SCOTT, Bart., in his Study at Abbotsford." See Illustrations, No. XXIX.

(3.) On examining carefully the fragment of the Original Manuscript of WAVERLEY, purchased by Mr. Hope Scott, and now at Abbotsford, we are informed that it was a mistake (at p. 112) to suppose they were the first fifteen leaves, containing "the opening chapters of the Novel." The leaves, which are not consecutive, are stated to be chiefly unconnected pages of Chapters 18, 19, and 20 in Vol. II.

The interesting manuscript portion of IVANHOE, contained in the same volume, consists of 59 leaves, all in Walter Scott's autograph.

(4.) No. 235. The notice of a facsimile of the MS. of ROKEBY was inserted by mistake.

(5.) At page 26, No. 4, in justice to Mr. KNIGHT, R.A., whose Portrait of Sir Walter Scott is mentioned, there should have been added, that the Artist at the time it was painted was still a Royal Academy student. On looking at the finished engraving in the larger edition of Lodge's Portraits, it may, as a likeness, bear comparison with others by Artists of higher pretensions. Mr. Lockhart's criticism is too severe. There are, however, engravings from other and perhaps inferior portraits by Mr. Knight. In his Diary, 1826, January 7, Sunday, Sir Walter writes:—

"KNIGHT, a young artist, son of the performer, came to do a picture of me at the request of Terry. This is very far from being agreeable, as I submitted to that state of constraint last year to Newton, at request of Lockhart; to Leslie, at request of my American friend (Mr. Ticknor of Boston); to Wilkie for his picture of the King's arrival at Holyrood House; and some one besides. I am as tired of the operation as old Maida, who had been so often sketched that he got up and walked off with signs of loathing whenever he saw an artist unfurl his paper and handle his brushes. But this young man is civil and modest: and I have agreed he shall be in the room while I work, and take the best likeness he can, without compelling me into the fixed attitude and yawning fatigues of an actual sitting."

The following letter on the subject cannot be read without interest:—

"20 JAMES STREET, BUCKINGHAM PALACE,
25th July 1872.

"MY DEAR SIR,—In answer to yours of the 3d inst., it was during the Christmas season of the year 1825 or '26 that I painted the portrait of Sir Walter Scott for his friend Mr. Terry, the comedian; having been invited to Abbotsford for that purpose. The portrait, as part of the property of Mr. Terry, was sold by public auction after his decease.

"Some years afterwards I was invited to dine with Mr. Harding of Finchley, and on taking my place at the table I saw and claimed my portrait of Sir Walter Scott on the opposite wall, with the name of Sir Henry Raeburn conspicuously painted on the frame. Mr. Harding said that his plot had succeeded, for having casually heard that I was the author of the work, he thought the best way to test the truth would be to place me face to face with the picture; he therefore promised that thenceforward the picture should carry my name. As a young man I felt highly complimented with the appreciation thus expressed of my work, and grateful to Mr. Harding for so promptly acknowledging my claim.

"At the same time, viz. 1825 or '26, I made many little characteristic sketches, with the view of aiding me in painting the larger picture, one of which, in the year 1828, was placed in the hands of Mr. R. J. Lane, the eminent engraver, who produced a beautiful lithograph of it: but in the printing it was utterly spoiled, and I never saw an impression of it.

"Some years afterwards Mr. Harding informed me that the kitchen chimney, which passed close behind the wall on which the portrait of Sir Walter Scott was hung, had taken fire the day previous, and that the portrait was much injured. On examination I found the work was utterly and hopelessly destroyed. This was the only damage done by the fire; and by a curious coincidence Sir Walter Scott died on that day.—I am, etc.,

"JOHN P. KNIGHT.

"*To* SIR WILLIAM STIRLING MAXWELL, Bart."

JOHN PRESCOTT KNIGHT, R.A., was born in 1803; and became a student of the Royal Academy in 1823. He was admitted an Associate in 1836, and R.A. in 1844. Three years later he was elected to the important office of Secretary to the Academy, which he still continues to hold.

(6.) THE EVE OF ST. JOHN, a Border Ballad. 49 Verses. 12mo.

Lent by
MISS MUIR.

A transcript in the handwriting of Mrs. Charlotte Scott, afterwards Lady Scott, and presented by her to Captain Scott of Rosebank. 12mo. ten leaves. It has a small vignette drawing of Smailholm Tower.

(7.) LETTER to WILLIAM STEWART WATSON, Esq., Artist. No. 408.

The following copy of this letter is here added by favour of Mrs. Stewart Watson.

"DEAR MR. WATSON,— Your packet reached me in perfect safety, and the contents gave us great pleasure, both on account of the strong resemblances of the Miniatures and the stile of execution. I am particularly pleased with my wife's picture, as her features and expression are not easily hit, and I think you have been very successful. I have no doubt that, by continuing to bestow much pains (for that is everything in all difficult arts), you will soon place yourself high in your profession.

"My Wife is greatly obliged by the two screens so beautifully pencilled, and begs me to make her best acknowledgement. I am not less obliged by your attention to my blazonry, which is in no sort of hurry; if you look at it at a perfectly idle moment it is quite enough. Hoggle nam Bo [*in modern Gaelic*, 'Thogail nam bo,' to the lifting of the cows] will I dare [say] cast up among the M'farlanes in due time. I am, dear Mr. Watson, your obliged humble servant,

"WALTER SCOTT.

"ABBOTSFORD, 4 *October* 1825.

"I will be much obliged to you to look in upon the Glass-painter now and then."

LIST OF ARTISTS.

In the References, the figures refer to the No. in the Catalogue, the p. or pp. to the Illustrations.

LIST OF CONTRIBUTORS.

HER MAJESTY THE QUEEN, 55, 82, 86, 290.

ABBOTSFORD LIBRARY, 281, 282, 381, 393.

ADAM, William Patrick, of Blair-Adam, M.P., 60, 485, 592.

ADOLPHUS, Mrs., 23A Connaught Square, London, 38, 91.

ADVOCATES, THE FACULTY OF, 242.

AITCHISON, Thomas S., 74 George Street, Edinburgh, 509.

ALEXANDER, Sir James E., 418.

ANDERSON, David B., W.S., 8 Regent Terrace, Edinburgh, 528.

ANTIQUARIES, THE SOCIETY OF, Royal Institution, 36.

ARCHER, Thomas, Director of Museum of Science and Art, Edinburgh, 25.

ARMSTRONG, George, Alnwick, 460.

AYTOUN, The Misses, 28 Inverleith Row, 598.

BUCCLEUCH AND QUEENSBERRY, The Duke of, K.G., Dalkeith Palace, 49.

BREADALBANE, The Earl of, Taymouth Castle, 27, 426, 427.

BALLANTINE, James, 42 George Street, Edinburgh, 20, 452, 462, 507.

BALLANTYNE, John, R.S.A., Totteridge, Herts, 93.

BALLANTYNE, Robert M., 6 Millerfield Place, Edinburgh, 94.

BAYLEY, Isaac, S.S.C., 13 Regent Terrace, Edinburgh, 415, 416.

BEDFORD, Rev. W. K. R., Sutton Coldfield, Warwickshire, 407, 413.

BLACK, Adam, of Prior Bank, Melrose, 108, 115.

BLACK, Messrs. A. and C., Publishers, Edinburgh, 283, 313, 533 to 538.

BLACKLOCK, John, Dumfries, 18.

BLACKWOOD, John, 45 George Street, Edinburgh, 64, 75, 89, 95, 102, 110.

BLAIKLY, James, 135 Buchanan Street, Glasgow, 480.

BLATHWAYT, Rev. Raymond, Chaplain, H.M. Prison, Worthing, Surrey, 92.

BOHN, Henry G., Northend House, Twickenham, 74, 97, 107, 270, 589.

BONNAR, Thomas, 137 Princes Street, Edinburgh, 23, 96, 112, 453, 459, 542, 543.

BONNAR AND CARFRAE, Messrs., 77 George Street, Edinburgh, 28.

BRODIE, William, R.S.A., Cambridge Street, Edinburgh, 42.

BRUCE, Daniel, 12 Greenside Place, Edinburgh, 155, 499.

BRYCE, David, R.S.A., 131 George Street, Edinburgh, 484.

BUTTI, James, 7 Queen Street, Edinburgh, 449.

CARTWRIGHT, Lady Elizabeth-Jane Leslie-Melville, Melville House, Ladybank, 435, 593.

CLINTON, Right Hon. Lord, Trefusis Castle, Falmouth, Cornwall, 101.

COLQUHOUN, Lady, Strathgarry, Pitlochrie, 434.

CALLANDER, Mrs. Burn, Prestonhall, 4.

CARFRAE, Robert, 19 Pitt Street, Edinburgh, 495.

CARRE, W. Riddell, of Cavers-Carre, 117, 198, 403.

CLARK, James, Clackmannan, 461.

CLARK, William D., 1 Knox Place, Mayfield Loan, Edinburgh, 20, 510.

CLARKSON, James Barnet, M.D., Avenel, Colinton Road, 600.

COCKBURN, A. D., 6 Athol Crescent, Edinburgh, 524.

CONSTABLE, Thomas, 11 Thistle Street, Edinburgh, 99.

CORSAR, David, Arbroath, 517.

COWAN, John, Beeslack, Penicuik, 249.

MACKAY, Charles, LL.D., Fern Dell, Boxhill, Surrey, 37.

MACKAY, Mrs., 17 Lutton Place, 104.

MACLAGAN, Professor Douglas, 28 Heriot Row, Edinburgh, 447.

MACLAURIN, Mrs., 9 Randolph Cliff, Edinburgh, 412.

MACLEAY, Kenneth, R.S.A., 3 Malta Terrace, Edinburgh, 521, 563, 564.

MEIK, Miss, 22 Greenhill Gardens, Morningside, p. 200.

MEIK, Thomas, C.E., 7 Newbattle Terrace, Morningside, 411.

MELVILLE, Mrs., 8 Newbattle Terrace, Morningside, 489.

MERCER, Robert, of Scotsbank, Ramsay Lodge, Portobello, 492, 493, 496.

MURRAY, James Wolfe, of Cringletie, 35.

MURRAY, John, 50 Albemarle Street, London, 53, 58, 87, 401.

MUSPRATT, James, Seaforth Hall, Seaforth, Liverpool, 477.

NATIONAL PORTRAIT GALLERY, London, 66.

NAPIER, Right Hon. Baron, Thirlstane Castle, Selkirkshire, 54.

NAPIER, Mark, 6 Ainslie Place, Edinburgh, 258.

NICHOLSON, Alexander, Kelso, 39, 604, 606.

NICHOLSON, Mrs., 6 Henderson Row, Edinburgh, 50.

ORR, Sir Andrew, of Harvieston, 508.

POLWARTH, Right Hon. Lord, Mertoun House, St. Boswells, 394.

PATON, Sir Joseph Noel, R.S.A., 33 George Square, Edinburgh, 12, 29.

PATERSON, Dr. A., Bridge of Allan, 24.

PATERSON, William, 23 Hope Terrace, 545. Also volumes of the Waverley Novels.

PEAT, Mrs. Cumine, Welnage, Dunse, 471.

PEEL, Sir Robert, Tamworth, p. 47.

PENDER, John, M.P., Minard Castle, Argyleshire, p. 87.

PRINGLE, Mrs. William, Portobello, 404.

ROYAL ASSOCIATION FOR THE PROMOTION OF THE FINE ARTS IN SCOTLAND, 8, 577 to 583.

ROYAL SOCIETY, The, Edinburgh, 63.

RUTHVEN, The Dowager Lady, Winton House, Tranent, 68.

RAEBURN, John P., Charlesfield, Mid-Calder, 59.

RAMSAY, R. B. Wardlaw, of Whitehill, Lasswade, 450, 502.

RENNY, James, 22 Picardy Place, Edinburgh, 114.

RICHARDSON, Francis, Mickleham, Surrey, 233, 239, 240, 247, 270, 273, 277.

ROBERTSON, Robert, 5 South Lauder Road, Grange, Edinburgh, 494.

ROSE, John T., 11 Duncan Street, Edinburgh, 5, 135, 139, 151, 161, 168, 188, 192, 200, 204, 205, 224, 610.

SCOTT, The Dowager Lady, 85.

SCOTT, James R. Hope, Q.C., Abbotsford, 45, 47, 88, 90, 235, 237, 248, 253, 269, 284, 389, 398, 400.

STRATHMORE, The Earl of, 20 Rutland Gate, London, 436.

SCOTT MONUMENT, The Trustees for the, 21.

SIGNET, THE SOCIETY OF WRITERS TO THE, Edinburgh, 307; also several of the Nos. from 207 to 304; from 315 to 340, 348, 352, 358, etc.

SPECULATIVE SOCIETY, The, 73, 395, 396.

SALE, W. F., Irwell Bank, Kersal, Manchester, 455.

SANSON, Mrs. Margaret, 24 Minto Street, Edinburgh, 456, 511, 565, 567.

SCOTT, R. T. C., J.P., Melby, Shetland, 414, 599.

SHAND, A. Burns, 3 Great Stuart Street, Edinburgh, 479.

SIMPSON, George B., Seafield, Broughty-Ferry, 482, 500, 501, 504, 505.

SIMSON, David, 25 India Street, Edinburgh, 518.

SIMSON, James, M.D., 3 Glenfinlas Street, Edinburgh, 601.

SKENE, A., 22 Regent Quay, Aberdeen, 262.

SMITH, Colvin, R.S.A., 32 York Place, Edinburgh, 62, 103, 106.

SMITH, John A., M.D., 7 West Maitland Street, Edinburgh, 162, 191.

SMITH, Mrs. Stewart, 6 Marmion Terrace, Morningside, 519.

SPENCE, A. Blair, Dundee, 498.

STEVENSON, Thomas G., 22 Frederick Street, Edinburgh, 199, 406, 608.

STEVENSON, R. HORNE, D.D., 9 Oxford Terrace, Edinburgh, 2, 98, 257.

STIRLING, Gilbert, of Larbert House, Royal Horse Guards, London, 475.

SWINTON, Archibald Campbell, of Kimmerghame, Dunse, 13, 111, 123, 285, 343.

SWINTON, Miss, Kimmerghame, Dunse, 602.

THOMSON, Lockhart, S.S.C., 20 Coates Crescent, Edinburgh, 100

WALKER, Mr., Peebles, 596.

WATSON, Henry G., 123 George Street, Edinburgh, 30, 65, 69, 473, 474.

WATSON, William Smellie, R.S.A., 10 Forth Street, Edinburgh, 527.

WATSON, Mrs. Stewart, 21A Broughton Place, Edinburgh, 77, 408, and p. 200

WELLS, William, M.P., 22 Bruton Street, London, 72

WELLWOOD, Allan A. Maconochie, Meadowbank House, Kirknewton, 1.

WHITE, John, Netherurd, Peeblesshire, 467, 514

WHITE, William Logan, Kellerstain, Hermiston, 81.

WILLIAMS, T., Elm-Tree Road, London, 607.

WILLIAMSON, John, The Deans, South Shields, 478.

YOUNG, James, of Kelly, 113

PRINTED BY T. AND A. CONSTABLE, PRINTERS TO HER MAJESTY, AT THE EDINBURGH UNIVERSITY PRESS.

CPSIA information can be obtained
at www.ICGtesting.com
Printed in the USA
LVHW08s2107011018
592013LV00013B/1457/P